WE ARE HERE

We Are

Here

MEMORIES *of*
the LITHUANIAN
HOLOCAUST

Ellen Cassedy

University of Nebraska Press, Lincoln & London

Acknowledgments for the
use of copyrighted material
appear on pages 272–73,
which constitute an extension
of the copyright page.

Publication of this volume
was assisted by a grant from
the Tides Foundation.

Library of Congress
Cataloging-in-Publication Data
Cassedy, Ellen.
We are here: memories of
the Lithuanian Holocaust /
Ellen Cassedy.   p. cm.
ISBN 978-0-8032-3012-5
(pbk.: alk. paper)
1. Jews — Lithuania — History.
2. Cassedy, Ellen — Travel.
3. Lithuania — Description
and travel. 4. Lithuania —
Ethnic relations. I. Title.
DS135.L5C37 2012
940.53'1807202 — dc23
[B]   2011032474

Set in Arno by Bob Reitz.
Designed by Nathan Putens.

For my family

Contents

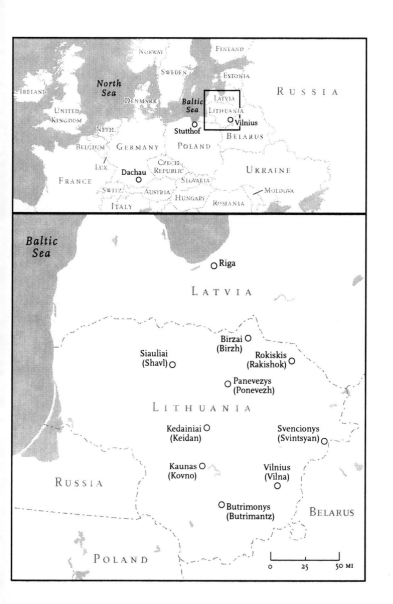

Family Tree

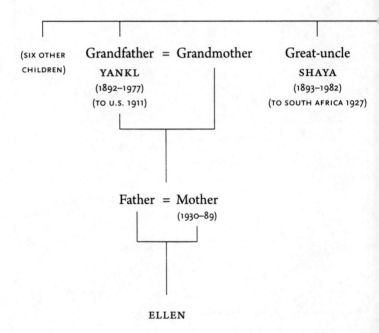

(SIX OTHER CHILDREN)

Grandfather = Grandmother
YANKL
(1892–1977)
(TO U.S. 1911)

Great-uncle
SHAYA
(1893–1982)
(TO SOUTH AFRICA 1927)

Father = Mother
(1930–89)

ELLEN

Great-grandmother Great-grandfather

(1) ASNE = DOVID-MIKHL = (2) SOREH*
(1859–1900)   (1854–1924)   (1876–1944)

Great-uncle Great-aunt   Great-uncle Great-aunt

AARON* = SONYA*   WILL* = MANYA
(1894–1971) (1902–88)   (1917–2009)
                          (TO U.S. 1949)

ASYA*
(1928–)

* = in Shavl ghetto, 1941–44

WE ARE HERE

Preparations

1. Sv. Ignoto gatve (St. Ignatius Street), Vilnius.

A soft summer rain was falling as a white-haired woman made her way to the microphone. "Tayere talmidim!" she began. "Dear students!" Through the pattering of drops on my umbrella, I leaned forward to catch her words. The old woman's name was Bluma, a flowery name that matched her flowered dress. She was a member of the all-but-vanished Jewish community in Vilnius, Lithuania, the city once known as the Jerusalem of the North. "How fortunate I am," she said in a quavering voice. "I have lived long enough to see people coming back to Vilnius to study Yiddish."

Seventy-five of us — students of all ages from all over the globe — huddled on the wooden benches that were clustered together on wet cobblestones. Around us, the damp walls of Vilnius University rose into the heavens. As the rain continued to fall, I shivered. It was a complicated place, this land of my ancestors — a place where Jewish culture had once flourished, and a place where Jews had been annihilated on a massive scale.

My reasons for being here were not simple. I had come to learn Yiddish and to connect myself with my roots — the Jewish ones, that is, on my mother's side. (On my father's side, my non-Jewish forebears hailed from Ireland, England, and Bavaria — hence my name, Cassedy, and my blue eyes and freckles.) But I had other goals, too. I wanted to investigate a troubling family story I'd stumbled upon in preparing for my trip. I had agreed to meet a haunted old man in my ancestral town. And I planned to examine how the people of this country — Jews and non-Jews alike — were confronting their past in order to move forward into the future. What had begun as a personal journey had broadened into a larger exploration. Investigating Lithuania's effort to exhume the past, I hoped, would help me answer some important questions.

When my mother was alive, I could count on her to keep hold of the past. But after she died, all those who'd gone before seemed to be slipping out of reach. I found myself missing the sound of Yiddish, the Jewish *mame-loshn*, or mother tongue, that she had sprinkled into conversation like a spice. At the window on a rainy day: "A *pliukhe* (downpour)!" In the kitchen: "Hand me a *shisl* (bowl)." On the telephone: "The woman's a *makhsheyfe* (witch)."

Once my mother was gone, I felt bereft — of her, and of the homey sounds that had once resounded in Jewish kitchens, lanes, meeting halls, and market squares on both sides of the Atlantic. My desire for Yiddish developed into a craving. I wanted to speak it and read it, to understand, write, sing. I signed up for evening classes at the nearby Jewish community center, worrying that at forty, I was too old for language study. The Germanic sounds felt comfortable in my mouth, though, and the Hebrew alphabet was daunting but not impossible. While my children did their homework at the dining room table, I did mine, plodding through textbooks, copying out grammar exercises, thumbing my dictionary till the binding broke.

Raised in a mixed marriage by secular parents, I had never attended Hebrew school or recited blessings on Friday nights. Now, studying Yiddish felt like an act of devotion. Yiddish was the everyday Jewish idiom, not the language of religious texts. Yet to me it embodied sacred values. Yiddish was the language that great writers had used to convey stirring humanist ideas to an audience of "common folk." It was the language that had united activist Jews in movements for social change in Europe and North America.

Studying Yiddish signified that ordinary life mattered, that humble people and their humble daily lives had meaning and would not be forgotten.

Once described as "the linguistic homeland of a people without a home," Yiddish began to offer me the sense of continuity that had been ruptured by my mother's death. My husband, who'd been raised in Baltimore's Jewish community, sensed how important it had become for me, and so did our two children. Yiddish became a cherished presence in our household.

My mother would have been surprised, to put it mildly. In the neighborhood in New York City where she grew up, Yiddish was about ignorance and poverty. English — perfect English — held the place of honor. Yes, she enjoyed pronouncing the occasional Yiddish phrase. But what was most important to her was to break free of the world of *yidishkayt* (traditional Jewish culture) with its Old World accent and inflections and the immigrant culture they represented. Now here I was, training my tongue to master that very idiom.

I was not the only one. A robust community of Yiddish enthusiasts in Washington DC welcomed me with open arms. I joined a reading group that tackled the classic tales by Sholem Aleichem and Y. L. Peretz; we did our best to speak only Yiddish, from the first "gutn ovnt" (good evening) to the final "gute nakht" (good night). I became a member of the National Yiddish Book Center, visited the Workmen's Circle bookstore when I was in New York, and logged on to "Mendele," the Yiddish e-mail club. Within a few years I had progressed to translating Yiddish short stories for publication.

And in 2004, when I learned about an intensive Yiddish summer program being offered in Vilnius, I decided to enroll.

I had to consult an atlas to find out where I was headed. There it was: Lithuania. One of the three Baltic republics, with Latvia and Estonia to the north and Poland to the south. Geographically the size of Maine. Population three and a half million, about the same as Connecticut. "Drink bottled water," said the brochure from the travel agency; "please avoid shorts."

In my childhood, the Old Country had seemed utterly inaccessible, as if it existed in another dimension, like Atlantis or Narnia. No one from my family who'd crossed the Atlantic Ocean to America had ever gone back. Yet now I was on my way, preparing to look up into the same sky that had sheltered my great-grandmother Asne and her dairy farm, my great-grandfather Dovid-Mikhl and his study house. Under this sky, my grandfather Yankl (later Jack) had been a *yeshive bokher* (religious student) and a socialist before fleeing to America to escape the czarist draft. Here, my great-uncle Will had been imprisoned behind barbed wire in a ghetto during the Nazi era. And here, another great-uncle, Aaron, after surviving the concentration camp at Dachau, had been arrested by the Soviet regime and exiled to Siberia.

Of all of them, only Uncle Will was still alive. Shortly before setting off for the Old World, I paid a visit to him and his wife, my great-aunt Manya, at their New York apartment.

The two of them were waiting in their doorway as I stepped off the elevator. With his small, trim stature, his silver hair and twinkly eyes, Uncle Will closely resembled my grandfather. His high cheekbones were the same as my grandfather's, my mother's, my own. Aunt Manya, even tinier than my uncle, stood beside him with her proud, perfect posture.

With great ceremony I spread out the two maps I'd downloaded off the Internet. The first showed the streets of Rokiskis, the town in the very northeast corner of Lithuania where my family tree extended back into the early 1800s. Uncle Will had lived there until he was thirteen years old. The Lithuanians pronounced it ROCK-*ish-kiss*, my uncle said; the Jews called it Rakishok. The second showed the city of Siauliai (*show-LAY* to the Lithuanians, Shavl to the Jews), 130 miles northwest of Vilnius. Here, Will and his mother and other family members had been confined in the ghetto during the war.

Where should I go? I asked. Where did you live?

My uncle was almost ninety years old. Some sixty years had passed since he'd left Lithuania in a boxcar in 1944. The world of his youth was nearly beyond reach.

"You had to cross the road to get to school," he said slowly. "You took a right turn out of the square."

His hand hovered over the little grid. Finally he pressed his finger down. "Here," he said. "We lived here." He sat back in his chair and smiled, then reached under the table and took a nip from the bottle of vodka next to his foot.

Then something unexpected happened. My uncle felt in his pocket and pulled out a worn photocopied page. He unfolded it and put it in my hand. "Read this," he said.

When I did, I learned something about my uncle and his wartime actions that I had never known before. Something that had been hidden from me. Something I had never suspected.

Growing up, I'd heard heroic stories about Uncle Will during the Holocaust. In the ghetto, he'd saved two little girls by hiding them in a cupboard. On the death march out of Dachau, he had carried Uncle Aaron when he was too weak to walk. I treasured these stories. But now, as I headed for the scene of the great tragedy of the twentieth century, he'd decided it was time to reveal something else.

By the time I left my aunt and uncle's apartment later that afternoon, the view of the past that I'd grown up with had broken apart, and the course of my journey to Lithuania had been radically altered.

Soon after the encounter with my uncle came another surprise. I'd written to an official in Rokiskis to ask about the museum there. She wrote back encouraging me to visit. The old manor house boasted a magnificent collection of goblets and golden plates, she said. And there was something else. Something important. An old man in town named Steponas wanted to talk to a Jew before he died. Would I be that Jew?

Would I? As I read and reread the official's words, I tried to imagine myself face-to-face with this man, this Steponas. Here was *another* old man who wanted to talk to me about his role in Lithuania's Holocaust. What had *he* done, and what did he want from me?

It took me a long time to write back. If not for what I'd just heard from Uncle Will, I might have said no. I might have turned away. But now the ground was shifting. Old certainties were dissolving, new complexities emerging. Something was expected of me. I wrote to the Rokiskis official. Yes, I said, I would meet with Steponas.

A desire to strengthen my ties with my origins had drawn me to the Old World. Now I felt my mission expanding. The old man in Rokiskis, I quickly learned, was only one of many people in the land of my ancestors who were seeking to engage with a complex past. With the fall of the Soviet Union, a newly independent Lithuania had gained the right — indeed, the responsibility — to shape its own historical understandings. A new public discourse about the Holocaust had begun. As the country prepared to join NATO and the European Union, some in Lithuanian — non-Jews as well as people in the forty-five-hundred-member Jewish community — were holding up long-buried truths for examination. They were questioning cherished assumptions and challenging age-old prejudices. Only in so doing, they felt, could Lithuania hope to build its future.

The way forward was not easy. The murder of the Jews of Lithuania had been among the most brutal in all of Europe. The German invaders had issued the orders, but in most cases Lithuanians pulled the triggers. In the forests surrounding Lithuania's towns and villages lay hundreds of mass graves where Jews had been shot and hastily buried. In the three major Lithuanian cities, including my uncle's Siauliai, tens of thousands of Jews had been confined in ghettos; most were eventually killed. By the end of the war, out of an estimated prewar Jewish population of 240,000, fewer than 20,000 remained alive.

Nor did the end of World War II bring peace to Lithuania. The

incorporation of the Baltics into the Soviet Union brought an eco-
nomic and social upheaval, a guerrilla resistance struggle, and tens
of thousands of deportations to Siberia. Between 1940 and 1952,
historians say, as much as one-third of the Lithuanian population
was lost to massacre, war casualties, deportations, executions, and
emigration.

By 1991, when the Soviet Union collapsed, half a century under
two regimes had turned Lithuania into a cauldron seething with
competing martyrdoms, hatreds, and resentments. Nonetheless,
a brave cadre of leaders began to extend hands across cultures,
reach out across radically disparate views of history, search for
ways across seemingly unbridgeable divides. They followed in the
footsteps of people in many other countries — Germany, Poland,
South Africa, Chile, Argentina, and Haiti among them — who had
launched concerted public initiatives in the wake of conflict. Their
aim was to extend the bounds of empathy, to bind up wounds, and
even, perhaps, to prevent future genocides.

The more I learned about the Lithuanian endeavor, the more
intrigued I became. If the effort was fragile, struggling to take root
in less-than-hospitable soil, that vulnerability only increased my
interest. Maybe what was happening in the land of my ancestors
could help me make sense of Uncle Will's disclosure and of whatever it was that Steponas wanted to tell me. Maybe, I thought with
increasing excitement, my stay in this country would turn out to
be not only a journey of return but an encounter with the future.
Maybe a homeland could be a place to stretch myself, to grow.

As I immersed myself in Yiddish and walked through the streets
that once pulsed with Jewish life, I vowed, I would connect deeply
with my own heritage. But I would also look beyond that heritage.
Drawing on my background as a journalist, I arranged to meet the
people who were leading Lithuania's Holocaust education programs
and other efforts to engage with the past in order to build a better
future. I planned to seek out the chafing of differing worldviews, the

tectonic shifting of different histories. I would allow all the elements of my journey — my encounter with Yiddish, my questions about Uncle Will and Steponas, and Lithuania's collective engagement with its twentieth-century history — to collide.

All of this, I hoped, would help me answer a set of questions that had come to seem increasingly urgent. How do we judge the bystanders and the collaborators, the perpetrators and the rescuers — and ourselves? Where should my sympathies lie in this place where some had killed, some had resisted, and many had suffered? Could I honor my heritage without perpetuating the fears and hatreds of those who came before?

As societies around the globe struggle to recover from war-torn histories, the moral dilemmas of the Holocaust will not fade; in fact, they will always be with us. What I hoped to learn in the land of my ancestors could have relevance far beyond the borders of Lithuania. Observing how people in the land of my ancestors were seeking to open the minds and hearts of their fellow citizens might open my own mind, my own heart.

I tried to imagine how Uncle Will and Aunt Manya would respond upon learning that I had set up appointments with Lithuanians who were working to exhume the past, and that I had a hunch that Lithuania had something to teach about moving forward from tragedy.

They would be highly skeptical, I felt sure. Be careful whom you trust, they would warn, and whom you forgive. Lithuania's engagement with the past might be nothing more than a cynical ploy, a charade designed to impress the West. Keep an open mind, they might say, but don't let your brains fall out.

IN the damp courtyard of Vilnius University, the heavy Baltic sky darkened and the rain fell harder. The white-haired woman in the flowered dress stepped away from the dais, and the director of the Yiddish program, Mendy Cahan, took her place. Dressed in a white linen shirt and a black jacket with an antique cut, he looked as if he had stepped out of a bygone era as he combed his fingers through longish dark hair and then gripped the podium.

We were about to travel back in time, he said. "I invite you to taste the borscht, the herring, and the latkes. Taste this long tradition."

Guided by the last Yiddish speakers of the region, we would explore the streets of this beautiful city. We would plumb the riches of Yiddish poetry and prose. We would study the styles and structures of writing, meditation, and understanding that had flowered in this part of the world. "And we will touch on terrible destruction."

Suddenly a great black cawing thundercloud of crows filled the heavens. All of us — students and white-haired Bluma and the Vilnius residents who had come to welcome us — peered up into the drizzle. Harsh cries echoed off the stone walls. The director, too, looked up. He waited until the birds were gone and the sky was blank.

"You must listen to the silences as well as to the sounds," he said.

PART ONE

Mir zaynen do

(YIDDISH FOR "WE ARE HERE")

A tfile iz yeder shteyn,   Each stone is a prayer;
a nign yede vant . . .   a hymn every wall . . .

MOYSHE KULBAK, FROM THE POEM "VILNA"

Here, on This Spot

THE sky was a brilliant blue, with puffy clouds, as I hurried through the iron gates of Vilnius University. (Founded in 1579, it is among the oldest in Eastern Europe.) I crossed the cobblestoned courtyard where we'd gathered the evening before and climbed a steep staircase. High up under the eaves was a classroom just big enough for twenty students, with a blackboard and four rows of battered wooden tables. Through the open window, a light breeze carried the sounds of voices, honking horns, and clattering silverware from Pilies gatve (Lithuanian for "Castle Street"), the busy thoroughfare down below.

We students introduced ourselves. We were young, old, and in-between. Most were Jewish, but many were gentiles. Among us were two German teachers from Japan, a Soviet dissident now living in Israel, an American man whose dying father had begged him to study Yiddish. There were a Dutch librarian, a tango singer from Argentina, a white-haired Holocaust survivor from Australia, and a German psychiatrist who'd started learning Yiddish when her psychotic patient refused to communicate in any other tongue.

From our seats, we took stock of the instructor we would be facing for two hours every morning. Yitskhok Niborski was a distinguished scholar from a Yiddish institute in Paris. (Pronouncing his name, *YITS-khok*, with its guttural traffic jam of consonants, was a Yiddish lesson in itself.) He did not carry a whip like the *melamed,* the teacher in the one-room Jewish schoolhouse of old, but his rules were strict. In a voice as soft as his fluffy reddish beard, he announced that he would answer questions only about words that did not appear in our dictionaries — and having written more than one of the dictionaries himself, he knew exactly what was in them. Not a word of English or any language other than Yiddish would be permitted.

We read aloud a poem by Eliezer Schindler:

Undzer yidish,
undzer shprakh
farmogt dokh
oytsres gor a sakh . . .

Our Yiddish,
our language,
possesses such
a wealth of treasures . . .

Linguists traced the beginnings of Yiddish to the eleventh century, our teacher told us, when Jews began to migrate from France and Spain into what is now Germany, and from there eastward into the Slavic lands. Written in the Hebrew alphabet, Yiddish developed as a fusion tongue. Its base was German, with discrete, recognizable chunks of Hebrew, Slavic, and Romance languages stirred into the stew. The earliest works of Yiddish literature were directed at women. Among these was a sixteenth-century romance called the *Bova bukh,* whose name was thought to be the origin of the phrase *bubbe mayses,* meaning "old wives' tales." There was a seventeenth-century book of biblical stories known as *Tsena urena* (Come out and see). There were also popular booklets of Yiddish prayers, and the famous story book of folktales called the *Mayse bukh,* and a seventeenth-century memoir written by a wealthy woman named Gluckel of Hameln.

Our class, Niborski said, would concern itself not with these but with the modern era of Yiddish literature, which began in the mid-nineteenth century, when several important Jewish writers stopped writing in Hebrew and Russian and switched to Yiddish — not because they thought or dreamed in that language, but for a purely strategic reason: they wanted to reach the Jewish masses. Three writers rose to special prominence. Mendele Moykher Sforim (1835–1917), the earliest of the trio, became known as *der zeyde*, the grandfather of Yiddish literature. Y. L. Peretz (1852–1915) was called *der zun*, the son. And Sholem Aleichem (1859–1916) was dubbed *der eynikl*, the grandson. (A fourth writer, Avrom Reisen [1876–1953], though a man, was sometimes known as *di mame*, the mother.) All became enormously popular, and so did other Yiddish writers. The golden age of *mame-loshn* lasted for about a century. Between the mid-nineteenth century and World War II, some thirty thousand Yiddish books were published. After that, Yiddish literature declined, felled by emigration, by assimilation, by the embrace of Hebrew in Israel, and, of course, by Hitler.

All this information Niborski conveyed in Yiddish. Desperately I struggled to keep up. I'd been placed in this next-to-most-advanced class on the strength of the textbooks I'd plowed through and the translations of Yiddish fiction I'd published. Had a grievous error been made? I slid sidelong glances at my fellow students. It was hard to tell whether they were managing any better than I was.

We took turns reading aloud from a memoir by Kalman Marmor. At the end of the nineteenth century, a *yeshive* student stands in a classroom high above the courtyard of the Great Synagogue — right here in Vilnius, just blocks from *our* classroom high above the street. Using a copper coin, the young man scrapes a peephole in the frost that covers the pane. Down below, thousands of Jews have gathered for the funeral of a famous Talmudist. So large is the crowd, and so great its collective heat, that the ice begins to melt from the glass. Now, in our own attempt to see, we students scraped away at the difficult text. And as the young man in the story threw open the window and leaned out to survey the scene, we leaned out and surveyed it with him.

I kept a finger glued to the page. If my concentration faltered for a second, I was lost. At the end of class, as we received our homework assignments and closed our notebooks, I felt so drained I could barely stand.

Next came grammar class, taught by Khanan Bordin, a fortyish Latvian Jew who lived in Israel. Stocky and broad-shouldered, with close-cropped hair topped by a crocheted yarmulke, he leaned forward with his whole body in the effort to make us understand. He started at the beginning, with the alphabet, just like in the old days, when little Jewish boys began their lessons at the age of three. On their first day, the letters in their primers would be sprinkled with sugar, to show that learning was sweet.

Bordin's huge eyes played over our faces. To end the lesson, in a sonorous and elegiac voice he read us a poem by Moyshe Kulbak:

Gezen hob ikh yidishe verter vi fayerlekh kleyne, vi fayerlekh kleyne . . .

To my eyes, Yiddish words are like little fires, little fires,
Sparks extracted from black ore.
To me, Yiddish words are like pure-white doves, white doves,
Doves cooing and cooing in my heart.

Affection for Yiddish — Kulbak's, our teacher's, and our own — flooded the room. What could be more consoling? To be nestled in the bosom of this beloved language was a *mekhaye*, a joy.

ON the sunny steps of a university building, several dozen of us assembled for a walk through *Vilne fun amol*, the Jewish city of old, before the ghetto, before the destruction, when the Jewish community of Vilnius numbered in the tens of thousands, many times more than the current figure of only two thousand. Our guide was a tiny woman in her eighties with steel-gray hair and a proud bearing. Fanya (at her request, we addressed her by her first name) spoke in Yiddish, and one of the advanced students translated. She began in olden times, when, in the words of an evocative Yiddish memoir, Lithuania was a land of "dense forests laden with bewitching secrets . . . bears, wolves, foxes, and millions of birds of all sizes. The earliest inhabitants lived in small, widely dispersed hamlets. . . . If a stranger stumbled into such a hamlet, he could find his way to the next one only by following the far-off barking of a dog or the crowing of a rooster." By the Middle Ages, Lithuania had become the largest kingdom in Europe, extending from the Baltic Sea all the way to the Black Sea — fourteen hundred miles as the crow flies. In the sixteenth century, Lithuania and Poland united to form a Commonwealth that lasted until the end of the eighteenth century and then disappeared from the map, partitioned among the Russian, Prussian, and Austro-Hungarian empires. The northern region where we were now standing had gone to the czar.

Jews, who arrived in the thirteenth or fourteenth century, called the region by a name of their own — "Lite" (pronounced LEE-*teh*) — and referred to themselves as Litvaks. The city was known as "Vilne" (now more commonly "Vilna") among Jews, "Vilna" among Russians, "Wilno" among Poles, and "Vilnius" (pronounced VIL-*noose*) in Lithuanian (a language that, amazingly, shares some common traits with Sanskrit). In time, it became a jewel in the crown of European Jewish culture, so highly esteemed that it was known as "yerushalayim de lite," the Jerusalem of the North. What made the place so renowned was not the size of the Jewish population. Some sixty thousand Jews lived here before the war (a third of the total population), but Warsaw had five times more. Nor was this city's Jewish community the oldest in Europe. Jews arrived here later than in other regions. No, this city was a Jerusalem because it was without peer as a center of Jewish culture, learning, and political activity. By the eighteenth century it was a hub of religious scholarship, led by the scientifically oriented wing of Jewry known as the *misnagdim*. In the nineteenth century it became a focal point of the Jewish enlightenment movement known as the *haskalah*. At the turn of the twentieth century it emerged as a hotbed of Zionism, the movement that fought for an independent Jewish state and favored the Hebrew tongue. Simultaneously, it birthed the pan-European socialist organization known as the Bund, which promoted Yiddish language, the rights of Jewish workers, and Jewish national autonomy. With its distinctive architecture of narrow, twisting lanes spanned by dark stone archways, Jewish Vilna deserved its reputation as "the capital of Yiddishland."

For an encounter with Yiddish, Fanya said, there was no better place for us to be. She fixed us with a penetrating look. "We Litvaks have a very huge heritage to pass on."

The words hung in the air. We students exchanged glances. This was our task: to receive the heritage.

With her short, strong legs, Fanya set a fast pace down Universiteto gatve. In front of an outdoor café awash in pink petunias, she stopped and waited for us to catch up. This was Zydu gatve, Jewish Street, or in Yiddish, *Yidishe gas*, near where I was sharing an apartment with my roommate Minette. Zydu gatve: the name sent chills down my back. How, I wondered, could people bear to pass by such a sign every day, with its reminder of mass murder? When Fanya was young, she said, rabbis brushed up against fish peddlers here on this spot. The streets were full of Jews, and the nearby library — there, in that building — was packed with patrons. Fanya had been there, and now we were here with her. How close the past was, so close we could nearly touch it, and yet how absent, how utterly distant. The traces of the old life were all around us, in full view, yet without Fanya as our guide we would have missed them.

There was so much to tell, so little time. Fanya's words tumbled out as she marched us through the mostly empty streets, where elegant baroque facades — some lovingly restored, others blighted by crumbling plaster and teetering balconies — alternated with no-nonsense Soviet-era buildings, all square angles and straight lines. Here, she said, was the Yiddish theater, where the famous Vilna troupe performed; here Lipovsky performed, Tsirele Lipovsky, who was a schoolmate of Fanya's sister. Here operas were produced, including Verdi's *Aida* in Yiddish. Here was the conservatory; Gershteyn, the teacher, once stood on the *bine*, the theatrical stage, looking exactly like Y. L. Peretz. The Jewish technical institute, where Fanya's father was an instructor in electromechanics, stood here. Over there were the offices of the newspaper *Der tog*. Here was the Talmud Torah, the Hebrew school for orphans.

I struggled with my camera, my notebook, my pen. I tried not to stumble on curbs and cobblestones. Fanya's words came faster. We pressed closer. The city had never had a mainstream, a dominant culture. Russians, Poles, Lithuanians, and Jews had rubbed elbows. No one culture achieved supremacy. As one people among many, Jews had not been pressured to shed their ethnic identity. As a result, the Jewish community here was unusually cohesive.

All the Jews spoke Yiddish back then, even those who went to Polish or Hebrew schools. If a teacher caught you on the street speaking Polish or Russian or Lithuanian instead of Yiddish, you had to pay a fine. Here was the famous Romm Publishing House. That pink building was the *kinder-bibliotek*, the children's library. Here Marc Chagall himself came and mounted an exhibit in honor of Sholem Aleichem. Over there, on the day the high school term ended, the students would walk in a procession, and from that balcony people would toss flowers.

Here was Sophia Gurevitch's gymnasium, where Fanya went to high school. Here, at the end of this street, lived the *shtarke*, the tough guys of the Jewish underworld. The beggars had their own street, and each one rattled his own *pushke*, his collection box. You had to put a coin in each box; if you skipped one, the beggar would curse you heartily. Karpinovitch, the writer, used to come down here and record the curses. "An umbrella should open in your stomach."

After two hours, I tore myself away and peeled off down Traku gatve, heading for my dinner appointment. Hurrying through the neatly swept streets, I caressed with my eyes the textures of brick and mortar, granite and plaster on the walls around me. The lost civilization was so densely layered. In Moyshe Kulbak's long poem "Vilna," he addressed the city:

Du bist a tilim oysgeleygt fun leym un ayzn . . .

You are a psalm, spelled in clay and in iron . . .

I didn't want to leave. I wanted to remain in the lost world of Fanya's childhood, the realm where Yiddish words cooed like doves and three-year-old scholars tasted letters sprinkled with sugar. I wanted to hold on to those bygone days, the time when the world of *yidishkayt* was still robust and vibrant, not yet a collection of shattered remnants. I wanted to keep listening to tough, sturdy Fanya as she poured out her love for the Jewish Vilna of old. (The tour went on for *another* two hours, I heard later.)

But I couldn't stay. To answer the questions I'd carried with me across the Atlantic, I had to wrest myself out of this cozy world. I had a dinner appointment with Violeta, a Lithuanian chemist, and now here she was, waving at me from an outdoor restaurant across Pilies gatve — a middle-aged woman with a broad, fair face and blond hair, her solid body squeezed into a tight, fashionable jacket and matching skirt. We sat down at a checkered tablecloth and ordered a decidedly un-Jewish meal of shrimp salad, then raised our wine glasses.

"L'chaim!" I said, offering the traditional Jewish toast. To life!

"I sveikata!" she responded in Lithuanian. To health!

A friend back home had connected me to Violeta, who was neither Jewish nor a professional history-confronter. I'd written and asked if she would talk to me about how her country was exploring its twentieth-century history, especially the Jewish tragedy, and she'd responded warmly, eager to help. Now I told her a little about the walking tour with Fanya, then took out my notebook and the questions I'd prepared.

"Hmm, the Jewish tragedy," she said, chewing. "I will think about that."

I waited, pen poised, as she took several bites of salad, then put down her fork. The real problem, she blurted out, was her husband. Recently he had taken up with another woman. "He says he does not anymore love me, but he will not move from the house." She took a quick peek at my face, her eyes stricken. "His woman I believe is prostitute."

I moved my chair back an inch or two. Surely she knew that I hadn't come all the way to Vilnius to hear about her marriage. I glanced again at my list of questions. In my work as a journalist, this would have been the moment when I'd have tried to take control of the conversation, steering it firmly to the topic we were supposed to be talking about. But now I hesitated. The stream of marital woe flowed on. And on. I ate my salad, scraped up the last morsels. I buttered a roll, then another. I waited for her to finish.

At last she took a deep breath. "I will be okay," she said. "Maybe it is better this way."

Quickly I picked up my pen. Growing up in the Soviet era, I asked before she could say another word, what had she learned about what happened to the Jews during the war?

She squeezed her eyes shut and furrowed her brow. "We knew about Auschwitz and Buchenwald," she said. "We learned in school that many Jews died." As a child, with her parents, she had visited the Ninth Fort, an old garrison near the city of Kaunas (Kovno in Yiddish) where tens of thousands of Jews had been shot. "I knew it was Jews who were killed there."

"Did you learn about the pits in the forests" — I made a digging motion with my hand — "where the Jews were shot and buried? The mass graves?"

Yes, she had learned about this, too. She looked away, then met my eyes. "But . . . but no one taught us in school how many Lithuanians were sent to Siberia by the Soviet power, in 1940, in 1941, and also after the war. Pregnant women and children — they died in Siberia!" Her voice grew louder. Many Jews had been involved in the Soviet system, she said heatedly. Many Jews had worked in the KGB. It was they who had sent her people to Siberia.

Here it was, the tangle of resentments I had come to investigate. I looked around at the nearby tables where other city residents were talking and eating. Some of them, too, were no doubt seething with such feelings. I, too, was seething, I found. I didn't like hearing the massacre of my people placed side by side with the suffering of hers. I hated hearing my people blamed for the suffering of hers.

She sliced the air with her hand. "I want to say," she declared, "that the Lithuanian people through all of history loves other nationalities — Jewish people, Russian people, Polish people!" She paused. That is, she clarified, *normal* Lithuanian people loved others. The White Armbands — the local men who had helped round up Lithuania's Jews for execution in 1941 — were not normal people. "But," she said, "every nationality has some like this. Some abnormal people. Lithuanians as a whole should not be blamed for the actions of these few."

She fell silent, then spoke in a quieter voice. "My son's music teacher was a Jew," she said. "She was a fantastic woman."

After a moment she looked up, her face changed. She would like me to meet her mother, she said, who lived in her childhood town of Kedainiai. She would take me there. She named a weekend.

Kedainiai was not far from Siauliai, where Uncle Will and other members of my family had been confined in the ghetto. "I had family near there," I said. "In Siauliai."

"You have?" Violeta asked. "You have family in Siauliai?"

"I did," I said.

"They are there now?"

"No, they *were* there," I said.

"They are?"

"They *were*," I said, sharply this time.

She looked confused. "But they are not there now."

"No." Of *course* they aren't there now, I wanted to say, or scream. They were Jews! The Jews were killed or sent to concentration camps! Don't you understand?

Were we simply struggling over grammar? Past tense, present tense? Or was Violeta unaware of the sheer magnitude of the Jewish annihilation? Did she not know that only a tiny percentage of the prewar Jewish community had survived?

I looked at my watch and stood up. Violeta rose with me, and we shook hands.

"When we visit my mother," she said, "she will tell you how my family rescued Jews during the war."

My mouth opened in amazement.

She shifted her purse onto her shoulder. "My mother cannot believe what my husband, he is doing," she said. "His mother too does not believe. He . . ."

Frowning, I rushed off toward Rudninku gatve, where one of my fellow classmates and I were to meet for a study date. As I threaded my way through the winding streets, I struggled to grasp what I'd just heard: Violeta's complaints about her husband, her seeming lack of comprehension of the Jewish tragedy, her accusation that Jews had been responsible for sending her people to Siberia — and then the revelation that her family had rescued Jews! Who was this woman? And what kind of investigator was I? I'd let her prattle on far too long about her cheating husband and barely made a start on getting "the story." Yet, come to think of it, I'd taken in quite a lot — more, in fact, than I could sort out all at once.

Ringing the bell at my fellow student's apartment, I reminded myself that what had happened with Violeta was exactly what I had hoped for when I set out on my journey. My intent was to allow disparate voices to swirl around me. To lose my balance. To let the confusion build. To gather information in bits and pieces without trying to decide right away what it all meant. To recognize that the path ahead would be full of twists and turns, without trying to avoid the bumps and jolts. I *would* go to visit her mother, I decided.

My classmate and I settled ourselves on her balcony with our textbooks and our dictionaries. The sun was down, but gold still tinged the pastel facades, the church spires, the warm textures of the stone walls and the terra-cotta rooftops. Slowly, we made our way through a story by Zalman Shneour called "Misnagdishe kishkes brenen," "The Guts of the *Misnagdim* Are Burning." In a little town not far from Vilna, a bitter feud is raging between two groups of Jews. Members of the stern intellectual wing of observant Jewry known as *misnagdim* are wrangling with the ecstatic wing known as Hasidim. Mischievous young boys take up the battle, tormenting their foes by stealing pine branches off the roofs of their *sukkahs*, the ritual booths built for the Jewish harvest festival. Whooping and hollering, the boys use the stolen boughs to build an enormous bonfire. Sparks fly as they engage in a rowdy, uncontrollable dance and threaten to burn down the whole town.

My friend and I helped each other, taking turns looking up words we didn't know, until the stars came out and it grew too dark to see. Then I made my way home. Even late at night, it was safe to walk through the narrow lanes. My head was full to bursting. First the classes with their precious freight of linguistic lore. Then Fanya's walking tour through the Jerusalem of the North, whose star-studded sky was spread out above me. The hour with Violeta across the checkered tablecloth, with its surprises. And finally, the tale of the howling boys and their wild conflagration.

I reached the corner of Stikliu gatve (Glassworker Street, or in Yiddish, *Glezer gas*) and Zydu gatve. From my bag I extracted an old-fashioned iron key and opened the heavy door into the courtyard where my apartment was located. As I climbed to the second floor, the image of the boys and their bonfire was joined in my mind's eye by another fiery image — this one from Czeslaw Milosz, the Polish poet who grew up in Lithuania and went on to win the Nobel Prize. In an early poem, Milosz describes himself as a rapt child standing in the doorway of a blacksmith's workshop. Not only horseshoes are being forged, but also the poet's very being:

> At the entrance, my bare feet on the dirt floor,
> Here, gusts of heat; at my back, white clouds,
> I stare and stare. It seems I was called for this:
> To glorify things just because they are.

I, too, felt poised on a threshold.

In the morning, I sat at the kitchen table with my roommate Minette, a retired teacher from Los Angeles who had grown up speaking Yiddish with her parents, who were Holocaust survivors. Through the long, filmy curtains that covered the kitchen window, we could see creamy walls and boxes of ruby-red geraniums glowing in the sun. Between us sat a loaf of dense black bread. We sawed off thick slices and slathered them with butter, then ate them with chunks of cheese and small, knobby cucumbers. To my delight, the dairy products came from Rokiskis, where a hundred years ago my great-grandmother had managed a dairy farm belonging to a Polish landowner.

Minette's goal for the summer, she said, was to learn to read and write. I told her about my dinner with Violeta, about the other appointments I had set up, and about my plan to explore how Lithuanians were engaging with the Jewish past.

She pursed her mouth. "You mean how they're *not*?" she said.

On the way to class, we went to throw out our trash. Our landlord had scribbled a map on a scrap of paper, which brought us to an empty lot, its scuffed grass bisected by a dirt path that led to a row of rubbish bins. It was the former courtyard of the Great Synagogue, we realized with a start — the very place I'd read about in class, where the *yeshive* student had scraped the frost off the window in order to look down on the huge crowd of Jews assembled for a funeral. The Great Synagogue was bombed by the Nazis. After the war, its ruins lay open to the elements before being bulldozed by the Soviets. Now, where the temple had once stood, three slender birches leaned over a bust of Elijah ben Judah Solomon Zalman (1720–97), the Vilna "Gaon," or genius, who had been the towering spiritual leader of the intellectual *misnagdish* wing of Jewry.

Along Zydu gatve we stopped to decipher a granite plaque inscribed in Lithuanian and Yiddish. How extraordinary to stand on a city street and read an official sign in *mame-loshn*. Together we sounded out the words:

Oyf dem ort iz geshtanen der toyer fun der kleyner vilner geto . . .

"Here, on this spot," we translated together, "stood the gate of the Small Vilna Ghetto. Through it, between the 6th of September and the 29th of October, 1941, 11,000 Jews were driven to their deaths." Pictures spun through my head, and through Minette's, too, I felt sure as I saw her face go pale. Men, women, and children had been marched five miles out of town to the forest of Ponar. There they were ordered to undress before being shot. Their bodies fell into giant pits.

We were living in the Small Ghetto, then. Our building, with its charming courtyard and the view of the red geraniums, was once home to hundreds of doomed Jews.

AT 1:00 in the afternoon — 13:00, as they say in the Old World — I walked up the broad sidewalk of J. Basanaviciaus gatve, the grand avenue that was once home to numerous Jewish institutions, including YIVO, the center of research and scholarship that moved to New York in 1940. I was on my way to see Irena Veisaite, a Jewish woman who was at the heart of Lithuania's effort to confront the past. Everyone had told me I had to meet her. She was a controversial figure. "A saint," said some. "Universally hated," said others. But everyone agreed: "You must meet with Veisaite." (Her name was pronounced *veh-SIGH-teh*. In the Lithuanian and Russian manner, people here often referred to women by their last names alone. At the root of "Veisaite" was the Jewish surname "Veis," or "Weiss." Single women's names end in *aite, yte, ute,* or *iute,* married women's in *iene.* Irena had made the unusual choice of keeping her maiden name through two marriages.)

I passed through iron gates into a crumbling courtyard and climbed up four flights to a flat on the top floor. The woman who greeted me at the door, with straight dark hair in a simple cut, looked younger than her seventy-six years. Her calm, watchful expression lent her a regal air as she ushered me into a parlor crowded with heavy pieces of furniture, paintings, photographs, and honorary plaques.

We began by discussing the reasons behind the wartime massacre. Why had Lithuania exploded into genocide? Perhaps there could never be a full explanation. Yet historians agreed that several factors helped to pave the way.

For centuries, I knew, Jews and their non-Jewish neighbors had coexisted relatively peaceably in Lithuania. On the brink of World War II, Jews made up one-third of the population in Lithuanian cities and about one-half in small towns. But if there were few outbreaks of violence against Jews, nonetheless relations between the two cultures were not particularly warm. When World War II broke out, the tensions that had been simmering for centuries helped set the stage for carnage.

Among the specific precipitating events of the prewar period, Veisaite named the Molotov-Ribbentrop Pact. In August 1939, Nazi Germany and the USSR signed a secret agreement allowing the Soviet Union to annex Lithuania, Latvia, and Estonia. (The three

Baltic states, which had been part of czarist Russia throughout the nineteenth century, had been independent since the end of World War I.) "You will hear about the Molotov-Ribbentrop Pact many times during your visit here," she predicted, and this would turn out to be true.

Under the terms of the pact, the tanks of the Red Army rolled onto Lithuanian territory in 1940. Some Lithuanians supported this move, hoping that Soviet military power would provide a bulwark against German invasion. Others were enraged. Lithuanian notions of a stolen destiny had begun to take root centuries before and had intensified during the years of the Lithuanian-Polish Commonwealth, when Lithuanian peasants had worked as virtual serfs on the vast estates owned by Polish aristocrats. Resentment grew during the suppression of Lithuanian culture under the czar during the nineteenth century. By czarist edict, for example, parents were forbidden to teach their children to read Lithuanian. The Soviet tanks were the latest in a series of blows to Lithuanian independence.

It wasn't just tanks. Along with the army came a wholesale Sovietization of Lithuanian society. In the space of a single year, Jewish and non-Jewish social institutions alike were turned upside down or disbanded. New government institutions were created. Elections were held, and new leaders took control at every level. The total disruption of civil society, Veisaite said, created fertile conditions for the lawless and violent behavior that was to break out when the German invasion came.

Few Jews had served in the previous Lithuanian government. But under the new Soviet order, Jews occupied more administrative posts than before, and this, Veisaite said, was a second precipitating factor. Although Jewish government officials were a minority, in the eyes of non-Jews they stood out.

A third factor, Veisaite said, was the Nazi propaganda that flooded the region. The propaganda promoted the notion that Jews were Communists, Communists were Jews, and Jews were to blame for the Soviet takeover. In fact, only a small fraction of Jews were Communists. But the presence of Jews within the Communist Party was easily exploited. "I'm absolutely sure the Holocaust would never have happened the way it did here," Veisaite said, "if this terrible propaganda hadn't seemed so convincing."

Massive Soviet deportations to Siberia were the final and perhaps the most decisive factor that laid the groundwork for the massacre, Veisaite said. Tens of thousands of people — Jews along with non-Jews — were sent into exile. A knock at the door, and entire families — men, women, and children — were ordered to pack what they could carry, herded onto freight trains, and resettled in the east. "It was a shock to everybody," Veisaite said, "the first experience of a totalitarian regime." For this, fingers of blame were pointed at Jewish Communists.

As it became clear that Lithuania was trapped between the Nazis and the Soviets and the prospect of German invasion loomed, Jews and non-Jews found themselves in very different situations. Nazi rule was clearly a grave threat to Jewish survival. Yet for many non-Jews, Soviet rule appeared the greater danger.

In June 1941, Germany abrogated the Molotov-Ribbentrop Pact of 1939 and pushed into Lithuania with planes, tanks, and troops. As the Red Army retreated, an orgy of bloodshed broke out. Assisted by Lithuanian locals, special German forces — the Einsatzgruppen — swept through the countryside in search of Communists and Jews. For the most part Lithuania's Jews were not shipped off to distant camps. Instead, they were rounded up and marched into the woods to their deaths, or herded into urban ghettos, where they were confined under extreme conditions of deprivation and terror.

Veisaite became one of the ghetto residents. "When the Germans came in 1941," she said, " — I mean the Nazis; I don't like to use the word 'German' in such a case, as one can never blame an entire nation — " her mother was ill and in the hospital; a few days later she was taken away to prison, never to be seen again. Veisaite's father had earlier divorced her mother and left the country. At thirteen years old, she was without parents. She entered the Kovno ghetto with her aunt and her grandparents.

The invaders made it clear to the population at large that helping Jews was strictly forbidden and would be severely punished, even with death. As the columns of doomed Jews filed by on the way to ghettos or forests, most Lithuanians peeked from behind their curtains or turned away. Some helped the Gestapo to hunt down Jews and took the vodka or tobacco offered as a reward. Some moved into the houses of the murdered Jews, appropriated their furniture, wore their clothing.

Yet some Lithuanians took a different path. Some helped their Jewish neighbors by hiding their valuables and making them available when they were needed to pay for food or life-saving favors. Some provided Jews with false documents and helped them escape from the ghettos. Some hid and fed Jews in barns or back rooms or specially constructed hiding places, sometimes for long periods, sometimes at considerable expense. Some saved Jewish books from the Nazi fires. Some became couriers who visited the ghettos to relay messages.

After Veisaite had lived in the ghetto for two and a half years, gentile friends managed to come to her rescue. One evening, carrying false papers, she mingled with a work brigade as it exited the ghetto gate. Once outside, she was spirited away to Vilnius, where she moved from house to house, one step ahead of the Gestapo. In one household, a visitor arrived carrying a book about Van Gogh. Veisaite, who had been introduced as an orphan from the countryside, forgot herself. "Oh, how wonderful!" she exclaimed. "I like Van Gogh so much!" The visitor was suspicious. Who was this girl from the country who knew about Van Gogh? Veisaite was quickly packed off to another hiding place, but soon the Gestapo showed up there, and she had to move again. Finally, she was taken in by the widow of a Lithuanian general with six children. This woman, a gentile, Veisaite came to refer to as her second mother. "She was an absolutely outstanding person."

She leaned forward in her chair and fixed me with forceful gaze. "To kill thousands of people," she said, "you need only several people with guns, and these people don't risk anything except their souls. But to save one person, you need the tremendous courage of many people. All the rescuers were saints."

By the time Veisaite went into hiding, most of the Jews of Lithuania were dead. In 1944, as the Germans retreated from Lithuania, they emptied the ghettos and transported the remaining residents to concentration camps outside the country. There, most perished.

When the war ended, the Allies divided Europe into spheres of influence based on whose army had ended up where. Once again, the Baltic lands came under Soviet rule. Among many non-Jews, the years *after* the war were remembered as being far more difficult than the years of the Nazi occupation. "De-Nazification" proceeded apace. Some fifty thousand Lithuanians were put on trial and convicted of collaboration with the German occupation and crimes against the Soviet Union. The deportations to Siberia began again on a massive scale. From deep in the forests, armed Lithuanian guerrillas launched forays against Soviet power.

A postwar Jewish community began to take shape, a shard of its former vibrant self. Some Jews who had fled east into the Soviet Union crept back. Some emerged from hiding places in the cities and the countryside. A small number of concentration camp survivors returned. And some Jews moved to Lithuania from other parts of the Soviet Union.

At first, the survivors were permitted to honor their murdered brethren with numerous rituals. Monuments commemorating the perished were built at the massacre sites in the forests, and a Jewish museum opened in Vilnius. But it was not long before Soviet policy toward Jews underwent a radical change. As Stalin targeted Jews through a nationwide campaign against "cosmopolitans," the plaques at the mass-murder sites were altered so that they no longer referred to the dead as Jews but instead as "victims of fascism" or "innocent Soviet citizens." The museum in Vilnius closed down. The reality of the Holocaust went underground.

At that point, Veisaite said, opportunities for dialogue about the Holocaust were few. The handful of Jews who had survived the war "were full of outrage and hatred," and for their part, non-Jewish Lithuanians "insisted first of all it was not they who had killed the Jews, and second of all, even if it was, the killings were justified" because — they claimed — the Jews had betrayed *them* in 1940 by supporting the Soviet takeover. During this period, Soviet policies allowed neither Jews nor Lithuanians to speak in their own voice. "There was no possibility to take up the Jewish question — but of course it was always inside somewhere."

Inside everyone? I asked. Or just inside Jews?

For a moment she was silent. "I don't know," she said finally. Some scholars maintained that between the traumatic disruption of society and the official suppression of Jewish culture, it was possible that the Holocaust did not exist in Lithuania's collective memory. "I would say it did exist," Veisaite said. "Everybody knew. But it was not vivid."

Lithuania was not the only place that buried a history that couldn't be faced, I pointed out. In Western Europe and the United States, just as in Lithuania, countless ceremonies and other rituals of commemoration took place immediately after the war. But as the 1950s began, just as in Lithuania, a "latency period" took hold. A decade went by before the West found itself ready to hold up the facts of the Holocaust for public examination.

In Lithuania, Veisaite said, the process of truly facing the past began in earnest only in the late 1980s. The truth about what had happened in Lithuania was there all along — somewhere. The memories were always there. With the end of the Soviet era, buried truths were unearthed, and denial began to give way to recognition.

Little by little, the story of the war years began to be described in a new way. Scholars and others began to assert openly that while it was Germans who organized the destruction of the Jews, in region after region it was Lithuanian individuals who helped by rounding them up, guarding them, selecting the mass-murder sites, and readying the pits. Only after this "preparatory work" had been completed did German officers arrive to oversee the massacres themselves.

It was not only a question of who actually pulled the triggers. The shooters themselves may have been relatively few in number, but the actions and inactions of the Lithuanian population at large, the "supporting cast," played a critical role, and so did the failure of political leaders and clergy to oppose the massacres. The German occupation as a whole was administered mostly by local people.

"Germans comprised only 3.3 percent of the occupation administrative staff," one prominent historian concluded in an essay I read later. The rest of the staff, well over 90 percent, were Lithuanians. The rules that were put forward by the occupation — requiring Jews to wear yellow stars on their clothing, to walk in the street rather than on the sidewalk, to turn over their property, to move into sealed ghettos — were implemented for the most part by Lithuanians, people who had lived side by side with Jews as neighbors.

Among the influential voices in the new discourse was Saulius Suziedelis, a Lithuanian American historian, who offered guidance as to how Lithuanians should respond to the truths that were emerging into the light of day. Accepting a terrible past, he wrote, was "not the same as accepting collective guilt, any more than contemporary Americans are responsible for slavery." But "the legacies of such crimes, the historical burdens, remain." And so, "the only way for Lithuanians to lighten the load of the difficult history of 1941 is to embrace it."

One of the first acts of the newly independent government, Veisaite told me, was to rebuild the steps leading to the Palace of Trade Unions in downtown Vilnius. Just after World War II, gravestones from the old Jewish cemetery had been used to build these steps. Now the old stones were removed. The new government also replaced the plaques at the mass-murder sites that dotted the countryside. The new plaques — like those that had been installed right after the war and later altered — made clear that the victims were mainly Jews. The killers, too, were accurately described, as "Hitlerists and their local helpers." And in the same spirit, Lithuania's president, Algirdas Brazauskas, visited the Knesset, the Israeli parliament, in 1995 to deliver a formal apology for Lithuanian collaboration with the Nazis.

Veisaite went to the kitchen and returned with a tray, black with pink and green flowers. She poured tea into delicate glasses, offered sugar and cookies.

People like her, she said, had a special role to play in Lithuania's effort to embrace the burden of a difficult history. She was a person with two identities, she said — Jewish and Lithuanian. "My first mother, my biological mother, was an absolutely wonderful person. I adored her," she said, "and I miss her to this day. My second mother, my Lithuanian mother, was also outstanding. I loved her very much, too. My whole family was killed. I was saved. I believe my experience gives me the right to build bridges of mutual understanding, to promote the dialogue that can help us overcome the painful past."

Understanding the past, Veisaite stressed, was not a "Jewish project." In the effort to create a civil society, to foster democracy, it was equally important for Jews and non-Jews alike. "As long as you are hiding the truth, as long as you fail to come to terms with your past," she said, "you cannot build your future."

Jews themselves, she believed, needed to work harder to reach out to their non-Jewish fellow citizens. She did not mean to suggest undervaluing what had happened during the Holocaust. "Of course, the Holocaust was unique," she said. "A civilized country — Germany — made an industry out of mass murder." As she knew deeply from what she herself had lived through, "it was horrible, horrible. But we are not the only ones. There have been other genocides."

Her approach took root during her last visit with her biological mother in 1941, she said. She went to her mother's hospital room, bringing clothes, and found her alone — the guard was flirting with the nurses. As she said good-bye, her mother offered this counsel: "Always live with the truth. Never take revenge."

Veisaite never saw her mother again. Ever since, she'd sought to live by her creed. "I try to understand people, to love people," she said. "I believe that hatred destroys you, destroys the world. You should not live with this feeling."

Recently, she said, a Holocaust survivor had visited Lithuania from Israel and traveled around the country speaking at high schools. At one lecture, a student came up to the old man in tears. "My grandfather was a killer of Jews," the student said. "What should I do?" The survivor embraced and kissed him, saying, "It is enough for you to understand."

This young man would remember that his grandfather was a killer, Veisaite said, but he would also remember the goodness of the survivor, and he would live up to that goodness in his own way.

Veisaite was encouraged by the efforts of Lithuanian scholars, some government agencies, and nonprofit organizations. Yet she acknowledged that public opinion had been slow to change. Age-old prejudices had by no means been stamped out in her country, she said. "Of course there is still anti-Semitism here — just as some Jews, unfortunately, are also very biased. Of course everyone sees his own suffering first of all. This doesn't contribute to an easy dialogue." Festering conflicts flared up again and again — over what should be done with the Jewish property seized during the Nazi and Soviet eras, over who should be defined as a war criminal and who should be prosecuted, over whether Nazi and Soviet collaborators should be legally rehabilitated. Jewish cemeteries and community buildings were desecrated, and prejudice exploded on Internet sites. At times the forces of hatred rose up with such fury that they seemed to overwhelm the fragile forces of tolerance.

Not long before, for example, "an appalling series of anti-Semitic articles" had appeared in a Vilnius newspaper. Yet in response, many organizations and individuals spoke up in protest, which Veisaite considered a cause for optimism. "This," she said, "is a very big achievement."

In May 2004, when Lithuania joined the European Union, Veisaite represented her country at an outdoor ceremony in Berlin. Standing at the Brandenburg Gate, she reminded members of the crowd that they were gathered not far from the Reichstag, where as a child she had been condemned to die. Against all odds, she had survived, and so had her deep feeling for her native land. "Today," she told the assembly, "I speak proudly in the name of my country."

It was late afternoon when I left Veisaite's apartment and turned onto noisy Pylimo gatve, Ramparts Street, with its crush of cars and trolleys. Friday, the end of the work week: people were on their way home. In my bag, my notebook was full of Veisaite's words — words I found astonishing. "Never seek revenge." "Hatred destroys you, destroys the world." And the Holocaust survivor's message to the weeping student: "It is enough for you to understand."

People like Veisaite, people who had lived through terrible times, had a right to their hatreds, I believed. Yet she had chosen to use her authority, garnered at enormous cost, to preach dialogue and understanding. As she prodded Jews and non-Jews to follow her lead, I could see both why she would be considered a saint and why she would be hated.

During my visit, I would not speak with Veisaite again. Yet her name would come up repeatedly, and I would think of her often. As I stepped through new doorways, she would be my guide.

THE doorway I was about to step through now was that of a synagogue — the only one remaining in Vilnius. Before the war, the city had been home to 110 synagogues. The Chor Shul, the choral synagogue, had survived the Nazi era because it had been used as a warehouse. We Yiddish students had been invited to attend the Friday-night service by the president of Vilnius's Jewish community, Shimon Alperovitch, a tall, hulking giant of a man with bushy white eyebrows.

As I approached the entrance, three old men came near.

"Shabes — do?" I asked in my primitive Yiddish — the service would be here?

They plucked at my arm with gnarled hands, their faces pinched with disapproval. "Nisht keyn tash," they said. According to Orthodox custom, a woman was not permitted to carry a *tash*, a purse, into the *shul*.

I understood and apologized. I would leave my bag — the one full of Veisaite's words — *bay mir*, at home.

"Nayntsn draysik," said one of the three, assuaged — the service would begin at 19:30 — that is, 7:30 p.m.

On my way to my apartment to drop off the bag, I thought of my grandfather, Uncle Will's brother, and of his limited patience for pious men like these. When my mother was small, he taught her to stand up in front of company and sing a song that poked fun at the Hasidic religious leaders known as *rebbes*, whom his own father, my great-grandfather Dovid-Mikhl, had greatly revered:

Der rebbe tut vunder,
hob ikh aleyn gezen . . .

The *rebbe* works wonders —
I've seen it myself.

Miracles and wonders!
He jumps in the water —
and comes out wet!

He causes the blind man to walk
And the deaf man to see. . . .

"Little Grandpa," we called him. He was small and pink and had a high-pitched voice. When he helped in the kitchen, he wore an apron, a woman's apron with a frilly hem, tied around his waist. He liked to press his scratchy white whiskers against my cheek and croon to me in a delighted falsetto: "Hee-hee-hee."

About the Old Country he said only the bare minimum: that his father, Dovid-Mikhl, had sired many children but had done nothing to support them. That his mother, Asne, had single-handedly managed the dairy farm they leased while also caring for the ever-expanding brood. That after she died of tuberculosis at the age of forty-one, the children had been parceled out among the relatives. My grandfather, then eight years old, was sent off with his brother Shaya (pronounced SHY-*eh*) to live with an aunt. "We had to sleep with the animals in the stable," my grandfather said bitterly. Curiously, my cousins told me that when Shaya told the same story, he phrased it differently. "We *got* to sleep with the animals," he said — as if the beasts were welcome bedfellows.

In 1911, when my grandfather arrived in New York as a nineteen-year-old draft dodger, he was briefly a revolutionary, running up and down the stairs of tenement buildings clutching handfuls of leaflets. He liked to tell about the time a man opened the door and hollered, "Get lost, you little Jew bastard, or I'll break your legs!" My grandfather's eyes would twinkle. "How that fellow knew I was a Jew," he would say in his pungent Yiddish accent, "I will never know."

My grandfather worked hard at the drugstore he acquired, keeping it open for business six days a week, including on the Sabbath. In the evenings, like his father before him, he devoted himself to his studies. But the texts my grandfather pored over were not the ancient sacred tomes of the Jewish faith. Instead, he favored a biography of Abraham Lincoln, the essays of Mark Twain, and liberal magazines such as *The Nation* and *The New Republic*.

He hated rabbis along with racism and Republicans. No doubt he would have scoffed at the myths I was hearing here in Vilnius about the Gaon, the spiritual "genius" who had been so revered by generations of Jews in this city. Could the Gaon *really* write with both hands, different sentences at the same time? Unlikely. Had he *really* memorized the *entire* Talmud by the age of four? Doubtful. My grandfather rejected the strictures of orthodoxy with such passion that he could be cruel. Every Yom Kippur he made a point of calling Uncle Will, his brother, on the telephone, precisely because he knew that no observant Jew would pick up the receiver on this most holy day.

Near the end of his life, barely moving, my grandfather sat in an armchair in his apartment in Brooklyn or in a lawn chair in our backyard on Long Island. He looked to me like a relic brought up from the deep. One day he asked to be taken to a Friday-night service. He came home early. "The rabbi was a *nudnik*," he said. (According to the early-twentieth-century poet Morris Rosenfeld, a *nudnik* is "a man whose purpose in life is to bore the rest of humanity.")

My mother inherited Little Grandpa's aversion to religious services, and although my father was raised in a different faith, as a nominal Christian who intermittently attended whichever Protestant church was closest at hand, the two of them ended up in pretty much the same place. Although my mother described herself as Jewish and my father described himself as "not," both were ardent secularists, and thus my "mixed" background was in some ways not so mixed. I had my moments of embarrassment as a child — Sunday mornings, for example, when little girls on my block emerged from their doorways wearing stiff crinolines, white gloves, and polished shoes while I cowered inside in my play clothes — but in time I came to cherish my secular upbringing. It was not simply a rejection of religion, an absence of creed, but a system of belief in its own right, one that affirmed the worthiness of human beings and valued the never-ending struggle for justice and equality. Throughout my childhood, I saw my parents gracefully adopting customs and rituals from each other's cultures. No doubt the boundary-crossing they modeled was among the factors that propelled me across the Atlantic for, among other things, an investigation of efforts toward tolerance.

The sky was shading from white to lilac as once again I approached the entrance to the Chor Shul, this time without my purse. Until recently, even this one remaining synagogue had been closed because of a bitter dispute within Vilnius's tiny Jewish community. Tonight it was to open for a trial run. Shimon Alperovitch wanted all of us Yiddish students to be there. "A show there will be," he promised.

Ten years earlier, in his role as president of the Jewish community, Alperovitch had invited an American rabbi to move to Vilnius and lead services at the Chor Shul. His pick was not just any rabbi, but one from within the ranks of Chabad, the well-endowed Hasidic sect with branches all over the world. It was a strange choice. Historically, Hasidim had not been welcome in Vilna. In the eighteenth century, in fact, the venerable Gaon had been so offended by these fervent dancing-and-singing Jews that he had sought to excommunicate them and drive them out of the city.

At first, when the American rabbi arrived and began holding forth from the pulpit, Alperovitch was pleased. Although, like most of the city's Jews, Alperovitch himself was a secularist whose views probably paralleled those of my grandfather, he liked having the Chor Shul in use. The ranks of the community had been thinned and thinned again during the Soviet era by periodic waves of emigration to Israel and the United States. The Jews' common language was no longer Yiddish; nearly all community activities were conducted in Russian. The new rabbi helped to further the Jewish revival that had begun to blossom with the fall of the Soviet Union. He set up a kosher kitchen that distributed meals to the needy, started a school and a youth group. Alperovitch's work proceeded, too. The Jewish museum, a Jewish high school, a quarterly newspaper, clubs and social services moved ahead.

For a decade, the two men got along without any serious difficulties. But when the Lithuanian parliament took up the issue of restitution — the return of religious property that had been appropriated from the Jewish and Catholic communities by the Nazi and Soviet regimes — problems arose. It was not difficult to figure out how to return the Catholic property: the church had a clear and orderly chain of command, from the pope on down. But the Jewish religion had no such hierarchy. One rabbi was equal to another. Even the word "Jew" meant not a worshipper but a member of a people, a culture. If restitution was owed to the Jewish community, to whom should it flow? Shimon Alperovitch could trace his roots in the area back through the generations. He was a genuine Litvak in the tradition of the Gaon, as well as a Holocaust survivor and a leader of the Jewish revival on both the cultural and the political front. The American rabbi was a newcomer. But there was no denying that the rabbi was an ordained religious leader, qualified to conduct services at the synagogue. Alperovitch was not.

Suddenly, what went on in the Chor Shul mattered a great deal to the future of the community as a whole. Who should get the property? And who should decide? The conflict escalated. Fistfights broke out between the two factions. The police were called. "The fewer Jews, the more problems," Alperovitch sighed. He recalled the old joke about the solitary Robinson Crusoe living out his life on a desert island. Why does he build two synagogues? "In this one I pray, and in that one I will not set my foot."

In keeping with Orthodox custom, we women were required to sit apart, high up in the balcony, near the ornate ceiling. My fellow students and I leaned over the railing. Down below, a row of security guards in light-blue shirts lined the walls. The rabbi stood facing the congregation. On one side of the aisle sat several dozen of his supporters; on the other sat twenty of Alperovitch's. We could see our male classmates milling in the back, trying to avoid taking sides by not sitting down at all. As the Hebrew prayers began, welcoming the Sabbath bride, the men on the rabbi's side chorused along loudly in the Hasidic manner, as my great-grandfather Dovid-Mikhl would have done, while those on the other side held their hands over their ears to show their disapproval of such vulgar behavior.

All at once the lights went off. A man from Alperovitch's side had flicked the switch. Now he was slamming down the blinds with a loud clatter. A man from the rabbi's side ran over and began to pull them back up, one by one. The guards closed in. But the service went on. The hearty chanting continued, and so did the ear-covering.

Afterwards, we women clustered around the rabbi's glossy-haired wife, his *rebbetsin*, who was eager to articulate her view of the dispute. "Shimon Alperovitch doesn't care about the *shul*, he just wants the restitution," she said heatedly. "But we're the ones who've been doing the work all these years."

We students exchanged uneasy glances. I thought of my notebook full of Irena Veisaite's words about love, dialogue, and understanding. How difficult it all seemed.

Following the service we students made our way down Pylimo gatve to the Jewish community building, a massive stone structure that had been the *Tarbut shule*, the Hebrew-language high school, before the war. A giant iron-studded door swung open and we climbed a grand stone staircase. In a spacious hall, tables were spread with snowy cloths for the weekly *shabes tish*, the Sabbath meal. We greeted one another with the distinctive Yiddish inflection, "gut sha-a-abes, gut sha-a-abes." Bottles of wine, vodka, and juice sparkled in the candlelight. A hundred of us — summer students and local residents alike — raised our glasses, and two enormous braided challah breads made their way from hand to hand, followed by platters of fruit and nuts, cheese and steaming buckwheat groats and mushrooms and herring. Far into the night, we sang endless *nigunim*, old melodies by turns mournful and full of joy.

That night in bed, in my flat in the Small Ghetto, the notes of those age-old *nigunim* were still sounding in my ears as Uncle Will came vividly to mind. I remembered the time, some fifteen years ago, when my mother and I had shown up in his New York apartment with a tape recorder. My aunt and uncle brought out old maps and photos, and my mother and I posed questions that seemed so basic, so necessary, it was almost beyond belief that they had never been asked before.

When we came home, I played and replayed the tape. I listened to the clatter of spoons and teacups, my mother's soft alto, Uncle Will and Aunt Manya interrupting each other with their Old World accents. I wrote down all the words I could make out, and as I typed them up they seemed to arrange themselves into a poem with its own rhythm, a *nign* of sorts:

who was *bubbe blumtse*
your father's mother's mother
and this one was your mother
my mother yes
what was her name
sarah
soreh
soreh

and when did your father die
1924
i was seven
and did your mother ever remarry
no
she died in a concentration camp
and what was her name
soreh
soreh

my father had eight children
he had nine children
he had ten children
one died
one boy
we counted ten
ten

taybe
soreh
rikle
lube
menakhem mendel
aron
pinkhas
yankl
shaya
and then later
me
he had ten
one died, i don't know if you know

i'll nibble on that
decaffeinated
decaffeinated
herbal tea
reba was the first cousin to your father
reba's father and your father's mother
were sister and brother
asne's brother
was the father of *reba*
asne's brother
no *asne*'s mother's brother
asne's mother's brother was married to *reba*'s mother
reba's father
no no no
asne's mother was married to *reba*'s father
asne's mother
brother and sister
his mother
his brother
his sister
asne's mother's brother
was *reba*'s father
okay
okay
okay

1930 i moved to shavl
what is shavl
a city in lithuania
your tea
i baked
i got home late today
another cup of coffee
some candy
some more tea
thank you no
in '41 the war broke out
the war broke out
and so they took
who did
the germans
8,000 were killed immediately
5,000 went into the ghetto

my mother
we were hiding her
1943
november
a big *aktsye*
aaah
no no no
catching people
roundup
roundup
roundup
children
i hided
i hid
what is the past of hiding
i hid my mother
two girls
i put them in the attic
i put a cupboard over it
a door
they used to come into a house

a blanket
stabbing into it
a child in there
the two girls are now in israel
so they survived
yes

but in '44
in '44 they took us to germany
i couldn't
my mother
so she was
she went with you
but we were separated
in july '44
she was in stutthof
and where were you
they took the men to dachau
thank you no
so i didn't see her anymore
and don't you ever wonder how. . . .

In the years since, the tape had haunted me with its jumble of genealogy and ghetto, dessert and Dachau, and the heartbreaking way Uncle Will's words trailed off as his mother went up in smoke. But now I had learned that what Uncle Will had told us that evening was only a piece of the story. Not until years later, as I prepared to visit the Old World, had he revealed another piece.

Tomorrow I would begin my investigation. I would meet with a man who carried a complex Holocaust legacy of his own. I would tell him what I knew about Uncle Will, and I would try to find out more.

The Nazi Era

RAIN clouds were gathering overhead as I shook hands with Emil on the corner in front of my apartment. At the outdoor café with the pink petunias, we sat down in teetering chairs across a tiny wrought-iron table. Cautiously we looked each other over. He was about thirty years old, with a stern brow and a tense jaw line, his collarbones protruding sharply from beneath a pale silken shirt. He carried a slender briefcase. Someone at the Holocaust Museum back home in Washington had suggested that he might be able to help me with archival research. In my correspondence with Emil, I'd conveyed the bare outlines of what Uncle Will had said to me in his New York apartment. Now he fixed his haunted green eyes on my face as I told him what I knew so far and what I wanted to find out.

Uncle Will, I said, was my grandfather's much younger half brother. I'd known him all my life. He and Aunt Manya had met at a displaced persons camp near Munich, he a survivor of Dachau and she of Auschwitz. They had immigrated to America just before I was born. I loved listening to the stories he told about my infancy. "Your parents were so poor," he'd say, "that they couldn't afford a crib. They put you to sleep in a dresser drawer." Then he would laugh, his high-pitched "hee-hee-hee" just like my grandfather's. He worked as a foreman in a ballpoint pen factory, and his pockets were always full of cheap pens for us kids. In our tiny extended family, he was one of my favorites.

But although Uncle Will and Aunt Manya lived not far away, we didn't see them often. Unlike the avidly secular wing of the family headed by my grandfather, they and their two sons observed the Sabbath and all the Jewish holidays and ate only kosher food. The difference in religious practice created a divide, and there were other tensions, too, which I sensed only dimly. A few stories about the Old Country, as elemental as fairy tales, made their way around the family, but face-to-face conversation about those days was minimal. Like many families in the postwar years, ours seemed afraid to touch the past. As the years went by, the silence hardened. The one time that my mother and I had visited Uncle Will and Aunt Manya with a tape recorder had been a sharp departure from the norm.

But when my mother died, my days of holding history at arm's length were over. I needed to touch the past. Soon after I began to study Yiddish, remembering that my aunt and uncle spoke *mameloshn* to each other at home, I wrote them a halting letter in the alphabet I was just starting to master. Delighted, they wrote back right away, and a new friendship blossomed.

On the day when I arrived in their apartment with the maps of Rokiskis and Siauliai just before my trip, the table in the dining alcove was loaded with a lavish dairy lunch — bagels, rolls, whitefish, smoked salmon, salad, olives, and pickles. As we ate, I savored my uncle's dear, familiar features, my aunt's brisk, tart demeanor, and the flavor of their Old World vowels. Uncle Will told the story about seeing me sleeping in the dresser drawer again, and we smiled and laughed.

When I spread out my maps, the two of them leaned in eagerly. They were excited about my trip. Nonetheless, I also sensed their uneasiness. After Uncle Will retired, they had traveled to Israel, to Spain, to Alaska, but never back to the land of their youth. For many years, the Iron Curtain had presented an impenetrable barrier, but even after the Soviet Union collapsed and it became possible to return, they'd chosen not to. Seeing Uncle Will's furrowed brow as he strained to remember the exact location of his house and his school, I felt as if he was cracking open a door that had been kept tightly locked for many a year.

It was after Uncle Will pointed to the site of his childhood home on the map that he surprised me by handing me the wrinkled page from his pocket.

The photocopied sheet, which had been folded and refolded, was a journalist's account of a single terrible day in the Shavl ghetto. On November 5, 1943, a *kinder-aktsye*, a roundup of children, had occurred there. Soldiers with snarling dogs and bayonets had rampaged through the narrow streets, ripping apart walls and floors in the search for every last child. A Jewish policeman stood at the ghetto gate as the sons and daughters of the ghetto — hundreds of them — were shoved into trucks and driven away, never to be seen again.

I shook my head. "Terrible," I said. I handed the page back.

My uncle sat silently, his head bowed.

I reached for the page and read it again. Ah. An idea crept into my head — from where, I didn't know. An idea that took me aback. I hesitated.

"Were you the Jewish policeman?" I asked.

He nodded.

In ghettos throughout Europe, I knew, the German occupation had required Jewish prisoners to form a Council of Elders and an internal police force whose job was to carry out Nazi orders. When the Nazi command needed Jewish ghetto workers to build an airfield or manufacture weapons, generally it was the Jewish police who formed them into columns and marched them to their labor. When the authorities demanded fifty or a hundred or a thousand victims to be sent to the killing fields, in some ghettos it was the Jewish police who played a role in deciding who would live and who would die. But the Jewish ghetto police also helped their fellow Jews by allocating food and housing. They saved people's lives by subverting Nazi orders, warning people, helping them to escape.

The Jewish ghetto police were controversial back then, and remained so in the years since. Did they play a beneficial role, or did they facilitate the slaughter? Were they collaborators or victims? Primo Levi, the eloquent survivor of Auschwitz, called them inhabitants of a "gray zone," where good and evil blur.

In setting off for the Old World, I knew I needed to prepare myself for painful encounters with the past. But I hadn't expected to learn this. My beloved uncle with his twinkly smile: a policeman in the ghetto, an inhabitant of the "gray zone"?

Once again I handed the page back to my uncle, and he folded it up and put it away. For a moment we sat at the table without speaking.

Did I really want to know more? Wouldn't I prefer to stick with the heroic stories and leave it at that? The one about how my uncle had saved the two little girls by hiding them in a cupboard, for example — it must have happened on this very day, the day of the *kinder-aktsye*. The one about carrying Uncle Aaron on the death march out of Dachau — how much easier it was to contemplate that tale, in which victims and perpetrators arranged themselves so neatly into two distinct columns.

But I opened my notebook and picked up my pen. Cautiously, I tiptoed into the unfamiliar terrain of the "gray zone." My uncle tiptoed in with me. Aunt Manya sat between us, her eyes darting back and forth.

As a policeman, my uncle began, he had been granted special privileges. His voice was high and thin, as if part of it had been drained away. From time to time, he said, he'd been allowed to leave the ghetto. Outside the gate, he was able to pick up food for friends and family, and nobody searched him on his way back in. His eyes crinkled up the way they always did, the way I loved. "Once," he said, "I even brought in a live chicken in my pants and took it to a *shoykhet*, a kosher butcher, to kill for my mother."

I laughed.

"We can laugh about it now," he said, but he had stopped smiling. Near the ghetto, he continued, was a public bath that Jews were not permitted to enter. "Normally, when we bathed, we used a *shisl* — how do you say?"

A word my mother had used. A bowl?

No —

A basin?

"A basin." On Sundays the public bath was closed, but the water was still hot. With his police armband, he was allowed in for a nice shower, he and his brother Aaron. "That hot water was worth a million dollars." He was smiling again.

How had he gotten the police job?

A silence, a fumbling.

"*Protektsye!* Connections!" Aunt Manya declared forcefully. "Everything was connections!"

My uncle waited for the next question.

What had his duties been?

Well, he said, Lithuanians would come to the gate offering to trade a pound of butter for a mink coat. He and his fellow policemen had to try to keep them away.

He waited again.

Any other duties?

There was only one grocery store, he said. People would push and shove. He helped make sure they stayed in line.

"It was much better to have the Jewish police do it," Aunt Manya put in. "Otherwise the Germans would have."

Did the ghetto residents cooperate with the police?

"Yes."

I waited for him to say more.

If there was a rumor that the Germans would be at the gate, he said, the Jewish police would run to the Jewish work brigade as it returned to the ghetto, warning people to avoid punishment by dropping any illegal food parcels they were carrying. "We protected people."

I scribbled in my notebook.

"There was a *komandant sho*," he continued. "How do you say it?"

A curfew?

"A curfew." Cousin Asya was running to the gate from her work assignment at the factory. Anyone caught violating the curfew was in danger of being shot. The curfew had begun and the Germans might shoot. "The Jewish police said, 'Hurry! Hurry! Go home, go home!'" Asya ran faster. The Jewish police saved her life.

Another silence.

"Tell me more about the *kinder-aktsye*," I said.

He spoke quickly now, the sentences tumbling out one after the other. "I was at the gate," he said. "Dr. Pace was with me." Two girls who were distant relations of the doctor's were thrown into the truck. Dr. Pace spoke to Forster, the ss commander. "Herr Forster," he said, "these two children are mine." The commander trusted the Jewish doctor because Pace had treated him for a dangerous infection. "You owe me," Pace said. "Save my children."

"Your children?" Forster said, " — but you're a bachelor!"

"My *illegitimate* children," Pace said quickly.

"Oh ho ho," said Forster. And he allowed the older girl to get off the truck. She was smuggled out to a gentile rescuer, and she survived, and so did her parents. But the younger girl was taken away with all the other children.

"The doctor died in New York," Aunt Manya said. "Pace. We went to his funeral."

That same day, Uncle Will said, he hid his mother and two girls behind a wardrobe. The soldiers did not find them. After the roundup, the girls were smuggled out to a Lithuanian family. Today they were grandmothers in Israel.

My uncle's eyes glowed with pleasure. This was the story I loved, the story I had grown up with. But I forced myself to push on. What else about the *aktsye*? I asked.

The chief of the Jewish police, he said — his boss, a man named Efroyim Gens — had carried his four- or five-year-old daughter to the trucks in his arms and handed her over to the Germans. He shook his head. "Efroyim Gens — we lived with him, you know." Eight people had shared a single room, with a *shmate* — a ragged curtain — between them. He shook his head again. "He was a very stupid man."

"Efroyim was the brother of Jacob Gens, the Jewish chief in Vilna," Aunt Manya said. "Believe me, they didn't love Jacob Gens in the Vilna ghetto."

"But Efroyim was different," Uncle Will said, "and over him was a Jewish Council with a good head." The Shavl ghetto was smaller than the one in Vilna, he said, and that made it easier to be a good head.

He nudged a plate of pastries toward me. "Eat something, Ellen," he said.

I took a bite, swallowed. So, I said, about the police. Were some jobs more difficult than others?

"Well, we worked in shifts," Uncle Will said.

Such as?

"Well, keep order, work here, work there. The administration would give orders." His voice trailed away.

Such as what?

"Such as the grocery store."

Silence.

And?

"And we would tell people to watch out because the Germans were coming to the gate, don't bring in any food," my uncle said. "We kept the gentiles out when they came trying to make deals. A mink coat for a pound of butter."

"Remember," Aunt Manya said in her firm voice, "you can't judge unless you were there." She stood up. "Ellen," she said, "when is your train?"

The interview had come to an end.

Now, sitting across from Emil at the café in Vilnius, I shivered. The rain had begun, a shroud of drizzle. What was I doing, digging into the dark recesses of this terrible era? Perhaps I should leave those bygone times alone. But the image of Irena Veisaite came to me, the crusader for dialogue who had inspired me in her parlor over tea and cookies. "As long as you are hiding the truth," she had said, "as long as you fail to come to terms with your past, you cannot build your future." Lithuanians were being asked to examine the past in all its complexity. Wasn't it incumbent on me to do the same?

I took a deep breath. How, I asked Emil, could I find out more about the police in the Shavl ghetto? What could I do to explore the choices they had faced and how they had handled those choices? Would a visit to the site of the ghetto tell me anything? Where else should I look?

Emil leaned toward me. Information about the Shavl ghetto was relatively scarce, he said. In contrast to the voluminous scholarship about other major ghettos, to a large extent the story of my uncle's ghetto remained to be told. The city of Siauliai as a whole had never developed into an intellectual or cultural center the way the other two had. And once the war came, the ghetto there had housed fewer than ten thousand residents, compared to Vilna's initial eighty thousand and Kovno's thirty thousand. Perhaps for these reasons, the Shavl ghetto lacked the extensive documentation that had been produced in other Lithuanian ghettos and in those in Poland's Warsaw and Lodz.

But, Emil said, he had some ideas about places to look.

The rain began to spatter the table. We moved our chairs farther under the striped awning, closer to the wall.

Emil's grandfather had been the chief of the Jewish police in the Kovno ghetto, he said. This was why my friend at the Holocaust Museum in Washington had thought to connect us.

Our eyes locked. No wonder he had struck me as haunted.

For years, he went on, he had been searching for information about his grandfather, reading everything he could put his hands on. Recently a new cache of information had opened up at the Lithuanian Special Archives. The outgoing Soviet regime had left behind the records of the Soviet secret police, which covered the period from 1940 to 1991. Among them were the records of tens of thousands of trials that had been conducted by Soviet authorities after the war. Certain Jewish ghetto residents from Shavl had been put on trial, including a man named Efroyim Gens.

My uncle's boss in the ghetto. The man who had shared a room with my uncle and six others. The man who had given away his child on the day of the *kinder-aktsye*.

The story of Efroyim's brother, Jacob Gens, was well known. He had been the head of the Jewish police, and then the chief Jewish leader overall, in the Vilna ghetto. His story had been examined and reexamined, told and retold. So had the stories of such Jewish ghetto leaders as Elkhanon Elkes of Kovno, Chaim Rumkowski of Lodz, and Adam Czerniakow of Warsaw. By contrast, the story of Efroyim Gens had never been told. His trial records had never been translated, his life never examined by scholars.

"The records of Efroyim Gens might tell you something about your uncle," Emil said.

A waiter began to roll up the awning over our heads with a long pole. The rain was still falling. We were the only customers at the café.

"Will you come upstairs?" I asked.

Emil ducked his head. "If it is appropriate."

At my kitchen table, he extracted from his briefcase a sheaf of notes in a precise, delicate hand. He straightened the sheets into a neat pile. "I propose to go to the archives for you," he said. "I have visited already to inquire and prepare."

Gaining entry to the archives was no easy matter. During the Soviet era, the files were top secret. Even now, only authorized scholars and those with a familial connection to the records were allowed in. Each trial protocol was hundreds of pages long, and the proceedings had been conducted in Russian, a language I didn't know.

The first step, Emil said, was to obtain the signature of the director granting permission for him to enter the archives on my behalf. Next, a stamp of approval was required from another official. After that, the volumes would arrive in the official reading room. Emil would read through them and select the pages I needed.

"For this work I will pay you?" I asked. After just a short time away from home, my hold on idiomatic English had loosened.

No, he said, he did not want money. I would pay only for the cost of copying.

He wrote out a letter, in Lithuanian, in an elegant European hand, saying that I, an American researcher, wished to deputize him, Emil, to examine documents relating to Shavl ghetto officials that bore significantly on my family history.

That's what he said it said, anyway. I signed the letter, then thanked Emil with flowery European courtesy — more evidence of my de-Americanization.

He turned to leave. "The two regimes were both evil," he said darkly. "The Nazi and the Soviet. Perhaps equally so."

After he left, I stood at the window until he disappeared into the rain. Who was this man? Why did he want to do this work for me without payment? Could I count on him to select the right pages? And what would I find out about my uncle?

THE friend from back home who had put me in touch with Emil was himself a survivor of Lithuania's Kovno ghetto. He had alerted me to an extraordinary document within the holdings of the Holocaust Museum — a 250-page record of the Jewish police in that ghetto that had been written by the police themselves at the very time that they were carrying out their duties. Carefully typed on a

Yiddish typewriter, it was a thorough and searching account of what the police did and how they felt about their actions. Buried in the ghetto in a tin crate during the war, the document was unearthed during a construction project in 1964. For decades, it languished in a closed Soviet archive. In 1998 it found its way to the museum in Washington, where my friend translated it into English. Between my visit to Uncle Will and my departure for Lithuania, I read through it feverishly, looking for clues as to what had happened in the Shavl ghetto, some ninety miles to the north.

"If we should not survive," the account began, "then perhaps the document we are writing here will fall into the hands of Jews, who will read it and be astonished." The first pages sketched the establishment of the ghetto in August 1941, when nearly thirty thousand Jews were settled into a congested warren of streets. Right away, upon Nazi orders, a Jewish Council was created to preside over housing, health care, and food distribution. Again upon Nazi orders, this body in turn created the Jewish police force, which came to be headed by Emil's grandfather.

The Kovno ghetto was sealed — enclosed behind barbed wire, with entry and exit tightly controlled — on August 15, 1941. That very day, the dreadful dilemma facing the police took shape. The Jewish Council received an order from the German command to provide five hundred young men "of good appearance" for "work in the city archives." Many volunteered, but when the German authorities and their Lithuanian assistants arrived to collect the young men, the number fell short. To meet the quota, the Jewish Council instructed the newly appointed Jewish police to grab more men off the ghetto streets and deliver them to the assembly point. The five hundred were then marched off, never to return. "And so," said the history, in my friend's translation, "by their assistance, the police helped to deliver five hundred Jews perhaps to their death, although, as they saw it, it was done with the best of intentions and with a clear conscience, that what they did was for the well-being of the ghetto."

A few months later, in October, what came to be known as the "Great Action" took place. Ghetto residents were ordered to gather at 6:00 a.m. in a large field called Demokratu Square. In the chilly darkness, German police, Gestapo leaders, and Lithuanian police stood guard as the Jewish police assembled tens of thousands of their fellow ghetto prisoners into orderly columns. The Gestapo sorted the Jews into two groups. Some went to the right and some to the left — some to be sent to their deaths, some to be spared. The process took all day. The Jewish police organized and reorganized the columns in an attempt to save their fellow Jews, but "the opportunities were few and the results . . . meager."

When night fell, the Gestapo ordered the Jewish police to search the ghetto for residents who had failed to show up in the square. This time the police did succeed in saving some lives. "The policemen checked and, to their delight, found people hiding in many places in attics and cellars. . . . All those found were immediately led through the fence [to safety]." The next morning, the ninety-two hundred people who had been sent to the left — one-third of the ghetto population — were taken to the Ninth Fort on the outskirts of town. There they were machine-gunned to death.

Having culled the ghetto population, the Germans put the remaining inhabitants to work. Some were forced to toil in local factories, others to construct a military airfield on the outskirts of the city. It was the job of the Jewish police to supply the daily quota of workers. Every morning before dawn, the police would begin banging on shutters, shouting, "Arise for the airfield!" To roust out shirkers, the police crawled under beds and broke into attics and sheds. By 6:00 each morning, thousands would be milling in the square, illuminated by searchlights. "The square is surrounded by our own Jews, so that no one will be able to avoid going to work. . . . There is confusion and turmoil, talking and shouting, people are hustling . . . Jews driving other Jews to crushing labor." The writers commented: "It is, of course, not good and not nice that one Jew should beat another for not wanting to go to slave labor. On the other hand, however . . . when the labor quota for the airfield was an issue of life or death for the entire ghetto of sixteen thousand Jews, one could not stand on ceremony."

At day's end, when the columns of Jews returned from work, many carried parcels of food they had bought illegally from Lithuanians. Everyone tried to push past the German guards without being stopped for inspection.

> The swarming thousands . . . would press, pull and push. The Germans would strike with their rifle butts and truncheons. The Jewish policemen . . . tried first to hold back the crowd with their own hands. . . .
>
> When this failed, they also took up truncheons, striking the shoulders and heads of Jewish sons and daughters. . . . at first partly ashamed, with pity, the second time somewhat more boldly, and later, when he has become accustomed to it, the Jewish policeman beats with brutality and strikes as well as the Germans.

"Truncheons." The word hit my ears with a thud. I could see the pushing and shoving, hear the heavy sticks as they connected with flesh and skulls — Jewish sticks on Jewish skulls.

The police force quickly became riddled with corruption. Everything came down to connections, to who knew whom — *protektsye*, the word Aunt Manya had used — which was known as "Vitamin P." Those with Vitamin P got the best houses, extra food, the easiest work assignments.

The German officials demanded that ghetto residents turn over their gold, putting the Jewish police in charge of the collection. "The innate craving for money and gold was very strong, and when a 'golden' opportunity presented itself, one took. One . . . ceased to be embarrassed for one's own actions or for those of others. Each one possibly had on his conscience something which he would not have allowed himself to do in normal times, and therefore had to tolerate the sins of others to some extent."

The authors of the police history did not attempt to pass judgment on their actions. "We are too deeply immersed in the ghetto to rise high above it," they wrote. Instead, they sought to record what they were doing with brutal honesty, vowing to try "with all [our] might to preserve objectivity, to convey all happenings and events in their true light, as they actually occurred, without exaggerating or diminishing them."

The way the police saw it, they were too close to the situation to step back and consider the moral implications of the situation. That stepping back and considering, as they saw it, would be the job of future generations, future readers. People like me.

Well, the project was under way. Emil was heading for the archives. What he found there would shed light on how the Jewish police had behaved in my uncle's ghetto. This, in turn, would help me step back and consider the moral dimensions of Jewish officials in general during the Holocaust, and even more broadly, to think about what should be expected of human beings under conditions of terror.

OUR walking tour with sturdy, steely-haired Fanya had focused on *Vilne fun amol* — the Jewish community before the war. Today we were to learn how that world had been destroyed.

On a little concrete island in the middle of Vokieciu gatve, German Street, my fellow students and I gathered around our guide, Rokhl. Like Fanya, she was a former ghetto resident and anti-Nazi partisan in her eighties who wished to be addressed by her first name. Unlike Fanya, she was soft and gentle in appearance, with pink cheeks and fluffy white curls. And whereas Fanya had painted a joyful portrait of Jewish Vilna in its prime, the tale Rokhl had to tell was a gruesome one, in which the Jewish police played a significant role.

The Germans arrived in Vilnius on June 25, 1941, Rokhl said, and right from the start "it seemed that they had nothing to do but go after the Jews." She spoke in Yiddish; Mendy Cahan, the director, dressed as always in his Old World garb, translated her words into English. Rules were posted on the walls: No Jews on the sidewalk. No Jews walking together. No Jews on the trams. Jews allowed to buy food only after 11:00 a.m., only at Jewish shops. Jews required to wear yellow patches that were to be sewn on tight with twelve stitches.

Within days of rolling into the city, the Nazi command seized sixty prominent Jewish men and held them hostage while the Jewish community struggled to raise an enormous ransom. The three-and-a-half-million rubles that were gathered were not enough. The men were executed.

One night Rokhl was awakened by the barking of dogs. Outside her window, long columns of people were passing by: thousands of Jews. "They had their children by the hand and their belongings tied up in bedsheets," she said. "White sheets in the black night."

The columns disappeared beyond the city borders, never to be seen again.

Over the next few days, tens of thousands of Jews were ordered to move into the old Jewish quarter, a handful of tiny streets: *Yatkever*, named for the meat market; *Strashun*, for Matityahu Strashun, the nineteenth-century Jewish book collector; *Shpitol*, for the hospital. We followed Rokhl into this cramped section, which had been known as the Large Ghetto.

A tall wooden fence and brick walls enclosed the ghetto, Rokhl said, and the windows of adjoining houses were covered. People lived thirty or forty to a room. The bread was like mud. Many, especially the older people, died of hunger. "Our teachers died."

A series of roundups began. On Yom Kippur, on their way home from synagogue, twenty-two hundred Jews were seized in the streets and taken away. Another day, fifteen hundred more were taken.

We turned down Rudninku gatve, passing a wall adorned with giant graffiti, in English: YOUR LIFE BECOMES MORE AND MORE OF ADVENTURE. Here was Number 8, the former Jewish high school, where the Jewish Council had had its headquarters. On

October 23, 1941, Rokhl said, "the worst thing happened." The Jewish police, headed by Jacob Gens (the brother of Uncle Will's boss in the Shavl ghetto), issued yellow passes to several thousand ghetto residents who were deemed to be skilled workers. They and their families were assembled in the Jewish Council courtyard. Then, Lithuanians acting on Nazi orders stormed the ghetto, removed the remaining thousands of Jews from their homes, and marched them away.

Again and again, here in this courtyard, the ever-diminishing ranks were ordered to assemble and present their papers. By December 1941, just a few months after the Nazi occupation began, the ghetto population had been greatly reduced. Of the original eighty thousand Jews, only seventeen thousand remained.

No one knew where the "selected" had been taken. One night, Rokhl's father came home from his job at the ghetto hospital and reported that two wounded girls had been admitted to the ward. They claimed that they had escaped from a massacre in the forest of Ponar, five miles out of town. They described how ghetto residents had been shot at close range by rifle-wielding Germans and Lithuanians. Wounded by gunfire, the girls had fallen into a pit with the others. When the shooting stopped, they said, they had clawed their way out and run back to the ghetto.

The doctors didn't believe them. They thought the girls had lost their minds.

But the truth began to sink in. Abba Kovner, a young activist in the ghetto, was one who came to understand that Vilna's Jews were slated for annihilation. On the last day of 1941, while drunken German guards were celebrating the New Year, Kovner called a meeting at the Jewish Council building and delivered a speech calling for armed resistance: "Let us not go like sheep to the slaughter."

The next month, in January 1942, Kovner and others set out to organize a resistance movement. "We tried to get the people to rise up," Rokhl said, "but they would not."

While the underground gathered weapons and debated what to do, the roundups continued. In July 1942, Rokhl said, "old people were seized."

Then she paused to rephrase what she had said.

"Actually," Cahan translated, "the Jews gave up the old people, let them be taken, because — because this is how things were." Gens and his police assembled a hundred elderly Jews in the yard of the Strashun Library and blocked the gate to keep them from getting away. The Germans took them. "May the aged among the Jews forgive us," Gens pleaded. "They were a sacrifice for our Jews and our future."

Then, for a time, the actions ceased. A kind of "golden period" began. Ghetto residents organized theater performances. There were two orchestras and two choruses. A puppet theater. A restaurant. Poetry readings. Gymnastics. A newspaper. A café. Rokhl worked in the ghetto library, which circulated seven hundred books a day.

Some ghetto inhabitants objected to singing and dancing under the horrendous circumstances, but others felt that the cultural activities were a vital form of spiritual resistance. "Our bodies are in the ghetto," Gens himself said, "but our spirit has not been enslaved."

Outside the ghetto, the Nazis closed all Jewish libraries and plundered their holdings, filling warehouses with mountains of rare manuscripts, documents, photographs, and letters. Out of one hundred thousand books collected, eighty thousand were considered waste, bundled as scrap and sold by the kilogram to a local paper factory. A team of ghetto intellectuals known as the Rosenberg Squad, or the Paper Brigade, was ordered to sort through the remaining piles and save the most important for shipment to Germany. After the war, according to the Nazi plan, these were to be made available to scholars specializing in the extinct race. The building that had housed YIVO, the Jewish research institute, which stood just outside the ghetto, served as the headquarters for the sorting operation — and as a secret hub from which both archival treasures and weapons were smuggled into the ghetto.

In April 1943 the German command announced that some Jews were to be resettled in the Kovno ghetto, sixty-two miles to the west. Upon the assurances of police chief Gens, hundreds of ghetto residents volunteered for the journey, hoping conditions would be better there. Gens himself joined them on the train. But a few miles outside Vilna, Gens disembarked. Moments later, the train stopped at the forest of Ponar, where all the passengers were shot. At a special session of the Jewish Council, Gens admitted that, yes, he had known beforehand that there would be a "selection."

In July the Gestapo ordered Gens to find Itzik Wittenberg, a ghetto leader who had helped to organize the resistance organization. If Gens failed to deliver Wittenberg for execution, said the Nazi command, the entire ghetto would be liquidated. Gens called a meeting of the ghetto population at large, and following his speech a crowd surged through the streets, howling for Wittenberg to surrender.

When Wittenberg did come forward, two-thirds of the underground — two hundred young people — escaped from the ghetto into the forest. There they planted mines, destroyed telephone lines, blew up bridges and railways.

Rokhl led us down the former *Shpitol gas*, now Ligonines gatve, Hospital Street, where the Jewish hospital once stood. In the dilapidated courtyard, she sat down heavily on a stone bench. "In this hospital was a wonderful order and cleanliness," she said. No one had to lie on the floor, the way people did elsewhere in the ghetto. There were beds, clean sheets, and food. Her father had been the radiologist here.

On September 1, 1943, she said, "a terrible thing happened here." German troops entered the streets of the ghetto and demanded two thousand Jews. Gens told them to leave the matter to him. Then, Rokhl said, the Jewish ghetto police came into the hospital yard. Here. They called out the sick and the staff. The doctors came out dressed in their white coats. The Jewish police surrounded them — "ringled," rhyming with "tingled," was the not-quite-English word Cahan used — and took them away. "The Jews took the Jews."

Three days later the Germans came again to Gens, demanding two thousand more. Gens gave a speech from a balcony. "Fellow Jews," he announced, "I have managed to obtain permission for the families of men who were deported to Estonia to join them there." Some thirteen hundred women and children came forward, and the Jewish police went through the streets and seized seven hundred more. All were taken away and killed.

As Gens put it: "When they ask me for a thousand Jews, I hand them over, for if we Jews will not give them on our own, the Germans will come and take them by force. Then they will take not one thousand, but thousands. With the thousands that I hand over, I save ten thousand. I did everything in order to . . . ensure that at least a remnant of Jews survive."

On September 14, the Gestapo came for Gens.

Ten days later, on September 23, 1943, the ghetto was once again surrounded by German tanks, and this time it was the end. The liquidation began early in the morning. Some Jews were sent to camps in Estonia, others to Latvia; some went directly to Ponar, some to gas chambers in Poland.

My fellow students and I drew closer to Rokhl's rosy face and snowy hair — "ringled" her, in Cahan's locution. Our faces were full of grief.

We followed Rokhl down narrow Mesiniu gatve, named for the old meat market. Right here, she said, had stood a little gate. On the last day of the ghetto, she and other members of the underground had torn off their yellow stars and slipped out to the forest to join the anti-Nazi partisan forces.

"Many wanted to go with us," Rokhl said, "but the Jewish police held them back with hands and sticks."

Her words, with their complex import — the Jewish police helping young resisters to get away while preventing others from doing so — fell like blows on my own head.

67

With this, Rokhl's lecture came to an end. Of the eighty thousand Jewish residents of Vilna in 1941, two or three thousand survived the war.

In the evening we attended a concert at the Jewish museum, where a soprano in a formal gown, accompanied by a chamber orchestra, sang the songs of the Vilna ghetto that had survived along with Rokhl and Fanya and the few thousand others:

"Vilna, my beloved city."

"Ghetto, I will never forget you."

"From among your white stars, Lord, stretch down a hand. In your embrace will I find solace."

"Hush, my child. Enemies surround us, graves sprout in our midst, but when you awake the light of freedom will shine upon your face."

The last song was the Partisan Hymn, composed in the Vilna ghetto, which had become an internationally revered anthem of remembrance. As was the custom, everyone rose. We sang together:

Zog nit keynmol az du geyst dem letstn veg . . .
Es vet a poyk ton undzer trot: MIR ZAYNEN DO!

Never say that you are walking your last way . . .
Our marching steps will thunder: WE ARE HERE!

Looking around at the backs of heads and the sides of cheeks, for a moment I felt myself transported back into the lost ghetto community, full of ragged tweed-covered shoulders, each one as irreplaceable as a book in the Strashun Library. Almost none of those who'd sung this defiant hymn in the ghetto had survived. Most of them *had* been walking their last way. "We are *not* here" would have been more accurate.

And the role of the Jewish police? As the last verse of the song came to an end, I squeezed my eyes shut.

From the Vilna ghetto, I had Rokhl's unflinching memories of the violent and often duplicitous operations carried out by the police under the command of Jacob Gens. And I had Gens's forceful justification for his actions: "With the thousands that I hand over, I save ten thousand." Of course, in the end, it was not so. Only a handful survived.

From the Kovno ghetto, I had the anguished account written by the Jewish police themselves. Were they wrong to drag their fellow Jews out of bed to work at the airfield? They believed that supplying labor for the Germans was all that stood between the ghetto population and annihilation. Yet after all the thousands of hours of work at the airfield, in the end less than 10 percent of the Kovno ghetto population survived. Rather than line people up for the work brigades and the selections, should the police instead have turned their truncheons on their oppressors — who were armed with machine guns?

From the Shavl ghetto, so far I had only the minimal words of my uncle. I tried to picture him at the gate, a young man with strong shoulders and a shock of black hair — and a truncheon?

AS the hot summer day relaxed into night, Minette and I sat at the kitchen table with our homework. In sleeveless housedresses, barefoot, hair pulled back off our sweaty foreheads, we whispered under our breath as we riffled the pages of our dictionaries. Joining ourselves to the Litvak tradition of scholarship offered a profound consolation.

It was tough going, though. Oy, the verbs, with their *umge*-this and their *oysge*-that, their *aroysge*-this and their *farge*-that! Every sentence was an ordeal. I divided the verbs and the compound nouns into their component parts. I underlined the words I didn't know. I double-underlined the ones I would stress when reading aloud. I enclosed phrases in parentheses. I numbered and rearranged the elements of especially convoluted expressions. After a couple of hours, the page of sinuous Hebrew characters resembled a sheet of matzo and the letters swam before my eyes. I was near tears. Why couldn't I understand? Why wouldn't this language — this comfortable old mother tongue — reach out to embrace me?

But I kept going, and after a while, alongside the literary characters on the page, I began to sense another set of characters coming to life as well. I could feel my mother beside me, with her love of a tasty turn of phrase; my grandfather, with his devotion to the American classics; my great-grandfather Dovid-Mikhl, whose beard once quivered over the Talmud; and finally, perhaps not a reader at all, my great-grandmother Asne, the dairywoman and mother of nine, who must have been possessed of a fearsome persistence.

Meanwhile, on the street below the open window, footsteps echoed on cobblestones, drunken voices rang out, and from around the corner, near the pub, the sound of vomiting could now and then be heard.

Precisely at 11:00, a cat began a piteous yowling. Minette looked up. "The lamentation of the ghetto," she said. She told me about a dream she'd had the night before, in which we, the Jews, were ordered to sew tiny beads onto our clothing in intricate patterns. The best designs would be selected, their makers spared.

It was about the Holocaust, of course. "And," I said, "about our homework." About how seriously we went at it, as if our lives were at stake.

IN the morning before class, we students sat sunning ourselves like cats on the warm stones in the university courtyard. The air was silken, and against the walls of the university buildings, window boxes blazed with bloom — magenta, wine, and pink. The staff of a nearby restaurant presided over a coffee urn and a tray of pastries. Every day they ran out of milk and had to run to the kitchen for more. Why not bring two pitchers, I wondered. But here in the Old World, you didn't just pour and pour and expect that there would always be enough. I liked this, I found. Did I dare say it? In some ways I felt very much at home in this land of bears and forebears.

In the tranquil setting, we chatted about the conflict at the Chor Shul. After Friday night's battle of the clattering window blinds, the building had once again been shut down, and now the American rabbi's faction had established a round-the-clock vigil on the front steps, with big posters demanding that the *shul* be reopened.

We went on to talk about Rokhl's tour of the ghetto. Several students began speculating about what they would have done if they'd been confined there.

"I would have joined the underground," said one.

"Not me," said someone else. "I would have been much too scared."

I turned my back. Toying with such questions rubbed me the wrong way. How could they even guess at what they would have done? How could anyone know?

One of my fellow students sat down beside me. He worked for an organization that aided impoverished Jewish communities throughout Europe. An expert traveler, he was accustomed to sizing up community leaders. I told him about Emil and the research he'd offered to carry out.

He listened carefully, then frowned. "I wouldn't have anything to do with the guy," he said. "You have no idea what he may be using you for."

Another student joined us. Her father was a survivor of the Kovno ghetto. I asked if she'd ever heard anything about Emil's grandfather, the Jewish police chief.

Yes, she recognized his name. He had a very bad reputation, she said. "He was an abomination. A monster."

Nothing was simple here, nothing at all.

As we filed into class, the back rows filled up with the younger people, while we middle-aged and older students vied for the front seats. Reading aloud, we leaned forward as if driving at night, squinting into the darkness. Niborski, our gentle, bearded teacher, sang corrections in a windy baritone and offered a piece of deadpan advice: "Leyent di oysyes vos shteyen geshribn un nit keyn andere," he intoned — read the letters that appear on the page and no others.

He had another helpful suggestion, too: "Tayere talmidim, men zol leyenen yidish nit nor mit di oygn — oykh mit der noz," he said — dear students, you must read Yiddish not only with your eyes but with your nose. Receiving a literary heritage was not only a skill but also an art, he meant. It required not only intellect but intuition.

I'd always been the kind of student who had a lot to say, and here, too, my hand was constantly flying into the air.

"Yo?" Yes?

Mouth open, I would realize suddenly that I had not the slightest idea how to say what was on my mind. In this unfamiliar language, I felt like two people. One was an impractical idealist who set off with supreme confidence into the unknown. The other was a benighted worker running ahead, frantically trying to build a road for the journey.

All of us envied the ease with which our fellow student Phyllis could make the words flow. As a child growing up in the United States, she'd spoken Yiddish at home, and she'd married into a Yiddish-speaking family. She made a lot of grammatical mistakes, though, and when Niborski tried to set her straight, she protested. "Mayn shviger hot geredt azoy," she kept saying — my mother-in-law said it this way. Her mother-in-law was wrong, Niborski insisted. But Phyllis was not convinced.

The student who'd studied with me under the stars on our first night was gone; she'd transferred to an easier level. I wondered whether I, too, should transfer. When Niborski spoke, whole paragraphs went by in a blur, and sometimes everyone laughed — everyone but me.

At the break, in the office of the Yiddish Institute, a hulking American in his twenties tried to console me. People pretended to understand more than they did, he said. They laughed at the jokes just because everyone else was laughing.

We talked about the essay we'd been assigned to write, based on the story about the roguish Hasidic boys with their bonfire. After scribbling pages of notes in English, I'd begun squeezing my ideas through the tiny funnel of my Yiddish vocabulary. I was halfway done with a pinched little piece, in pencil with many erasures, comparing the quarrel in the story with the ruckus at the Chor Shul on Friday night, the feud between the ecstatic shouting worshippers on one side of the aisle and their annoyed ear-covering rivals on the other side.

I asked the hulking American what he'd come up with.

"Oh," he said, "I wrote about Victor Turner's theory of liminality." The boys' wild ritual antics around the crackling fire, he explained, embody a liminal moment — a time of transition when things are *nisht ahin, nisht aher* — neither here nor there. A time when profound change can occur.

I sighed. I was a greenhorn in Yiddish, I thought glumly, as surely as my grandfather was a greenhorn when he arrived in America with no English and less than fifty dollars in his pocket. Maybe I would always be a greenhorn.

After class, at the Internet café, where you paid by the minute for the opportunity to write to your loved ones, I sat down in front of a computer screen but could think of nothing to say. I could picture my husband, my son, and my daughter, but words eluded me, just as they did in class after my hand flew up in the air.

As the expensive moments ticked by, my mind drifted to one of the relics of my family's diaspora that I'd studied before coming here — a postcard from the turn of the century. On the front was a sepia photo of my grandfather as a young man. In a studio setting meant to evoke the charms of the countryside, he's standing beside a spindly birch fence and a papier-mâché boulder. Next to him is another, taller young man — a cousin? a friend? Both are sporting mustaches (my grandfather's so feathery it looks as if he hasn't yet begun shaving) and three-piece suits. No traditional Orthodox side curls for them, and no hats. The little stamp in the bottom corner, in Russian, says "Birzai," a town not far from the family seat of Rokiskis. On the back, in a gorgeously flowing Yiddish script, my grandfather has penned a message to his sister, who'd immigrated to New York years before:

Ebige ondenkung
far mayn libende
shvester Taybe
fun ir bruder
Yankev Levin

Eternal remembrance
for my beloved
sister Taybe
from her brother
Yankev Levin

How thrilled I was when I learned enough Yiddish to decipher these words — and how perplexed. This was all he could think to say? He couldn't even use up half the space on the card?

When I was a child, my grandfather's silence about the Old Country puzzled me. Now, as I sat stymied, wordless, less than 150 miles from where he'd posed with the plaster boulder, I thought I understood — both why he'd sent such a diminutive message and why he so rarely talked about his native land once he got to the other side. I could feel how difficult it was to cross from one side to the other. And I could sense, too, that I myself had crossed over. I was on this side. I was here.

2. My grandfather Yankl (Jack) Levine (*left*), with a friend or relative, in Birzai, Lithuania, early twentieth century.

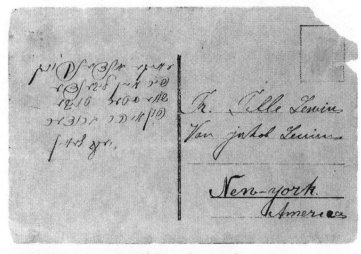

3. Postcard written by my grandfather, early twentieth century.

The Soviet Era

DURING the Soviet years, the KGB had established its Vilnius head-quarters in a massive building just off Gedimino Prospect, the city's grandest boulevard. After the fall of the Soviet Union in 1991, the structure was turned into a museum, and now I was on my way there for a tour.

My uncle Aaron — the brother of Uncle Will and of my grandfather — had spent a year imprisoned in this building. The story that came down to me from Uncle Will was this:

In July 1944, when the German army was retreating from Lithuania, the residents of the Shavl ghetto were loaded into freight cars and transported to the concentration camp at Stutthof, in the north of German-occupied Poland. There the weak were separated from the able-bodied. Will's mother Soreh went off to her death. Uncle Aaron's wife Sonya and their fifteen-year-old daughter Asya were settled into a tent at the camp and forced to work as slave laborers, digging ditches and subsisting on watery soup. Will and Aaron were shoved onto another train bound for the labor camp at Dachau, hundreds of miles to the southwest, near the German city of Munich.

Over the next months, the two men managed to survive. In the spring, when Germany was about to surrender to the Allies, they and thousands of their fellow prisoners were driven out of the

Dachau camp onto the road. In Uncle Will's telling, "if you can't walk, they shoot. I carried my brother on my back." On the night of May 2, my uncle remembered, the prisoners were allowed to rest in the forest. They pulled branches off the trees to form a makeshift shelter from the rain. In the night it snowed, and the heavy, wet branches fell down on the huddled prisoners.

When they awoke, the guards were gone. "There were cherries on the trees," Uncle Will said. "A man had a knife. We cut raw meat off a dead horse to eat."

The two brothers found their way to a displaced persons camp in Munich. Uncle Will met Aunt Manya and made plans to immigrate to America. Uncle Aaron set out in search of his wife and daughter. He went from *shtetl* to *shtetl*, *dorf* to *dorf*. The little towns and villages were crowded with refugees. After several months of looking, he succeeded in finding the two at a hospital in Lauenberg, some miles west of Stutthof. In January, they had been driven out of the Stutthof camp on a death march of their own — six or seven weeks of tramping through snowdrifts at gunpoint. Of the group of twelve hundred women who began the march together, only a hundred had survived.

By the time Aaron found them, his daughter had recovered her health and was standing guard — armed with an empty rifle — at a Russian military building close to the hospital. His wife was still very ill. When she saw her husband's face, she lost consciousness. Hours passed before she could be revived.

A month later, when Sonya was well enough, the three of them climbed aboard a freight train loaded with coal and cattle and returned home to Lithuania, which was now a Soviet republic. They were hoping against hope that they would find Vova, Aaron's son, who had been a student in Kovno when war broke out and hadn't been heard from since. In Siauliai, they found most of the city streets bombed beyond recognition, the ghetto destroyed, and their house in ruins. They squeezed into a flat with five other returning Jewish families. Aaron's daughter went back to school. Her classmates were eleven and twelve years old; it had been years since they'd seen a Jew. She was five years older and hungry, her head full of pictures from the ends of the earth. Once a fashion plate, Aaron's wife now was weak and fearful. The sight of a policeman frightened her; the sound of a truck with an idling engine set her to trembling.

Vova did not return. Aaron and Sonya never learned how he had died or the date of his death. "I don't know when to cry," Sonya would say, "so I must cry every day."

The women who had once patronized Aaron's chic hairdressing salon greeted him with delight: "Levin is back!" But Aaron was no longer the elegant charmer who had once been a runner-up in the citywide "Mr. Shavl" contest. With grim determination, he organized a small group of Jewish survivors to defy Soviet authorities by taking up the traditional charity collection for Passover. They refurbished the Jewish cemetery and even circulated a Hebrew-language newspaper.

One night in 1950 the police came for him. Just five years after Dachau, he was incarcerated again — this time in a cell in the KGB building in Vilnius. After a year behind bars, he was convicted of "crimes against the Soviet Union" and exiled to a labor camp in Irkutsk, Siberia, near the Mongolian border.

Why? I asked. Why was Aaron taken away?

Uncle Will shrugged. "Stalin persecuted so many innocent people," he said. "He killed millions. Who knows?"

In 1955, two years after Stalin's death, a telegram arrived. Aaron was on his way home.

He was never again a well man. Slave labor under not one but two regimes had broken his health. "It was too much," said Uncle Will.

THE KGB building was a soot-darkened hulk that took up a whole block on Auku gatve, Victim Street. In the dim lobby, Dalia Kuodyte was waiting for me. A practical-looking gentile woman in her forties, she headed the research center that ran the museum. She introduced a young khaki-clad colleague with a shaved head and linebacker shoulders who began to recite the museum's history in rapid-fire English. I took notes as fast as I could.

Erected in 1890 during the time of Czar Alexander II, the building was used first as a courthouse. Later it became the headquarters of the Polish secret police. Then it was a strategic planning center for the Gestapo. Finally it became the KGB's headquarters and prison. Since 1992, it had been a museum whose goal, said the staffer, was "to immortalize the freedom fighters and victims of the Soviet genocide." Hence its name: the Museum of Genocide Victims.

A couple of sentences went by while I lost my concentration. "Genocide victims" to me meant Jews killed by the Nazis, not Lithuanians victimized by the Soviets. Had there really been a Soviet genocide in Lithuania?

A Polish-Jewish legal scholar named Raphael Lemkin, I knew, had coined the word "genocide" in 1944 by joining the Latin word *gens,* meaning "race," with *cidium,* "killing." In 1948, the United Nations defined "genocide" as

> any of the following acts committed with intent to destroy, in whole or in part, a national, ethnic, racial or religious group:
> — killing members of the group;
> — causing serious bodily or mental harm to members of the group;
> — deliberately inflicting on the group conditions of life calculated to bring about its physical destruction in whole or in part;
> — imposing measures intended to prevent births within the group;
> — forcibly transferring children of the group to another group.

Had the Soviet regime truly tried to kill off an entire people, an entire culture in Lithuania? The regime had sought to eliminate Lithuanian political and military opposition. It had executed and exiled many Lithuanians. But genocide? Even if the word *could* be said to fit the Soviet crime in Lithuania, it was difficult for me to swallow the idea.

I struggled to focus on the staffer's words. He was talking about the Molotov-Ribbentrop Pact, the Nazi-Soviet agreement that had secretly ceded the Baltics to the USSR in 1939. In June of the following year, he continued, Red Army troops rolled in and Lithuanian society was reconfigured from top to toe. Russian was declared an official language. Traditional Lithuanian festivals were outlawed. Farms were collectivized, businesses nationalized, government officials removed and replaced. A year later, when the pact had frayed and a German invasion was expected any day, the authorities arrested tens of thousands whose loyalty was considered suspect and loaded them into cattle cars bound for Siberia.

On June 22, 1941, when German bombs began to fall and troops marched in, "the Lithuanians are not clapping," the staffer said — though in fact I'd seen pictures of women throwing flowers at the German troops — "but they thought at least it will be easier, we will get our independence back."

It was not to be. The Nazi invasion brought occupation, not liberation. And when the Nazis were defeated, in July 1944, the Red Army returned. At the Yalta Conference in February of the next year, the United States, Britain, and the USSR designated Lithuania, Latvia, and Estonia as Soviet republics. At that, thirty thousand Lithuanian fighters took to the woods and formed a guerrilla army known as the "Forest Brothers." The fighters' goal was to harass Soviet authorities until such time as military and diplomatic aid arrived from the West. During nine years of bloody skirmishing, authorities displayed the dead bodies of Forest Brothers in the town squares, the staffer said, where they were gnawed by dogs.

After several years of forays, the ranks of the guerrilla fighters were severely depleted. Although the West furnished the Forest Brothers with weapons and intelligence, hope of a dramatic rescue by Western planes and troops had long since faded. The fighters' military actions gave way to propaganda, whose goal, according to a museum pamphlet, was "to say to the population, *Mes dar esame* — we are still here."

Meanwhile, deportations were taking place on a massive scale, wave after wave. More than 120,000 — some say 300,000 — men, women, and children were sent away. According to figures cited in the museum pamphlet, the pre- and postwar deportations together exiled a full 50 percent of the elite sector of Lithuanian society. The deportees were Jews and gentiles alike. They were members of political organizations, police officers, Trotskyites, Zionists, clergymen, business owners, stamp collectors, members of the Esperanto Society, people with acquaintances in the West, writers, former Nazi collaborators, former Nazi resisters, and thousands of ordinary people — anyone who appeared to lack sufficient loyalty to the Soviet Union. Including Uncle Aaron.

When Stalin died in 1953, the deportees began to return, Uncle Aaron among them. But the scars within Lithuanian society lingered. Bitter feelings were widespread and persistent — about Soviet power, about the Jews who were believed to have welcomed the Soviets in 1940, about the Western nations that had failed to provide military support. The museum pamphlet in my hand lamented: "There is no grand museum in Washington DC dedicated to those whose lives were destroyed by the communists" — a pointed reference to the U.S. Holocaust Memorial Museum.

I felt Dalia Kuodyte and her colleague watching me as we left the entry hall and began our tour through the cold rooms of the prison. To them, I sensed, I was not simply an individual but a representative — of the West, of the Jews, of those who did not fully comprehend or acknowledge the suffering of their country.

Here was the intake room, with dirty walls and tiny barred windows, where the prisoners were photographed and fingerprinted.

Here was the room where parcels from home were weighed. The limit was five kilograms.

Here were the unheated cells where ten to fifteen prisoners slept in bunks. "Everyone had to turn together."

Here was the interrogation room, with hidden microphones.

Here was the solitary confinement cell, where the only food was bread and water.

Here was the isolation cell, where a small platform had stood in a pool of icy water. "If you dozed off, you fell into the water."

Here was the padded torture cell.

Here was the execution cell, with a drain for the blood.

On the wall was a chart showing how many people had been executed on which days of which months. While my hosts waited, I copied down these numbers: 10, 8, 9, 40, 45, 1, 15. Such small numbers. I felt sullen, resistant, defensive. "My" genocide had been bigger, worse. In "my" genocide, daily fatalities had numbered in the hundreds, the thousands, even the tens of thousands.

The Lithuanian American historian Saulius Suziedelis has written of this country's "heritage of mutually exclusive pasts." Within these cold walls, I could feel the challenge of that diverse legacy, and it seemed heavy indeed. Try as I might to concentrate on the terrible things that happened inside this building during the Soviet era, my mind kept migrating to worse things that happened under the Nazis. I struggled to open my heart to the tragedies of the Soviet era in Lithuania, scrambling for a foothold from which to absorb that pain. I tried to picture Uncle Aaron's yearlong confinement here. Uncle Aaron: Little Grandpa's brother, Uncle Will's brother, the uncle who looked so handsome in the old photos, with his long, slender face and high forehead. Elegant Uncle Aaron, the esteemed hairdresser of prewar Siauliai. Uncle Aaron, victim of a double brutality.

But no matter how hard I tried, the terrors of the Nazi era seemed close and the terrors of the Soviet era more remote. Somehow, taking in the reality of the Soviet depredations seemed to require that I let go of my hold on the horrors of the Holocaust. Yet letting go of the Holocaust seemed unbearable. And so embracing the reality of the Soviet "genocide," if it could be called that, seemed beyond my reach.

Lithuanians, like other Europeans, and like people in societies around the world struggling to confront painful histories, were being asked to do the very thing I was finding so difficult. They were being asked to imagine themselves into someone else's heritage while keeping hold of their own. As I felt the power of the "competitive martyrology" syndrome deep inside myself, I wondered how that mission could ever succeed.

In my time here I had fastened onto the Litvak spirit — the rigorous search for the truth, the "prove-it" mentality, the cleaving to reason and fairness — that defined the centuries-old ethos of northern European Jewry. That heritage had served me as I tackled the nooks and crannies of Yiddish grammar as well as the ins and outs of twentieth-century history. Now, however, as the stubborn facts of the past pressed up against me, that time-tested Litvak spirit seemed far too puny for the task.

Dalia Kuodyte looked at my face and seemed to understand. She touched my elbow. "We have had fifteen years to accept very complicated things," she said quietly.

After leaving the museum I passed an arty drawing scrawled on the side of a building near the university. It showed two hands, one pointing to the right and the other to the left. *Eik ten*, it said — Go this way.

EMIL called to say he had finished reading through the file of Efroyim Gens, the chief of the Jewish police in Uncle Will's ghetto, and had selected the most important pages. He asked me to meet him at the Special Archives building to pay for the photocopying. In the hushed reading room, a hugely fat volume was brought to us, its cardboard cover reinforced with cloth tape. The file ran to 330 pages, most of them handwritten in a flowing Cyrillic script.

The bulk of the record was devoted to Gens's trial, which began in June 1949. Like tens of thousands of others, Gens was called up before a tribunal behind closed doors. He was charged with

betraying the Soviet Union, both as a Jewish police chief during
the war and for his actions in Soviet Lithuania after the war.

Emil turned the thick pages. Then he glanced at the archivist
seated behind a glass wall at the front of the room and put his
mouth close to my ear.

"Your Uncle Aaron was a witness in the trial," he whispered.

Uncle Aaron!

Here was his signature, and his wife's, my aunt Sonya's. I stared and
stared at the names scratched in clumsy Russian script: "A. Levin,"
my uncle. "Leviniene," my aunt.

Having shared living quarters with the two of them in the ghetto,
Gens had called them as witnesses, Emil said, to help prove that
he had saved people from death in the ghetto. But as I would see
when I read their statements, they hadn't testified exactly as Gens
had hoped.

Emil turned to a neatly typed page. Here, he whispered, was
Gens's sentence, issued on December 10, 1949. "He got twenty-
five years."

Twenty-five years!

He was sent to Vorkuta, Emil said, one of the coldest, darkest
camps, on the Arctic Circle.

What had Gens done to receive such a severe punishment?

I would see, Emil said. To begin with, the authorities didn't like
the way Gens behaved after the war. And as for his actions during
the war? He waved his hand dismissively. "The KGB wanted to hear
that Gens beat people, but it was nonsense."

He hadn't beaten people?

Some witnesses did say Gens was brutal, Emil whispered, more
urgently this time, "but this was inevitable. The police themselves
were victims." The KGB didn't understand and didn't want to understand. That was why they considered Gens a criminal.

But —

From behind the glass wall, the archivist stood up and beckoned.

We scurried forward, and Emil filled out a form requesting that 40 of the 330 pages be copied. These were the pages I needed to see, he said, the pages I would find most interesting.

We returned to our table.

If Uncle Will had returned to Lithuania after he was liberated from Dachau, I asked, would he, too, have been arrested?

Quite possibly, Emil said.

After being freed from the concentration camps, many Jews, including Uncle Will, had left Europe and immigrated to Palestine, the United States, Canada, Australia. Uncle Aaron had come back to Lithuania to search for his missing son, Vova. But Gens may not have had anyone to search for. He had turned over his young daughter to the Germans on the day of the *kinder-aktsye*. His brother Jacob, the chief of the Vilna ghetto police, had been shot by the Gestapo.

Why had Gens come back?

"He was naive, like my grandfather," Emil whispered. The word "he," sounding like "khee," scratched my ear like sandpaper.

Emil's grandfather, the chief of the Jewish police in the Kovno ghetto, had managed to escape from the ghetto in its last days, during the liquidation in 1944, Emil said. But soon after, when the Red Army arrived in the city, he was arrested, as Gens was later, on charges of collaboration with the Nazis.

My fellow student, the daughter of a Kovno ghetto survivor, had dubbed Emil's grandfather "a monster." But Emil did not agree. His grandfather was a man of personal integrity, he said. "How," he whispered indignantly, "could they try a person who was forced into the ghetto?" If his grandfather should be tried by anyone, it should be by his fellow ghetto residents, not by Soviet officials.

At his trial, Emil's grandfather had presented a petition signed by fifty survivors of the Kovno ghetto who supported him and pleaded for his acquittal. The Germans had treated him like all other ghetto residents, the petition said. During one *aktsye*, his own mother was selected for deportation and he was unable to save her. He had not hurt or betrayed any ghetto residents. He had turned a blind eye to illegal escapes from the ghetto. And although he could have escaped, he had risked his life by remaining in the ghetto until the end.

At the trial, Emil said, no one had said anything against his grandfather except for one young woman. His English faltered momentarily: "She said that once she saw that he beated by his stick one Jew. But we must understand that nearby stood Germans and Lithuanians." The Jewish police *had* to keep order, Emil said. If they hadn't, Germans and Lithuanians would have intervened with greater brutality. Aunt Manya had said the same thing about the police in Uncle Will's ghetto.

Despite the support of his fellow ghetto residents, Emil's grandfather was not acquitted. Instead he was sentenced to fifteen years of hard labor and loaded onto a train headed for Irkutsk, in southern Siberia — the same camp where my uncle Aaron was to serve his sentence five years later. The transport lasted four and a half months. It was an unbearable journey, Emil said. "In September 1945 he reached the last station of his life." At the age of fifty, he perished at the camp.

For a long moment Emil and I sat together in silence, the fat volume about Gens before us on the table. Then the archivist beckoned us forward once more. I was to pay 141 *litai*, about $55. The pages would be ready in a week or two. Emil would collect them, bring them to me, and tell me what they said.

Hurrying up Gedimino Prospect, I reflected that Emil seemed to have made his peace with the way his grandfather had behaved in the ghetto. But I didn't feel at peace. In fact, I felt more uneasy than ever. What had motivated Soviet authorities to impose such a harsh sentence on Uncle Will's boss? And how would my uncle have been judged if he'd been put on trial?

IN the morning I woke up with my teacher's voice booming in my head. "A substantiv!" Niborski was insisting — a noun!

On the way to class I kicked a loose stone down the street. Stone: *shteyn* in Yiddish. Was a stone masculine, feminine, or neuter? In Yiddish, every *substantiv* — every person, place, and thing — had a gender, and so did pronouns and adjectives. Whenever I opened my mouth or tried to write a sentence, this nasty business caused me to stumble as if stones were strewn in my path.

Was it *der shteyn* or *di shteyn* or *dos shteyn*?

"Ah soob-stan-TEEV! Ah soob-stan-TEEV!"

In class, Niborski began handing back our essays. Had everyone else written longer, better ones than I? Anxiously I peered over my fellow students' shoulders, trying to see how many red marks appeared on the pages in their hands. My heart began to pound. But my essay didn't come back. Why not? After all the work I'd put into it, was it lost? Had the teacher not finished reading it? Or was it so wonderful that he was planning to shower it with special attention in front of the whole class the next day?

Some of our most common mistakes went up on the blackboard. Word order was a major sticking point. Perhaps because I grew up hearing traces of Yiddish syntax in the speech of my grandfather, my uncle, and other native speakers, this particular element of grammar seemed to come naturally to me when the sentences were simple ones. But when indirect objects and past tenses and other such complications entered the picture, I lost my ear. *I have to her it given? I have it to her given?*

In Bordin's class, we ran our tongues over long strings of adjectives formed from nouns: oaken door, woolen glove, golden ring, clay pot. We learned that *krenken* was to get sick, but *krenklen*, with an added "*l*," was to fall ill again and again in a less life-threatening way. And we lingered over the intricacies of verbs: *Me tut a kush*, we kiss. *Mir kushn*, we are kissing. *Mir flegn kushn*, we used to kiss. *Mir voltn gekusht*, we would have kissed. *Mir veln hobn gekusht*, we will have kissed. And finally, *lomir kushn*, let us kiss.

The breeze wafting through the open window was lovely, and so were the pleasures of language. There was something comforting about being a student. Even the anxieties were comforting.

IN the evening, the sky was aglow with delicate pinks and golds as my roommate Minette and I walked across town to the Friday-night dinner at the Jewish community building. Freshly showered, with wet hair, we felt *shabesdik*, purified for the Sabbath. Amid the candles, the heavy platters, and the flowing liquor, an antique merriness took hold. Niborski acted the straight man, stiff and wry, while Mendy Cahan, the director, clowned with the blue cloth napkin that covered the challah, tying it around his head like a babushka and holding forth in a shrill falsetto while we giggled helplessly.

In a memory book published after the war about Rokiskis, my family's hometown, I found a description of a turn-of-the-twentieth-century Sabbath evening:

> The little prayer house was bright and full of rejoicing. All the lamps were glowing. The table was full of various dishes and looked in a holiday mood. . . .
>
> The Hasidim took small sips of whiskey and munched on the rolls and herring. It didn't take long for them to become lively and jolly. The dancing began. . . .
>
> The revelry lasted late into the night.

With us at the table sat a stocky gentleman who was introduced as "the last Jew of Birzai." Birzai was the town near Rokiskis where my Little Grandpa had posed in the photograph on the face of the old postcard. His mother, my great-grandmother Asne, came from Birzai. Maybe this "last Jew's" ancestors once drank and danced with mine. And now here we were, a century later, lifting our glasses together in the candlelight.

THE next day, in the sun-splashed expanse of City Hall plaza, I spotted the couple I'd arranged to meet for lunch: Mindaugas, lean and tall, with a shaved head, and Aldona, dark-haired with a colorful scarf and a hearty smile. Friends of a journalist I knew back home, they were not officials but private citizens, non-Jews, who had grown up after the war. I hoped that like Violeta, the woman with the troubled marriage whom I'd met early in my stay, they would help me delve into what "ordinary" Lithuanians today were thinking about the Holocaust.

We ordered pickled tongue sandwiches, and Aldona began to speak. Her mother, she said softly, remembered the Jews with love. As a girl, her mother had worked in the gardens of a Jewish family, tending cucumbers. And during the war, she said, her family and their neighbors had helped to hide Jews. One Jewish family had given her mother a valise full of photographs and a coat. Aldona paused to consult her Lithuanian-English dictionary. "A karakul," she said. The word for the curly wool was the same in both languages. "Save this for us," the Jews told her mother. "If we come back . . ."

They did not come back. Years after the war, someone else, a member of the tiny community of Jews who had survived, showed up at the door. "My mother gave the photos to him, and they cried together."

Now Aldona cried, and the three of us sat together in the presence of her tears. For all I'd heard about how the truth of the Holocaust had been buried in Lithuania after the war, here at this table the tragic events were unquestionably close to the surface, and the emotions, passed along through the generations, indisputably raw.

I asked the two of them what they thought their country should do with the legacy of the Holocaust. Mindaugas answered first. One thing that should *not* happen, he said, was to push Lithuanians too quickly to say that they accepted responsibility for the Jewish tragedy "before they truly understand in their hearts."

Aldona went further. The notion of tarring all Lithuanians with the wartime misdeeds of a few did not make sense to her. Her mother's family, for example, had cared about the Jews and had helped them as best as they could. "You can't say a whole nation is a murderous nation," she said. Her face, so recently wet with tears, reddened. "Very few of our people took part in the Jewish Holocaust," she went on. "In every nation there are some bad people," but the majority were not guilty. In fact, "if you add up how many took part in murdering and how many took part in rescuing, the balance would be positive."

I recoiled from the toxic calculation. One percent murderers, 1 — or even 2 — percent rescuers, 97 or 98 percent doing nothing — and the tab was even?

Mindaugas began to talk about the sufferings of non-Jewish Lithuanians. After the Nazis were driven out, he said, Red Army recruiters had swept through the countryside conscripting young men. It was summer, he said, early July. He made a threshing motion with both hands. It was the time for cutting the wheat. His uncles were standing in the field when a Soviet army car drove up. "They began to run. The Soviets began to shoot. They stopped running and stood still. The Soviets came to them, and without asking any questions they shooted them."

Did I understand? He stuck out his index finger and wiggled his middle finger as if pulling a trigger. "In my family, two were shooted, and three died in Siberia," he said. "Every family suffered in one way or another in those years."

Aldona spoke up, this time more calmly than before. It was a misfortune for everyone, she said, when only one side accused and the other side was forced to apologize. "The main thing now should be to understand why everything happened and to forgive one another."

In her mind, Lithuanians were not the only ones who needed to express remorse. Her eyes flashed as she continued. In those days, she said, the very existence of the nation was at stake. When it came to the question of whether her country would survive as an independent state, "the Nazi and the Soviet times were the same — equally difficult, equally terrible." She held my gaze. "American radio promised to help us, but nobody helped."

She leaned toward me. "Why did you promise," she said, "if in fact you were going to compromise with Stalin?"

I blinked. *Me?* Why did *I* promise? What did I have to do with any of this?

Instead of accusing Lithuanians of war crimes, she pressed on, "would it not be better for Americans to think, aren't *they* responsible for the Lithuanian victims lying in forests and in Siberia?"

She had switched to *they* from *you*, but she still meant me. In her eyes, it was incumbent on me to ponder how I had contributed to Lithuania's oppression by the Soviets. The United States had failed to support her country's anti-Soviet resistance, and therefore it was my task to reflect on how I was complicit in the deaths of Lithuanians at Soviet hands.

After we parted, I walked away slowly. Aldona's words were ringing in my ears. So. Instead of traipsing around Lithuania investigating how others were or were not looking into their guilty souls, I should be looking into my own?

A complex business, this. My mind drifted to "Kapoyer" ("Upside Down"), a modernist poem by Aron Tsaytlin that we were reading in class, with verses full of murmuring leaves stirred by the wind. *Shushken*, to whisper; *shorkhn*, to rustle. Trees bend over their reflections in the water, and unexpectedly, it's the reflections, not the trees themselves, that speak. "We who shimmer in the water, unafraid of the ax," the reflections say, "are safer, more real. You who stand on the riverbank are the ephemeral ones: you could be chopped down any day."

A duality. As so often in my time here, all was topsy-turvy.

I would ask Leonidas Donskis, I decided, what he thought about Aldona's accusatory words. Donskis was one of Lithuania's most prominent public intellectuals. He was a professor at a Kaunas university and the author of innumerable books and articles, many of them in English, about nationalism, ideology, culture, and politics.

He was the host of a highbrow television show, and he worked with the European Union on efforts to promote tolerance. He was in Vilnius today to deliver a lecture at the old-fashioned Hotel Conti, off Pylimo gatve. When I arrived, his talk had just ended and he was surrounded by a clot of audience members, all talking at once. When he succeeded in tearing himself away, we sat down in the lobby in a pair of leather chairs pulled close together.

His eyes, as round as buttons, fixed me with an intense gaze as I asked what he had to say about Aldona's accusation. Should Americans feel guilty for abandoning Lithuania to Soviet oppression — or even Soviet genocide, as the museum would have it?

He frowned and ran his hand through his springy brown curls. It was not so simple, he said. "This victim complex — that Lithuanians were forsaken — it's simply not true," he said forcefully. The history of Lithuania included not only the hostility of outsiders toward Lithuanians, but also hostility among Lithuanians themselves. To say that all Lithuanians felt oppressed by the Soviet Union was a distortion. "Some of us, especially the dispossessed, joined the Soviet system with great enthusiasm," he said. "Lithuania was divided, not simply occupied."

What he referred to as the "theory of double genocide" was deeply misguided, he said. Irena Veisaite, too, had spoken of this view, which not only equated the suffering of Jews and Lithuanians but also tended to excuse the actions of Lithuanians who had collaborated with Hitler to massacre the Jews. According to this way of thinking, if Lithuanians did kill Jews in 1941, they were justified in doing so: after all, Jewish Communists had betrayed Lithuania a year earlier by facilitating the Soviet takeover of the country. "This symmetry theory is *profoundly* immoral," Donskis said.

And as for the idea that 98 percent of Lithuanians had been blameless because they neither killed nor rescued Jews?

"Bystanders are the crucial majority," Donskis said. "To describe them as morally neutral — I would never do that. To remain silent, not to lift a finger — that is to side with the killers."

It was no surprise, however, that such views had taken hold. "The Soviets isolated people from our own history," he said. During the Soviet era, it was forbidden even to make reference to relations between Lithuanians and Jews. In the Soviet telling, neither Lithuanians nor Jews existed as peoples: "there were only Soviet citizens."

When the facts did emerge into the light of day, it was natural for Lithuanians to feel defensive. "It is difficult to admit that one's sons and husbands were criminals — psychologically unbearable."

His insight into how people could deny an excruciating truth was based on personal experience, it turned out.

Even though his father was Jewish, he said, the Holocaust was not discussed at home when he was growing up. (His mother was a gentile. A mixed background, like mine.) It was not until he was twenty-seven, in 1989, that his father invited him to go for a walk and revealed the full story of what had happened in his *shtetl*, Butrimonys, during the war. Two thousand Jews were killed there; only six survived, his father among them.

"I started shivering," he said. "To say I was upset would be vastly understating the case. I did not quite suffer a nervous breakdown, but close to it. I couldn't *believe* that Lithuanians had slaughtered the Jews."

For a moment Donskis sat in silence, as if stunned anew. He shook his head. "The idea that Lithuanians killed my family members," he said, " — it was nearly unbearable."

At the thought of this inconceivable secret, I, too, felt myself beginning to shiver. I posed a final question. Were leaders like Irena Veisaite asking the impossible when they urged Lithuanians and Jews to engage in dialogue about the past?

No, he said, they were not. The expressions of anti-Semitism he observed in Lithuania filled him with sadness and pain, yet he also felt optimistic. "I used to think that never in my lifetime would I be able to discuss the Holocaust with ethnic Lithuanians," he said. "I was wrong." The dialogue had begun, and that in itself was cause for hope.

He urged on me an article he'd written in which he asserted his belief that Lithuania was on the way to becoming "a modern ... culture ... one that is open to itself and to the world ... is not rejecting or isolating of the Other, but is attempting to understand."

AFTER leaving Donskis, I walked over to Gediminas Tower, which stood at the head of the city's most stately boulevard, and climbed to the top. The old castle was a beloved landmark. In the fourteenth century, from within its thick stone walls, Lithuanians had beaten back the pike-wielding Teutonic Crusaders who had come to pillage their land and convert them to Christianity. Yet here was another duality. From atop the castle's lofty ramparts, the most prominent landmark, the Hill of Three Crosses, was a monument with a contrary meaning: it commemorated Lithuania's eventual *acceptance* of the Christian faith.

To the west, the broad straight line of Gedimino Prospect extended all the way to the Neris River. In the days of the czar, the avenue was known as Georgievskiy Prospect, in honor of St. George, the dragon slayer much revered in Russia. In 1920 it became Adam Mickiewicz Street, in honor of the nineteenth-century poet venerated by Poles and Lithuanians alike. In the 1940s it became Stalin Prospect, then Hitlerstrasse, then Stalin Prospect again. In 1956, after Khrushchev's denunciation of Stalin, it became Lenin Prospect. And after the fall of the Soviet Union it was renamed once again, this time in honor of the Grand Duke Gediminas, founder of Vilnius in 1323.

To the south, I could see the tiled roofs of Old Town, where I lived, and farther off, the modern apartment blocks that ringed the city. In the distance was the faint silver gleam of a television tower, where the most violent clash of the largely peaceful transition to Baltic independence had occurred. In January 1991 a crowd of Lithuanians had battled Soviet soldiers there; at least thirteen people lost their lives and hundreds were injured. Beyond was the dark forest of Ponar, where tens of thousands of Jews had met their deaths.

Down below I could see a pair of gnarled old women making their way through a throng of young people — the inheritors of this land with its complicated history. My head swirled with the diverse tales I'd been absorbing, the different ways of seeing. The years of Jewish cultural flowering, the ghettos and the massacres, the Soviet deportations and the guerrilla struggle — all had left their imprint.

Mir zaynen do, the Jews of the Vilna ghetto had sung. We are here.

A decade later, the anti-Soviet partisans in the forests had distributed leaflets expressing the same message: *Mes dar esame*. We are here.

My forebears must have inhaled this sharp sense of heterogeneity with their every breath. Now I was inhaling it, too.

Slowly I made my way down from the top of the tower and along Universiteto gatve to my flat. Was Lithuania making progress toward Donskis's goal of "not rejecting or isolating . . . the Other, but . . . attempting to understand"? And as my meeting with the elderly man in Rokiskis drew near, could I live up to that goal myself?

The Bystander

SATURDAY evening: *havdole*: the sundown that ends the Sabbath, dividing the holy from the profane. At the kitchen table, I sat composing a list of questions to ask Steponas, the old man I would be meeting the next day in Rokiskis, the man who wanted to speak to a Jew before he died. I knew next to nothing about this man, this "bystander" — only that he wanted to talk to me about the terrible things he had witnessed. I had not been brought up to warm to such a man.

I could see the two of us seated together in the count's manor house that was now a museum. We would look into each other's eyes across a heavy wooden table in a high-ceilinged room, I imagined, with my tape recorder whirring between us. Two strangers reaching out across the barriers of language, age, and culture. Two individuals, but also two representatives: I, a descendant of the perished Jews; he, a member of the neighboring population that had witnessed, resisted, collaborated, rescued, killed, acted and failed to act, helped and failed to help.

1. Name?
2. When and where born?
3. Occupation?
4. Father's and mother's occupations?

I felt nervous. More than nervous: afraid. I was afraid to hear what this man might say about the tortures that had been visited upon the Jews of Rokiskis, afraid I would be forced to listen to something I wouldn't be able to handle, especially not in his presence. I was afraid he would want to name names or confess a crime of his own, and that I would be asked to pronounce — aloud — some kind of judgment. I was afraid that in sharing his memories, he might want to shift a burden onto my shoulders. Would I be expected to forgive him? To reproach him, to punish him somehow? I sensed that he needed me as a listener because he had no others, aside, perhaps, from the museum official who had connected us. But maybe this wasn't true. Maybe he had a compulsion to tell his tale again and again. Maybe he wanted attention.

5. Why did the massacre happen?
6. Did everyone know about it?
7. Could it have been stopped?
8. After the fall of the Soviet Union, were people surprised by new information that emerged about the Holocaust?
9. What should happen now?

A heavy weight of dread had settled into my chest. But I had to meet this man — not only because I had agreed to, but also because the encounter promised to help me answer the questions that had woven themselves into my Lithuanian journey. Did I agree with my lunch companion Aldona, who believed that 1 percent of Lithuanians had killed Jews, 1 percent had saved Jews, and the other 98 percent were innocent? Or did I agree with Donskis, the political science professor who had talked to me about "understanding the Other"? Donskis was appalled at the idea of describing the bystanders as morally neutral. "To remain silent, not to lift a finger," he'd said, " — that is to side with the killers."

Outside my kitchen window, the pearly evening light was fading. Six years before, at just such a twilit moment, my daughter's bat mitzvah ceremony had been drawing to a close. I could see her sniffing the cinnamon in the ritual spice box and stretching out her hands to the flickering candles. I could hear her voice as she recited a *tkhine*, a Yiddish women's prayer:

Der liber, heyliker shabes geyt avek
Di gute vokh zol undz kumen
Tsu gezunt un tsum lebn
Tsu mazl un brokhe . . .

The precious holy Sabbath is departing
May the good week come to us
In good health and in life
In blessing and good fortune . . .

I had been delighted when she agreed to study Yiddish and *yidish-kayt* in preparation for her coming-of-age ceremony. My husband was glad, too. Although he treasured the values he'd absorbed as a child in Baltimore's Jewish community, the rituals themselves had left him cold. In synagogue every Friday night, he'd passed the time counting the ceiling tiles. He wanted something different for our children. When our son turned thirteen, we enrolled him in a humanist Sunday-school class that hosted a group mitzvah ceremony. Our daughter's Yiddish project seemed like another good way for us to pass on our values.

We found her a tutor, a lively college instructor who'd grown up speaking Yiddish in Montreal. Together, the two of them sang songs in Yiddish, made pickles in Yiddish, and went to the zoo in Yiddish to visit the *malpes* (apes), *helfandn* (elephants), and *bern* (bears). Our daughter was an eager student. She enjoyed the feel of Yiddish in her mouth, mastered the alphabet, and lapped up pages and pages of literature in English translation. One of her favorite stories was Peretz's classic "Oyb nisht nokh hekher" ("If Not Still Higher"), a profoundly humanist tale about an encounter between a skeptical Litvak and a Hasidic rabbi.

As the day drew closer, however, she began to have second thoughts about the secular, Yiddish-flavored ceremony in the works. What about prayers? she asked. Could she add some Hebrew prayers?

Prayers? Why?

She just liked them, she said.

A few weeks later: Would we mind if she studied the Torah?

Torah?

After a flurry of negotiations, we arrived at an agreement. She would read, in Hebrew, the portion of the Torah traditionally recited on the date of her ceremony. This turned out to be part of the story of the Jews' exodus from Egypt. Then, in Yiddish and English, she would present the story of another, more modern exodus — the immigration of a great multitude of European Jews to America.

Another tutor came onto the scene, a motherly Israeli woman with her own color-coded system of teaching trope, the age-old singsong in which the Torah is recited. As our daughter practiced diligently, my husband and I came to feel glad that she'd insisted on expanding her ceremony beyond the Yiddish study we'd proposed. She managed — gracefully — to assert what she needed while also embracing our ideas. She found her own way to bind herself to her Jewish heritage.

"I'm glad I connected myself with both the religious Jewish language and the more everyday one," she declared from the *bimah*, the platform from which the Torah is read. "These languages came alive for me. I found it very moving that the Torah has helped people for so long." She planned to pass on her knowledge of Yiddish to her children, who in turn, she hoped, would pass it on to their children.

Uncle Will sat beaming in the front row. After the ceremony, he offered the highest praise: "She doesn't even have an *eksent.*"

UP the road we went, heading for the northeastern corner of the country, almost as far as the Latvian border, where Rokiskis is the regional seat. Regina, my guide, sat with me in the back of the minivan, munching on a fish sandwich her mother had packed. Her friend Markas was at the wheel.

Mile after mile of gently rolling countryside went by. I saw tidy rows of cabbages, a solitary cow chained to a post in the middle of a field of Queen Anne's lace, a horse and wagon. A decaying collective farm from the Soviet era appeared, then another, and another, the long, low buildings dotting the countryside along with other abandoned places I couldn't see but knew were there — massacre sites from the Nazi era, and the "dead" Jewish cemeteries that were no longer in use, and the marked and unmarked graves of the fallen Forest Brothers.

Regina undid her hair, passed a wooden comb through long chestnut curls, braided them up again. She told me about her own background, which embodied some of her country's complexity. Her mother came from a Lithuanian Catholic family, many of whose members had spent time in Siberia, and her father had been a Russian Jew and a Communist. Over the past decade, Regina had become one of the country's leading "Jewish roots" guides, helping visitors from all over the world to touch the old places full of meaning.

Increasingly anxious, I no longer wanted to meet with Steponas. I wanted the drive to go on forever. But in a matter of a couple of hours — no time at all, it seemed — a sign by the side of the road announced that we were entering Rokiskis.

My ancestral home. Except for the trilling of birds, the town seemed hushed, suspended like a held breath. There was so much air. Somehow my images of the past hadn't allowed for so much blank space. Everything seemed inflated, spread out. The market square was spacious, lined on both sides with old-fashioned two-story buildings, with a green park in the middle. At one end, the Church of St. Matthew thrust its tall, skinny spire high into the heavens. On the cindery side streets with their ragged borders, the wooden houses wore thick coats of red, green, and ochre paint. The windowsills of the oldest ones almost touched the ground, and muddy vegetable patches ran right up to their back doors. A profusion of flowers smothered the yards — hollyhocks, foxglove, black-eyed Susans, nasturtiums, hydrangeas, lavender, roses. Giant frames crammed with firewood tottered beside gnarled apple trees.

Regina pointed to a small white rectangle nailed to the brown shingles of a corner house: Sinagogu gatve, Synagogue Street, it said. Here three Jewish houses of worship once stood, painted with the colors of the Lithuanian flag — a red house for the Jewish community at large, a green one for Jewish community leaders, and a yellow one for scholars like my great-grandfather Dovid-Mikhl, Uncle Will's father. I wondered how the townspeople could bear to pass by such a sign every day, and to refer to it in conversation: "Meet me on Synagogue Street." Did they even know what the word meant? Did it painfully evoke the lost community, or not?

We crossed a little bridge spanning a picturesque pond and entered the grounds of the count's estate. The endless green lawn was dotted with majestic trees. From inside the palace-turned-museum, the official who had written to me emerged. She greeted us warmly, then directed us down the lane toward a white cottage with a steep tin roof.

We pulled up in the yard, and out came Steponas. Here he was: the man I was afraid to meet. Under a green cotton cap with a visor, bright blue eyes peered out of an unshaven face. A long-sleeved work shirt, blue trousers. An aluminum cane with a blue handle. His wife followed: several silver teeth, a sleeveless blue housedress, white socks.

We were face-to-face, but he didn't look at me. Maybe he, too, was afraid. Maybe he, too, had come to wish that our meeting had been called off. With difficulty he climbed into the front seat next to Markas. I sensed his frailty, and the fragility of the moment, this brief and tenuous encounter between strangers. His wife got in back with Regina and me. Instead of facing Steponas across a table, I would be staring at the back of his head, at his green cap, while we drove slowly through the town. I wouldn't be looking at his face, and he wouldn't be looking at mine.

I wasn't sorry, I found. As Markas started the engine, Steponas began to talk. I had my tape recorder at the ready, and my prepared list of questions, but I saw that I wouldn't be using the list. I wasn't sorry about that, either. Steponas knew what he wanted to say. Instead of peppering him with questions, my job was simply to listen, to let his words pour out while I scribbled down Regina's murmured translations.

He was seventy-nine years old, he said, which made him eight years younger than Uncle Will. Most likely when they were little, the two boys had seen each other more than once on the street, up until 1930, when Uncle Will, then thirteen, and his mother went to live with Uncle Aaron in Siauliai. I had a sudden vision of my uncle now, at eighty-seven. What would he make of my sitting here in this van in Rokiskis, listening to this man in the green cap?

Steponas had grown up just a short walk from where he lived now, he was saying. His parents worked for the count's estate, his father in the stable with the horses, his mother in the milk house. Over the course of his lifetime, he himself had worked as a carpenter and a tinsmith.

He said something to Markas, and the van came to a halt by the bridge over the picturesque pond.

Steponas pointed into the dark, still water. The Jews were driven into the pond, he said. As they stood in the water, they were told that if they did not give up their valuables they would be drowned.

The van crept forward. After the Jews gave up their valuables, he said, they were driven over the bridge into this field. Here, to the right of this flower bed, was the camp. Here was the men's latrine, and over here was the women's. "All of these houses and barns were full of Jews."

He pointed to a stone building belonging to the estate. The killers had lived together there, he said.

The words kept coming, Steponas's husky rasp and Regina's low murmurs. I wanted to cover my ears, my eyes.

"I drove my wagon loaded with carrots past the camp," Steponas said. "I threw carrots over the fence to the Jews." For this the guards had threatened to kill him.

He pointed at a barn where Jewish men had been held. "They killed the young men first." After the barn had been emptied of Jews, grain had been stored there.

The Jews were marched down the road to the forest. The White Armbands — Lithuanians who assisted the Nazis with the massacre — lined both sides of the road. The White Armbands came from the villages and small towns all over the region, Steponas said. "You needed a lot of people to guard such a huge crowd of Jews. Thousands of Jews."

Day by day, the barns and outbuildings on the grounds of the estate were cleared of Jews. "They were killing, killing, killing."

Steponas began to weep, softly at first, then in short, harsh bursts. A policeman had tried to sell him a pair of shoes, he said, "all covered in blood."

He wept and wept. "They took all the people, marching," he said. "Even the children and the old people."

Regina leaned forward and stroked his arm.

"It was all on my eyes," he choked out. "I was watching."

The lament of the witness. I squeezed my eyes shut, then opened them. I forced myself to write down every word.

A Jew from Panevezys came to the door of his family's house, he said. His wife had delivered a baby and they were on the run. "My mother gave them food," Steponas said. "We are sure they were killed."

At last the stream of words subsided. As Steponas wiped his eyes, Regina asked me if I wanted to visit want to visit Bajorai, the killing field in the forest.

I said I did. We drove down the Akniste Road — the most important road to Latvia and Russia, Steponas said — taking the same route that the Jews had had to walk. A mile, another mile. All this way the columns had been driven — men, women, and children passing by the farmsteads of their neighbors.

"Akniste is very far," Steponas said. "Sixteen or seventeen kilometers."

We should be walking, I thought. We should be on our knees.

Cows bellowed in the fields. A sign: Village of Bajorai.

Until now, Steponas's wife had not said a word. All the time her husband was talking, she had stared out the window, her face turned away.

Now she asked the name of my Rokiskis ancestors.

"Levinas," I said, using the Lithuanian form for Levin or Levine.

"Oh, very rich," she said, and nodded to herself. In her mind, perhaps, all Jews were rich.

"No," I said, "not rich." My great-grandparents had struggled to feed their children. My great-grandmother had died young, probably of overwork. After her death, as I'd been told many times, my grandfather and his brother, Uncle Shaya, had been sent away. They had slept in a barn with the animals.

We bumped down a track into a clearing dappled with sun and shade. Steponas, with his cane, stayed in the car. His wife and Regina and I got out in front of a grassy rectangle. A plaque said, in Yiddish and Lithuanian:

Do ruen di umgebrakhte
yidn fun di litvishe
daytshe natsionaliste hent
av 22–23, 1941

Cia ilsisi zuvesieji
1941. VIII. 15–16
nuo lietuviskai —
vokiskuju
nacionalistu ranku

"Here rest the Jews killed by Lithuanian-German nationalist hands," read the Yiddish version. The date was expressed according to the

Jewish calendar — the 22nd to 23rd of Av. The Lithuanian version used the standard Julian calendar — August 15 to 16, 1941 — and the same strange expression for the killers — "Lithuanian-German nationalists." But where the Yiddish version identified the dead as Jews, the Lithuanian version said only "here rest those who were killed."

In this green glade, the Jews of the Rokiskis region, including some of my own distant cousins, had been lined up and shot. Now the wind stirred the leaves of the birch trees. I listened, and in my head I answered. *Ikh bin do*, I whispered. I am here.

Steponas's wife pointed out a road that disappeared into the trees. "This is the way to Obeliai," she said. She leaned on the railing and crossed her arms. During the Soviet times, she said, people had dug here at the pit. "They found gold teeth."

We got back in the van and returned to town. Steponas pointed out his childhood home, a bright green house surrounded by apple and cherry trees, and nearby, a miraculous well whose water made the finest lemonade.

A few minutes' drive brought us back to the steep-roofed white cottage near the count's mansion. "My wife and I are the only *dvariokai* (estate workers) still alive," he said.

The proud, lonely words hung in the air for a moment. Then everyone got out of the van, Steponas unfolding his legs with difficulty and leaning heavily on his cane. All of us were feeling the same way, it seemed to me: a little shaky, somewhat relieved. While Regina fielded a cell-phone call from a group of New York tourists detained at the border to Belarus, I went inside the cottage with Steponas and his wife. Wordlessly, I touched the green-painted chimney that rose to the ceiling and the cucumbers and battered pans on the table. The old people smiled, amused that I seemed to find these simple objects worthy of notice.

We went back outside. Finally, I asked a question, which Regina translated: After the war, had people talked about what had happened?

"Oh yes," Steponas said. Everyone had. Most people hated the killers. "We had a special name for them," he said, "a curse." After the war, the killers had not led good lives. Most of the leaders ran away with the Germans. Some of the rest retreated into the forest to fight the Soviets, and many died there. Some went insane. Many became alcoholics. Some committed suicide.

Was this true? I wondered. How many had melted back into the community and lived out their lives in peace?

At the end of the war, the pit at Bajorai was exhumed, Steponas said, but he had not been in town then. In 1944 he had been seized along with thousands of other young Lithuanian men and transported to Germany to work as a slave laborer for the Reich.

When it was time for us to go, the old man looked me in the eye at last. He held my gaze for a long moment, then tapped his chest. "I have shivers walking through these places," he said. "So much pain." He bent his head and looked at the ground. "Women carrying their babies."

I could feel the terrible images crowding in again, behind his eyes, behind mine.

"But why did they not fight back?" his wife asked suddenly.

He turned to her with a patient look. "They killed the young men first," he explained as he had before, in the van. "To make sure there would be no resistance."

I shook his hand. We left them standing in the doorway, beside the garden with the deep-red gladioli.

As we drove away, I stared out the window without seeing.

"A sweet man," Regina said after a few moments.

I tried to respond but found I couldn't speak. I held tight to my notebook and closed my eyes. In my mind I could see Steponas's stubbly face and hear his hoarse voice, his sobs.

"His wife was probably very frightened that he was talking to you," Regina said.

I nodded but still couldn't say anything. It would be a while, I

4. House in Rokiskis.

knew — hours? days? more? — before I would be able to look at the words I had scribbled down and think about what I had heard.

"It's too bad we had nothing to leave with them," Regina said. "You should send them something."

"What kind of thing?" I managed to ask.

"An apron," she said. "You should send them an apron."

THE day wasn't yet over. Before we left town, Regina wanted me to meet someone she referred to as "the last Jew of Rokiskis," who was waiting for us in a nearby coffee shop with her teenage daughter.

"The last Jew of Rokiskis" was a bit of a misnomer. Olga, a middle-aged woman with a nimbus of frizzy hair and a friendly smile, was a Jew, but not really "of Rokiskis." A native of Vilnius, she had been posted here after graduating from medical school. She ended up marrying a Rokiskis local, a gentile, and settling here to bring up

5. The count's manor house in Rokiskis, now a museum.

her children. Now she was the town psychiatrist. (The *real* "last Jew of Rokiskis," a barber who survived the Holocaust, had died some years back, I heard.)

Olga had lived in Rokiskis for nearly twenty years, she said, before learning of the town's Jewish past.

How extraordinary! She was an educated woman from the capital, a Jew, and a psychiatrist — yet she had lived here for twenty years utterly ignorant of the Jewish community that stretched back into the nineteenth century. She'd been oblivious of the bloody trauma of 1941. She'd been unaware of the demons that were haunting Steponas and presumably other town residents. (At the time of my visit, Lithuania had the highest suicide rate in Europe. Men who had lived through the war were among the most likely to kill themselves.)

A year ago, however, her eyes had been opened.

What had happened a year ago?

Olga's sixteen-year-old daughter, Tatiana, answered. Like her mother, she'd been brought up non-observant, she said. But a year ago, at the urging of a cousin, she'd attended a summer camp run by the American rabbi I'd seen presiding over the Friday-night service

6. The pond where the Jews of the Rokiskis region were forced to give up their valuables in the summer of 1941.

at the Chor Shul in Vilnius. At the camp, the rabbi gave Tatiana the assignment of writing to a former resident of Rokiskis, a one-hundred-year-old emigrant living in South Africa. The old man living at the other end of the earth had written back to her about the lost Jews of Rokiskis. From the old man's letters, Tatiana and her family learned that Jews had once constituted half the population of the town. They learned that the buildings still standing in the town square had once been occupied by Jews, and that the railway had been administered by Jews. From the old man, they learned, too, how the Jewish community was annihilated.

Tatiana now preferred to be addressed as Miriam. She ate only kosher food. She was leading a Jewish life, she said, and passing it along to her parents. She gave her mother's arm a squeeze. "Every Friday," she said, "we bless the *shabes* candles together."

So Olga was truly not the last Jew of Rokiskis. More than sixty years after the death march into the Bajorai forest, her daughter

7. The road that the Rokiskis Jews were forced to walk on their way to being massacred in the forest in August 1941.

was reaching back through all the years of shrouded truths and kindling the ritual lights.

BY the time Regina and I took our leave of Olga and her daughter, the market square was tinged with gold. In the doorways of the wooden houses, masses of marigolds glowed in the long rays of the afternoon sun. We stopped by the museum to say good-bye to the official who had connected me with Steponas.

"One more thing," the official said. She pulled two faded canvas-covered volumes off a shelf. During the Soviet times, she said, every regional museum was required to compile an official record of the Nazi era. These volumes contained the documentation collected in the Rokiskis region. Perhaps we would be interested in taking a look?

Regina and I moved closer as she turned the pages. Here were studio photographs of Jews who had been murdered, yellowed newspaper clippings, and signed statements from local eyewit-nesses, all neatly glued onto carefully numbered pages.

111

We were looking at a meticulous historical record of precisely the sort I had been told did not exist in the Soviet era.

Time and time again I'd heard that after a brief period of memorialization just after the war, the history of the Holocaust, and indeed everything having to do with Jews, had been banished from public view. Soviet authorities had their reasons for suppressing the true history. Lithuanians had reasons of their own. As a result, I'd been told, until independence came in 1991, the history of the Jews and the Jewish tragedy had been thoroughly obliterated. This, it was said, was why Lithuanians were shocked by the new information that emerged after the fall of the Soviet Union.

Thus went the story as I'd understood it, anyway. But as with so much I was learning here in the land of my ancestors, apparently things were not so simple. From the looks of the volumes before my eyes, it appeared that during the period when I'd been told the history of the Jewish tragedy had been suppressed, in fact Soviet authorities had *ordered* local officials all over the country to put together a painstaking account of the Nazi era. Could this be?

Regina touched the edge of a sepia-colored photograph. "These are treasures," she breathed. "Very important." She and the official exchanged a few words, and moments later the two of us were on our way out the door with the fragile volumes in hand, headed for a copy machine in the back room of the local supermarket. While Regina worked with the clerk, I wandered up and down the aisles. On a shelf of baked goods, I spotted something familiar. *Riestainiai naminiai*, said the label on the plastic bag. According to my Lithuanian dictionary, these words meant "home-style ring-shaped rolls." Bagels. A trace.

We left town bearing a stack of photocopied pages, all in Lithuanian, and the next day, back in Vilnius, Regina came to my apartment to translate them. For the first time, I skipped class. Whatever these pages — these "treasures," in Regina's view — turned out to say, they couldn't help but add to the picture I was putting together.

How had the Holocaust been characterized during the Soviet years? What kind of public discourse had Steponas grown up with?

We spread everything out on the kitchen table, and while I filled the kettle, Regina gave the side of the gas range a friendly slap.

"Made in the Soviet Union," she said. "The best in the world."

Unlike others, I'd noticed, Regina did not pepper her conversation with anti-Soviet remarks. While others referred matter-of-factly to Soviet rule as an occupation, she made big loopy quotation marks with both hands, referring to the Soviet "occupation."

I poured two cups of tea and turned on my computer, and Regina picked up the title page of the first volume, which was inked in a florid hand:

Liaudies gyneju veikla
ir burzuaziniu nacionalistu
piktadarybes Rokiskio
rajone karo ir pokario
metais

I typed while she translated:

The activities of the defenders of working people
and the wicked deeds of the bourgeois nationalists
in the Rokiskis region
during and after the Great Patriotic War

I stared at the screen. Even in English the words were beyond my comprehension.

Regina explained. "The defenders of working people" meant the Red Army and local Communists and their supporters. The wicked "bourgeois nationalists" were the Nazis and their local followers. "The Great Patriotic War" was the Soviet term for World War II.

We turned to an article that had been published in the local newspaper, *Tarybinis Rokiskis* (Soviet Rokiskis), in August 1945, after the German army was driven out and Soviet rule was reestablished.

A local man was writing of his wartime experiences. In the summer of 1941, he said, he and hundreds of others, whom he described as "Soviet activists," had been imprisoned in the basement of the Rokiskis municipal building. The room was knee deep in filthy water, and day after day the prisoners were beaten with iron bars and flayed with wire whips. But on August 16 they were removed from the basement and lined up outside, face-to-face with hundreds of local "nationalists." They were lectured and beaten again — and then released.

Released? August 16, 1941, was the day that thousands of Jews — men, women, and children — were marched into the forest of Bajorai to be murdered.

These particular prisoners were not Jews, Regina explained. They were non-Jews who were arrested under suspicion of being Communists. Some of them were killed by the Nazis and their local supporters, but some, like these, were spared.

The article made no mention of the massacre of the Jews.

Regina pulled a second article from the pile, this one published twelve years later, in 1957, again in a local paper. This one, too, concerned the events of the summer of 1941. When "the Nazi terror began against peaceful Soviet citizens," the article said, "Lithuanian fiends with white armbands went wild searching for Communists and Soviet activists in the town." The villains were described in sharp, if grotesque, relief. But nowhere was it mentioned that the vast majority of victims that summer were Jews — and not only "activist" Jews but Jews of all ages, executed by the tens of thousands.

A third article, this one from 1958, seemed even more obfuscatory. It stated that "citizens of *Russian* nationality" had been special targets for persecution by the Nazis. "Village peasants and workers," it continued, "fought together with all nationalities of poor people against the bourgeois exploiters."

I tried to imagine Steponas reading these articles in his cottage, perhaps by the light of a kerosene lamp. He had been there. He remembered what had happened to the Jews. What on earth would he have made of this bizarre vocabulary? No doubt he and many of his neighbors would have dismissed these and other official pronouncements about the war years as utter nonsense.

As the years passed, however, the fate of the Jews of the Rokiskis region began to emerge from the shadows. An article published in 1958 did not use the word "Jew," but it painted a vivid picture that would have rung true to Steponas and his fellow townspeople: "The crowd heads slowly toward Bajorai village on the unpaved road. Many carry heavy bundles. Others wear only pajamas — the murderers did not even allow them to dress. The residents of nearby farms say that they heard gunshots and screams for three days."

Finally, in 1965, the massacre came into full public view. Four Lithuanian men were arrested and brought to Rokiskis, where they stood trial as war criminals accused of mass murder. The chief justice of the Lithuanian Supreme Court came to town to preside over the trial. The high school gymnasium was turned into a courtroom, and local residents packed the hall.

The trial was publicized throughout the country. Articles appeared in the national paper *Tiesa* (The truth — "the *Pravda* of Lithuania," Regina said, referring to the organ of the Communist Party published in Russian until 1991). Once again, the thousands of victims were not described as Jews. Instead they were "Soviet activists," "Soviet people," "the doomed people," "the doomed." But here was something new. Although the word "Jew" was not used, for the first time all morning we saw two other words.

Did the word "ghetto" denote Jews? I asked.

It did, Regina said.

And the word "pogrom"?

Yes.

The prosecutor's remarks, too, communicated — to those who could decipher the code — that it was Jews who had been killed. The victims, he said, were "people who were guilty only because they had a different nationality . . . people who were destroyed only because of their different beliefs."

The four defendants were found guilty on all counts and sentenced to death.

"Just a little more," Regina said. She pushed three kitchen chairs together to make a bench, then lay down on her back, her chestnut hair hanging down nearly to the floor. She picked up a batch of pages that described another effort that had been carried out at the same time as the widely publicized trial. All over the country, committees of local people had been given the task of officially certifying the locations of the killing sites of the 1940s. In the Rokiskis region alone, four certification ceremonies took place. The documents describing these events made clear that the victims were Jews and that Lithuanians were among the killers. Carefully typed eyewitness accounts asserted that the killers had been drunk and singing. "When the killing was finished," said one, "they screamed 'Hooray' three times in Lithuanian" and tossed empty vodka bottles in among the bodies. Local community leaders and Jewish survivors had affixed their signatures.

We'd been translating for nine hours. The table was littered with the remains of the black bread, cheese, avocados, and almonds we'd been snacking on.

"One last thing," Regina said. She picked up a single page. Back in the office of the Rokiskis museum official, she'd spied a small black envelope pasted inside the cover of one of the volumes. Inside was a list, handwritten in black ink. "Here are the killers," she'd said softly. Now, together, we bent over the names that had been carefully gathered and inscribed by museum staff. Nineteen names of Rokiskis residents and their official positions: head of the prison, interrogator. These men — Steponas's neighbors — were not drunken hooligans. They had carried out their work deliberately and methodically. Their identities were known. The facts had been officially gathered.

My head was reeling.

How could Olga, the "last Jew of Rokiskis," not have known that *every* Lithuanian town had once been home to a sizable Jewish community, and that *every* town had been cleared of Jews in 1941? How could Donskis, the political science professor, who like Olga was the child of a Jewish survivor, have grown up not knowing that Lithuanians had participated in killing their Jewish neighbors?

People did know.

At least, some people did.

Or, at some times, some did.

Over the years, the Soviet presentation of the past had been replete with distortions. No doubt many Rokiskis residents had ignored the 1965 trial and the program of local commemoration, or dismissed it all as false propaganda. Yet there was no denying that in the Soviet Lithuania of the 1960s, at least on some occasions, the reality of the Holocaust had been brought into the open for all to see. As I looked at the pages spread out on the kitchen table, I found it harder than ever to understand how anyone could be surprised to learn of the existence of the lost Jewish community in a place like Rokiskis, or be shocked to find out that neighbors had joined with Nazi invaders to commit mass murder.

While Regina stacked up the pages we'd been working on, I poured two glasses of limeade from the mini-market. *Viva revolucion!* said the carton — "Juicy revolutionary fruit taste! Cuban ingredients!"

Why had Soviet authorities so often been careful not to refer to Jews as such? I asked. Were they seeking to erase the Jews and their history, just like Hitler?

Regina sipped her juice. "The Soviets were internationalists," she said. In an effort to unify a deeply fractured society, authorities had sought to play down, or even conceal, the "otherness" of the massacred. They took pains, instead, to stress the "otherness" of the killers, denigrating them as "fiends," "bastards," and "outcasts." By referring to the Jewish victims as "innocent citizens," they sought to fold them into the ranks of "all of us."

"It was probably just as well that Jews were not explicitly mentioned," she went on. In some ways, things were better in the Soviet times. "There was less opportunity for people to express their anti-Semitism."

What, I asked, explained the change that took place in the 1960s? Why the highly publicized war crimes trial of 1965? Why the nationwide campaign to gather Holocaust history and certify mass-murder sites?

The trial in Rokiskis was not the only one of its kind, Regina said. Similar trials had been held in Vilnius and Kaunas around the same time and received heavy press exposure. Maybe these proceedings were a response to the internationally sensational trial of Adolf Eichmann, the Nazi lieutenant colonel who oversaw the transport of thousands of Jews to concentration camps. Eichmann was condemned to death in Jerusalem in 1961. The trials in Lithuania were perhaps intended to demonstrate that the Soviet Union, too, could prosecute Nazi collaborators.

Maybe, too, I reflected, it wasn't until the 1960s that the Soviet Union began to emerge from a postwar "latency period" regarding the Holocaust. The same had been true in the United States and Western Europe. In the West, after the Nuremberg trials ended in 1946, many years passed before the Holocaust became the subject of public discourse.

But there was a difference. Having brought the Holocaust into public view in the 1960s, Soviet authorities did not follow the lead of the West and keep it there. Over the next twenty-five years, once again the wartime fate of the Jews sank into official obscurity.

Regina put down her glass and stood up. "Whoever is in power tells the story his own way," she said. "Every era produces its own historiography."

And then she left, in a hail of kisses and *litai*, the bills I was paying her with. When the door closed behind her, I stomped around the apartment in a rage. I ranted about the terrible things human beings did to one another and about how cursedly difficult it was to make sense of it all.

IN the university courtyard the next morning, someone asked about my trip to Rokiskis. I still hadn't begun to explore my thoughts about the meeting with Steponas — it occurred to me that I was experiencing a "latency period" of my own — but I was able to say a few words about him, and about his tears.

"Now he thinks he can die with a clear conscience," one student said, and made a sour face.

"How do you know he was telling the truth?" said another.

"Maybe he wanted money," said a third.

"Well —" I said. It hadn't seemed that way to me. But now Niborski, our teacher, was entering the courtyard with his briefcase, and we gathered up our books and followed him into the building.

On the staircase, he, too, asked — in Yiddish, of course — about my trip.

A lump formed in my throat.

"Der kop iz fardreyt," he said gently — your head is spinning.

I nodded.

He himself had never wanted to visit his ancestral town in Poland, he said. It would have been too painful.

"Dos hob ikh nit gefilt," I said — I hadn't felt that way. I was glad I'd gone. Glad to have touched the spot where my ancestors had lived and died. Glad to have seen the cows, the trees, the sky. Glad to have met Steponas. "Ober" — "But" — I faltered, unable to say more.

"Write something about it in Yiddish," Niborski urged. "Try."

That evening at the kitchen table, I read a short story by Esther Singer Kreitman, sister of the famed Nobel Prize–winner Isaac Bashevis Singer. The setting was a snug wooden house — a dwelling like Steponas's, I imagined. On a chilly *shabes* afternoon, the cottage is sunk in deep snow — just as, for me, the meaning of the text was buried under the blanket of a difficult alphabet. Inside, near the stove, a lumber dealer named Yidl is opening a holy book. He is a beginning reader, this Yidl, who holds his place with an index finger as he sounds out the words. Just like me. Together, the two of us made our way down the page.

After a few minutes, my mind wandered. Uncle Will came into view with his mild smile, his head tilted to favor his good ear. When I got home, I imagined, I would visit the New York apartment and tell him about my visit to Rokiskis — about the market square and Sinagogu gatve and the count's mansion. It would be a *mekhaye,* a joy, to sit with my uncle while he crossed over into the world of his childhood. If I couldn't cross over with him, at least I could linger on the threshold, peering in.

I'd had the same feeling at Steponas's cottage when I entered his kitchen and touched the table, the cucumbers, the rough plaster of the fat chimney that rose up through the roof. It was not my home. I couldn't stay. But it was a privilege to be allowed to come close.

I could see Steponas now, bent over his cane. I still knew little about him. I didn't know how he was regarded in his community, or whether he had been honest or dishonest in what he said, or precisely why he had wanted to reach out and connect with me. Whether out of a sense of courtesy, or fear, or my limitations as an interviewer, or a desire simply to accept what was given, I hadn't pushed to find out.

Contrary to my apprehensions, Steponas hadn't confessed to a grisly crime of his own. He hadn't wanted to name names. He had asked neither for absolution nor for reproach.

Instead, he told what he had seen, showed where he had seen it, and laid bare his unending anguish over what had happened. I could hear his cry: "It was all on my eyes."

When Uncle Will talked about his wartime experiences, in contrast, he was flat and matter-of-fact. The story flowed evenly through him without much emotion, at least in my company. There was something cartoonish about his ghetto anecdotes: the live chicken he'd smuggled into the ghetto in his pants, the hot bath worth a million dollars. The details about his being a policeman were all positive ones: he'd kept order in the food line, warned people away from the German guards, and hidden the two little girls, who were now grandmothers in Israel. About the *kinder-aktsye*, his statements were simple, declarative, minimal: "I was at the gate."

Had his fellow ghetto residents come begging for favors or offering bribes? Had they asked him for help that he couldn't or wouldn't give, and what had happened then? Had he beaten anyone with his truncheon? He didn't say.

About what happened after the ghetto, my uncle was equally undemonstrative. Of the concentration camp at Dachau, he said: "I had an easy job." And: "On the death march, I carried my brother on my back." I'd read survivor accounts that vividly described the bitter cold, the desperate hunger. Uncle Will said: "We ate raw meat from a horse," leaving it to the listener to imagine the extremity of the situation.

Steponas had wept in my presence — not my uncle. Why?

Whether my uncle was at peace with the past, I didn't know. But I did know that he'd had a community in which to move toward recovery. In the displaced persons camp, and later with his fellow survivors in New York, he had polished and ordered the meaning of his past. Steponas, it seemed, had not been able to do this. The trauma of witnessing had never been sufficiently acknowledged by his society. I didn't know whether he'd spoken before audiences other than me, but even if he had, it hadn't been enough for him. At this late date, he'd needed me, a visitor from overseas, to hear his tale and recognize his pain.

Was it easier for Steponas to unburden himself to a stranger than for my uncle to confide in a family member? It struck me that my extended family had never served as a safe haven for Uncle Will's memories. In 1949, when my uncle arrived on American shores, my grandfather, by then a well-established immigrant, had perhaps not greeted him with open arms — or open ears. Nor was I a risk-free listener. Alongside my love for my uncle was my drive to get at the facts, to wrestle with moral questions. No matter how respectful and compassionate I felt, I had my own needs, which were bound to make him uncomfortable.

Was the experience of observing someone else's suffering a torment all its own? It was clear that Steponas's experience of watching in relative safety while others were assembled to be murdered had inflicted a special kind of wound, and a deep one. It was this, not his own ill-treatment at the hands of the German invaders, that he needed to talk about. Toward the end of the war, he'd mentioned, he'd been forcibly taken to Germany. I'd heard that the young Lithuanian conscripts had suffered terribly. They dug trenches while subsisting on starvation rations. When Allied bombs fell, they were ordered to run into burning buildings to retrieve valuables for Nazi officers. Yet what made Steponas's shoulders shake with sobs was not the pain visited upon him personally but the agony of seeing others suffer.

I wondered what "speaking to a Jew" — me — had done for Steponas. Had I responded the way he'd hoped? Had telling the story helped him? Now that I had listened, would anyone else do likewise? What could his country do for people like him?

And what was I to do with what he had told me? Was I to judge, to forgive, to condemn?

Being a bystander, a passive witness, was perhaps a moral failing, even a moral crime. But listening to Steponas had shown me that the act of witnessing — forced witnessing — could also be a kind of victimization. And Steponas, the Lithuanian bystander, was not *only* a bystander. He had not just stood by. He had taken risks on behalf of the Jews. By throwing carrots over the fence into the ghetto, he had imperiled his own safety.

For that matter, Uncle Will, the victim, had also been a bystander of sorts. He had stood at the gate while children and old people were loaded into trucks and driven away into the unknown.

Had Steponas been a "collaborator"? In going about his daily business, driving his wagon past the tents and barns that held the incarcerated Jews (even if he did sometimes throw carrots), had he contributed to a general sense in the town that the incarceration was normal, acceptable?

And as for Uncle Will, simply by standing at the gate, had he added an aura of Jewish authority to the roundup?

If it seemed offensive to say that Uncle Will had "stood by," or even "collaborated," during the *kinder-aktsye*—if you claimed that the Jewish police were so victimized under the Nazis that they couldn't be said to have had choices—then what should be said about the seventeen-year-old Steponas, living in his green cottage next to the ghetto? Was it or was it not asking too much of ordinary Lithuanians to expect them to stand up against the Nazis and protect the Jews?

Of course, many Lithuanians didn't *want* to help. Some bystanders benefited from the persecution of the Jews. Some actively wished the Jews ill.

But Steponas had helped, a little, and it seemed to me that it was his anguish about whether he could have done more that had led him to want to speak to me, and then to weep before me. His mother had helped the Jew from Panevezys who was hiding with his wife and baby. Aldona, who met me for lunch with her husband, had broken down in tears while telling how her mother's family had tried in vain to protect their Jewish neighbors. Like Steponas, she was haunted by the tragedy, even though she was too young to have seen it with her own eyes. Violeta's mother, whom I'd be visiting in her hometown of Kedainiai, would soon be telling about how she, too, had helped to save Jews.

Where on the moral continuum did these actions, and these people, lie? And where did my uncle and his actions lie?

As I sat asking myself these questions at my kitchen table in Vilnius, on the site of the former Small Ghetto, I felt a bit like a traitor. What was I doing, poking and sniffing at the behavior of the Jewish police, and consorting with locals, in the land where my people had been murdered by the hundreds of thousands?

A similar uneasiness must afflict Lithuanians in their new era of public discourse, I reflected. In questioning the actions of people they loved, they, too, must find their sympathies pulled in new directions, beyond where they had ever ventured before.

Steponas was only one of the people I'd met who felt compelled to retrieve things from the deep. I thought back on others I'd encountered in my time here. Irena Veisaite, the Kovno ghetto survivor who honored her "two mothers," the Jewish one and the gentile rescuer, was promoting dialogue about the past and the future. The men on opposite sides of the aisle at the disputed Chor Shul were seeking in different ways to preserve their endangered heritage. Fanya and Rokhl, among the last Yiddish speakers in Vilnius, were dedicated to passing on their memories. Emil, my volunteer research assistant, was digging into the archives. Dalia Kuodyte, at the Museum of Genocide Victims, was remembering the suffering and resistance of her people during the Soviet era. Aldona recalled the vanished Jews alongside the travails of Lithuanians under the Soviets. Donskis, the philosopher, himself scarred by secrets, subjected Lithuanian bystanders to a severe moral judgment, yet he hoped that his country was capable of "embracing the Other." In Rokiskis, Tatiana-turned-Miriam was lighting the Sabbath candles. All of them felt an urgent need to exhume the buried truths of their country's past. Steponas, with his yearning to tell, belonged among them.

I put my homework aside. As my teacher Niborski had suggested, I began to write in Yiddish about my visit to Rokiskis. Using neither a dictionary nor a grammar book, I honed the experience to its essence. A man tormented by the past had emerged from the void. He had offered something of himself to me, then vanished back into the unknown.

S'iz do in dem shtetl an alter man.
There is an old man in town.

Er vil redn mit a yid.
He wants to talk to a Jew.

Ikh bin der yid.
I am the Jew.

Mir trefn zikh lebn dem palats funem graf.
We meet near the palace of the count.

Der alter man taytlt tsum rekhts un tsum links.
The old man points to the right and to the left.

"Do hot men zey getribn keyn bajorai."
"Here they were driven to Bajorai," he says.

Er heybt on tsu veynen.
He begins to weep.

PART TWO

Mes Dar Esame

(LITHUANIAN FOR "WE ARE HERE")

Kas, jei ne tu, kurs   Who, if not you, will determine
rytojaus Lietuva?!   the future of Lithuania?!

VILNIUS BILLBOARD

8. Billboard in Vilnius: "Who, if not you, will determine the future of Lithuania? Become socially active!"

Our Goal Is to Transform Ourselves

RUNNING late as usual, I rushed out of class and hurried up Universiteto gatve. Midway through my visit, I was about to begin a series of meetings with leaders of projects that encouraged Lithuanians to face their history. As I listened to these leaders, I would be thinking of Steponas, of Uncle Will, and of lessons I could glean for my own engagement with a complicated past.

My first appointment was with leaders of the Jewish museum, which was spread out over several locations. A green wooden house off Pamenkalnio gatve was home to displays about the Vilna ghetto and other aspects of the Holocaust. The Jewish community center on Pylimo gatve contained other holdings. Not far away, on Naugarduko gatve, was the recently renovated Tolerance Center, where a new exhibit was being installed. There, following a worker in paint-spattered overalls, I picked my way through drop cloths, ladders, and blueprints to reach the office of the director, Emanuel Zingeris, high above the red roofs of the old city.

Zingeris, perhaps the most prominent Jewish public figure in Lithuania, was singular-looking, with jet-black hair and high cheekbones in a chubby face, and widely known for his efforts to bring the Jewish past out of obscurity. In the late 1980s he was active in Sajudis, the Lithuanian independence movement; he had signed the Lithuanian declaration of independence from the Soviet Union.

He was an off-and-on member of Parliament — so far the only openly Jewish one. As a delegate to the Council of Europe, he'd pushed for recognition of Yiddish as an endangered language and *yidishkayt* as an official European culture. Like Irena Veisaite, he was controversial among Jews and non-Jews alike.

No one questioned his energy, though, and as he entered his office on the run and plopped into a swivel chair I could see why. His English, which was excellent, streamed out in such a forceful torrent that I had a hard time keeping up. When he was growing up, he said, his mother, a Holocaust survivor, had told him about the vibrant Jewish life in prewar Lithuania, but he had never been able to grasp what she was talking about. Only as a university student did he begin to understand. By chance, he happened upon an archive of prewar Yiddish newspapers and was astounded by the rich cultural life they revealed.

Then, in a book, he came across a passing reference to the tiny Jewish museum that had been established in Vilnius immediately after the war by survivors of the Vilna ghetto, including members of the so-called Paper Brigade, the ghetto residents who had been forced to sort through Jewish books and other treasures plundered by the Nazis. During the war, these men had risked their lives to save as many books, prints, and religious objects as they could, concealing them in their clothing and spiriting them into hiding places in the ghetto. When the war ended, they crept into the smoking ruins to search for the precious remnants.

Rokhl Kostanian, Zingeris's deputy director, who had survived the war as a Jewish child refugee in Russia, added to the story in a high, clear voice. Carrying Jewish artifacts out of the rubble on little carts, she said, the survivors would smile and say, "This is our Louvre."

But the little museum created to display these objects lasted only a few years. In 1949 it was closed down, a victim — as Irena Veisaite had said — of Stalin's "campaign against cosmopolitanism." Even in the years after Stalin's death, as the decades passed, Lithuania's magnificent Jewish heritage remained invisible.

Then, in 1986, Kostanian said, she was walking down a street in Vilnius when she spotted a giant Jewish star plastered to a pole. At first she was afraid it was a racial slur. Instead, to her astonishment, it was a poster announcing that for the first time since the war, an exhibit of Jewish cultural heritage was to be displayed at an art gallery in Kaunas.

On opening day, the gallery was packed. The chairman of the Lithuanian Cultural Foundation got up to address the crowd. "My dear sister and brother Jews," he began.

Everyone was shocked. "I almost fainted," Kostanian said. "We were in tears."

Soon after, two dozen intellectuals bravely wrote to the government to say it was time for public acknowledgment of Lithuania's Jewish history, and for explicit discussion of the wartime massacres. "*Nu, kinderlekh*, well, people, that was something," Kostanian said, her eyes shining in her mournful face. "*Gan eyden* had come to us" — the promised land was in view.

During the Stalin years, it turned out, the staff of various Lithuanian museums had secretly stored some of the artifacts from the closed Jewish museum in their own warehouses. Other pieces had gone on display, along with ritual objects from other faiths, in a mocking "Museum of Atheism" that had been installed by the Soviet government in the Church of St. Casimir. Still others had been sold to antique shops.

Zingeris and others took up the challenge of tracking down the dispersed pieces and bringing Jewish culture into the light of day. Kostanian eagerly joined in. During the course of a long life, she said, she had never been acknowledged officially, without bias, as a Jew. Now all that changed. "I began to learn about our enormous heritage." The reclaiming of her culture became her passion. "It is a healing to my heart."

Bit by bit, most of the original collection was reassembled. In 1989, after being shuttered for forty years, the Jewish museum reopened its doors. "We made this museum from scraps of nothing," Zingeris said. "From remnants of remnants."

He fairly bounced in his seat as the words gushed forth. Once, he said, the Jewish community was "a vibrant *mittel-european* nation, fully competitive with the Baltic and Western European cultures." The streets of the Jewish quarter, he went on, were thronged with "open-minded Mediterraneans." It was a nation of idealists: every sister, brother, and cousin belonged to a different movement. Here was an organization to study Darwinism, here a Zionist organization, here a Bundist workers' organization. The energetic Lithuanian Jews numbered fewer than a quarter of a million, but they produced as much as if they had been two million.

As we strolled through the gallery, Zingeris pointed to glass cases full of silver candlesticks and other objects dating back to the seventeenth century. "We are telling the story about the Jews, our great Europeans," he said, "who were so creative, brave, and free. They were cut down in their glory. Now we must pick up the pieces. We are trying to frame in a golden frame every piece of our history. Every artist. Every writer. In the emptiness of their physical absence, we are putting together a broken mosaic," restoring them to their position among the European nations.

Oils, drawings, and woodcuts by dozens of prewar artists covered the walls. As these Jews strove to express themselves within the European artistic movements of their day, Zingeris said, they studied the carvings in wooden synagogues and the tombstones in cemeteries. The Jewish folk tradition fed their imagination.

He pointed to an elaborate miniature court of King Solomon, with wooden birds and animals dressed in tiny costumes trimmed with faded bits of lace and gold braid. This was but a trace of what used to be, he said. Once, Jewish homes had been filled with such crafts, including the intricate paper cuttings known in Yiddish as *shnitseray.* Now this womanly craft was gone. "We have searched village by village," he said. "Finally just now I have received a phone call from a rural museum that might possibly have one single example."

New acquisitions were being added one by one. The new exhibit, called *The Lost World,* covered seven centuries of Jewish life in Lithuania. It was aimed not only at local Jews and foreign tourists but also at the mainstream of the Lithuanian population. Zingeris dreamed of seeing local schoolchildren, students, intelligentsia, Lithuanians of all walks of life coming to the museum to get to know the thousand faces of Lithuanian Jewry.

But he wasn't waiting for Lithuanians to come to him. Instead, he was bringing the museum to them. Twenty-eight colorful panels, crammed with maps and texts and photographs, had been designed to travel to towns and villages throughout the country. I stopped in to see Ruta Puisyte, a young gentile woman who had spent two years driving the exhibit around the country in a truck.

The young woman's pale face glowed as she described how, upon arriving in a town, she would jump out and set up the panels for local people to see. All notables were invited, members of organizations, "and of course," she said softly, "the Jewish community, if there is one." The panels drew extensive coverage from local media, usually positive, Puisyte said. Some local museums reported that the exhibit attracted more visitors than they normally drew in an entire year. All in all, more than fifteen thousand people, mostly students, had viewed the panels.

In every town, a training session was offered to local teachers. Often, so many signed up that some had to be turned away. The word "Holocaust" was new to many of the participants, or they weren't sure exactly what it meant. Most of the teachers had never met a Jew. They asked Puisyte, "Please, show us a real living Jew." Some teachers asked if it was true that matzo was made with the blood of Christian children. In nearly every session, Puisyte heard remarks about Jews being Communists or avaricious financial wizards.

But, she said, "you plant seeds. You go and do it, you go and do it, and you believe." Teachers who came to the seminars full of prejudice saw that many of their colleagues had more open-minded viewpoints. Puisyte counted this as an important step forward.

The complexity of knowing and not knowing continued to baffle me, I told Puisyte. How could it be that the story of the Holocaust was new to the people she was teaching?

Puisyte nodded and leaned forward. Once, she said, she had asked a sixty-year-old woman whether, while growing up, she had ever noticed that half of her town was empty. No, the woman said, she hadn't noticed. But Puisyte felt sure that she had. "People seem to be concerned only with their fields, their pigs," she said. "But of course they know. All generations know."

She herself, she said, had heard part of the story as a young child, when her father had explained to her that innocent people had been killed by bad people. Bad local people. But in school she heard nothing. She was eighteen when she first met a Jew, in 1992, as a university student. Only then did she learn the full story. "All the blood and terror — I approached this with open heart and open mind." Behind her glasses, her eyes began to glisten. "I was crying and crying."

Now Puisyte was at work on an educational booklet that was to be distributed in high schools. She showed me the text she was carefully crafting:

> Most of the Lithuanian people didn't participate directly in the Holocaust. They saw the tragedy that the Jews were experiencing, felt sorry for them, but didn't aid them or attempt to save them. All they did was watch.

Four questions followed:

> What do you think of Albert Einstein's saying, "The world is a dangerous place, not because of those who do evil, but because of those who look on and do nothing"?

Why did only 6 percent of Lithuanian Jews survive? Could it have been different?

Have you ever been in a situation where someone needed your help and you didn't provide it? If so, why did you behave like others, rather than following your conscience?

Is there a connection between your answers and the behavior of people during the war?

Tough questions, I thought. Searing questions.

The museum was closing for the day. Downstairs, as we paused in the doorway, I could see tears on Puisyte's cheeks. I put down my bag and gave her a hug. "Thank you for what you do," I said.

Kostanian, the deputy director, escorted me out of the museum. Before we parted, she lifted her face into the late afternoon sun and asked what I thought of her city.

I looked around me at the light glinting on the curved iron balconies. It was beautiful, I said.

"Beautiful," she agreed — "and sad."

THE next day after class, I made my way to the Gallery of the Righteous, a branch of the Jewish museum located in the Jewish community building, which honored Lithuanians who had rescued Jews during the war. I found Viktorija Sakaite, a middle-aged gentile woman, at her desk high up on a top floor. Through the large bare windows, sunlight poured onto her strong features, the blond hair that cascaded to her shoulders, and her bright red blouse. Outside, the city with its pale walls and terra-cotta roofs stretched away into the hills.

She had been working on the Righteous Gentiles project for twelve years, she said in Lithuanian as my interpreter translated. In 1992, just after independence, she had teamed up with a Jewish professor from Siauliai University. Beginning with a single box of photographs, they had written hundreds of letters and set out to gather oral histories.

The research was not easy. Many of the rescuers, as well as the rescued, were no longer alive. Names and details had been lost. Sakaite showed me an essay that her project had published. "The facts related to the rescuing of Jews could have been the water of life for us," it lamented. "Alas, alas. All this has been scattered, not collected, and it is too late to turn back."

Over time, however, Sakaite's files had grown to contain the names of some three thousand rescuers. So far she had published three volumes containing reminiscences and photographs.

Who, I asked, were the rescuers?

People from all walks of life, she answered. In the big towns, the rescuers came from the ranks of the intelligentsia, including teachers and doctors. In the small towns and in the countryside, they were farmers.

Were they unusual people? I asked. People with a special spirit?

There were three kinds of rescuers, she answered.

First were Catholics who believed it was a good deed to convert the Jewish children they rescued.

Second were farmers who needed extra workers for their farms. It was hard to get workers during the war. So long as the German officials didn't find out about them, Jews were a useful source of labor.

Third were childless couples looking for children to bring up as their own. Girls were preferable, while boys were more difficult to adopt because circumcision marked them as Jews.

I looked at my interpreter. Had I lost something in the translation? Was that all?

Well, Sakaite said, perhaps there was one more factor. She drew herself up tall. She was from Zemaitija, she said, referring to the northwest quadrant of the country. The region had an independent tradition, she declared. "If the Germans say, 'Do not rescue,' we say, 'We *will* rescue.'"

A silence fell. I thought of Steponas, who had thrown carrots to the hungry Jews in Rokiskis, and of his mother, who had helped to hide a Jew on the run and his pregnant wife. I thought of Aldona, my lunch companion, who had cried when she told me that her mother's family had safeguarded photographs and a karakul coat for a Jewish family who did not survive. Surely it was compassion, fellow feeling, that had guided their actions.

I looked again at my interpreter, then back at Sakaite. Were any of the rescuers motivated by moral considerations, I asked — by a sense of right and wrong?

This, Sakaite answered, was hard to say. During the war, people tended to keep quiet about such things. If you got caught and the Nazis sensed that you actually cared about the Jews and their welfare, you were in trouble. But if you could plead that you'd taken in a Jew simply for the money — many Jews paid their saviors for the food they ate, and others paid much more — or to help out on the farm, then your punishment might be less severe.

But what about after the Nazis were gone? What about now?

Rescuers still didn't like to talk, Sakaite said. Many were still afraid. After the war, two-thirds of the rescuers ended up being sent to Siberia — not so much because they were rescuers per se, but because they were deemed "bourgeois." Rescuers *were* more likely than others to be bourgeois — to own property, to be better off than their neighbors. They were the ones who had the extra room, the barn, the wherewithal to take on such a responsibility. When the Soviet era began, many of these people were considered hostile to the regime.

Sakaite's goal was to break the long silence. "I am a teacher," she said. "I am glad when I can encourage people to talk."

She had personal experience with secrets, she said. Before she was born, during the Soviet era her father had been sent to Siberia for ten years, punished for the "crime" of directing a theater in the city of Panevezys. She had learned of his exile only in 1987, when she was thirty-four years old. And about the other great secret, the story of the vanished Jews, she had heard nothing as a child. She had had no education about Jews at school, nor had her parents told her anything.

She was beginning work on her fourth volume full of rescue stories, she said. Her plan was to make ten books, maybe eleven.

This gentile woman working for the Jewish museum, stubbornly publishing one volume after another, was herself a rescuer, I realized — a rescuer of rescuers. Despite her rigorously unsentimental characterization of the "righteous," she was a crusader.

And a resister. For one reason or another, her position at the Jewish museum had not always been easy, she said. "But I have the strong character from Zemaitija. I will not leave."

When tourists came, all they wanted to know was whether or not she was Jewish, she said. She rolled her eyes, then straightened her shoulders defiantly.

The words she said next may have fallen short grammatically, but they bespoke a shining moral vision:

"I am people of world."

A torrential rain pummeled the tile roofs as I made my way home from Sakaite's office. Thunder crashed. A *pliukhe*, a downpour, my mother would have said — a *mabl*, a flood. I splashed through puddles, and back in my apartment, as water streamed down behind the filmy kitchen curtains, I picked up *Hands Bringing Life and Bread*, the volume Sakaite had autographed for me. The introduction, by a Jewish leader, praised the rescuers as "people who preserved true humanism and risked their own lives and those of their loved ones." Yet in talking to me, Sakaite had described ordinary people responding to extraordinary circumstances in ways that had little or nothing to do with morality.

Slowly, I began to read the simple, folkloric stories she had gathered.

"Genovaite's mother asked her to go to the barn for eggs," I read. "Genovaite shrieked with horror when she saw a head sticking up from the hay." A Jew had found shelter in the barn — a teenager who'd been marched into the forest along with his fellow villagers. Before the first shots were fired, he fainted and fell into the pit. He awoke covered with blood, climbed out from under the dead bodies, and began to run. Fourteen kilometers later, he arrived at Genovaite's house. "Although the shadow of looming danger darkened their future life," they agreed to hide the young man. He remained in the barn for two and a half years.

An accident? An inspiring tale of moral courage? A bit of both?

"I left my horse in Lieporiai," another rescuer remembered, "and walked to the [Jewish] men's ghetto. " Finding it deserted, he realized that all the men had been taken away and shot. He hurried on to the women's ghetto, where he helped four prisoners to crawl through the barbed wire. By night, the women slept in his barn; by day they hid in the forest, where his children brought them food. All four survived the war.

This rescuer offered no reason for his actions. He had not wanted to convert the Jews to Catholicism. He hadn't needed help on the farm or wanted to adopt a child. Perhaps he was simply a stubborn Zemaitijan. But what about his neighbors, also Zemaitijans, who had not acted as he did?

In the small town of Radviliskis, a Jewish woman and the baby she'd borne with her gentile husband were passed around from family to family. The two had to stay on the move because hostile neighbors were constantly denouncing them. "It took only one executioner to kill a hundred Jews," the text said, "but the enormous efforts, understanding, spiritual power, and resolution of more than twenty people were necessary to save two people from death."

Irena Veisaite had used similar words in describing her own rescue. "To save one person," she'd said, "you need the tremendous courage of many people. All the rescuers were saints."

139

Were they saints?

"Very few of those who help us really like us," Aba Gefen wrote in *Hope in Darkness*, his memoir about hiding in the Lithuanian countryside for three years. Some of those who helped him to move from barn to barn, rye field to wheat field, he felt sure, were motivated solely by the fear that he would turn them in after the war if they refused — a fear so strong that it overrode the fear of punishment by the Nazis.

But some *were* truly righteous, it seemed to me. Here was a priest who had hidden more than a hundred children from the Vilna ghetto in his orphanage. Before long, word of the children's presence found its way to the authorities. German army nurses arrived at the orphanage, intent on identifying the Jewish children by checking to see which boys were circumcised. But the priest sent the circumcised Jewish boys into the forest for the day, substituting uncircumcised gentile boys to be checked in their place. A truly horrible story to contemplate — and surely a "righteous" tale. Hadn't a sense of moral obligation led the priest to help the Jews? And wasn't that different from helping Jews out of fear of reprisal after the war, or simply for the money?

Yet many rescuers must have had not a single, pure reason for their actions, but instead a tangle of reasons, some noble and some perhaps not so noble. Perhaps Sakaite was right to avoid characterizing them as paragons of virtue. Instead, she had ticked off a list of opportunistic motivations. I could feel the tug of her view, a kind of leaden fatalism. The banality of good.

In a way, though, her list of purely circumstantial reasons why some people had rescued Jews could be seen as protecting the great majority who had *not* rescued Jews. If being a rescuer was largely the result of simple happenstance, then perhaps the same could be said of *not* being a rescuer.

What was the answer? If these few individuals had managed to come to the rescue in defiance of the German occupiers, then why couldn't thousands or even tens of thousands more have done likewise?

In a time when decent behavior was risky in the extreme, I wondered, what did we demand of a person like Steponas, the old man who had talked to me in Rokiskis — or of a person like Uncle Will?

What, the American Jewish writer Cynthia Ozick has asked, is "the ordinary human article": a rescuer or a bystander?

Did it matter if there had been as many rescuers as perpetrators, or more, or fewer? The rescuers were "a drop in the ocean," one Lithuanian leader wrote, "that did not change the essence of things."

The rain drummed onto Stikliu gatve. Outside my window, all was murky. Whatever the answers to all these questions, perhaps Sakaite was right to enshrine the *actions* of the rescuers, rather than sanctifying the rescuers themselves. The acts and impulses of rescuing were for the good. It was good to remember and honor them.

THE International Commission for the Evaluation of the Crimes of the Nazi and Soviet Occupation Regimes was established by Lithuanian president Valdas Adamkus in 1998. It had a big name and a big mission — too big, some said. Critics worried that lumping the Nazi and Soviet eras together under one roof would lend credence to the idea that Lithuanian suffering under the Soviets was fully equal to Jewish suffering under the Nazis. This was the "symmetry theory," the theory of "double genocide" that Professor Donskis had inveighed against.

Snieguole Matoniene, a gentile woman who worked in the commission's education wing, had agreed to meet me at a restaurant near the former Lenin Square. She brought along a coworker, a quiet young gentile woman named Indre. As we slid into a shiny red banquette, Matoniene, who had the reassuring manner of an experienced teacher, started in about the commission's goals and its challenges.

In the words of a commission pamphlet, she said, the aim was "to analyze and evaluate critically historical events, eliminating prejudices and old stereotypes [and] promoting tolerance, equality, and human dignity." When independence came in 1991, Lithuanians were eager to air the history of the Soviet era. At last they could talk openly about the deportations to Siberia. But their understanding of the Holocaust was limited. "Lithuanians were used to viewing themselves as victims," Matoniene said. "The notion that the Jews were the real victims seemed impossible."

Schools were furnished with new textbooks full of facts and figures about the Jewish catastrophe, but six million (the number of Jews who died in the Holocaust) was just a number. Most young people had never seen a Jew. Jews and non-Jews had lived side by side for centuries in Lithuania, but even so, Matoniene said, "it is hard for us to think of Jews as 'ours.'" Jews were "others."

Little by little, however, as a commission leader put it, there came "an awakening from a long slumber of mind, spirit and conscience."

As they began to engage with long-buried facts about the Holocaust, people — "even the intelligentsia," Matoniene said — were unprepared. They were astonished, Indre said. "Mass killings, and their neighbors did it!"

Once again I wondered: How could people not have known? All over the country, the Jews had been rounded up right under the noses of their neighbors. Most had not been sent away to far-off death camps, as was the case in other parts of Europe. Thousands and tens of thousands had been killed on the spot, within earshot of their neighbors, in the beloved Lithuanian forests. Some of those who had seen what happened, like Steponas, and some of those who had done the shooting, were still alive. Even accounting for the twists and turns of the official Soviet line, how could it all have been so thoroughly erased from the national consciousness?

Matoniene looked at the table, then off into the distance, struggling for the words that would help me understand. "People knew," she said, "but they didn't know."

She looked at Indre, who made a different point. The older

generation did know, she said. They did remember. "This one had a carpet from a Jewish house. That one wore a Jewish dress." But the younger people — people like her — even in *post*-Soviet society, she said, truly had little or no knowledge of the Holocaust. As a girl, she had not heard of Anne Frank's diary, for example. To this day, her best friends still didn't know, didn't understand. Even her sister still didn't know, not really.

An image came to my mind: a Lithuanian writer travels to the United States to interview white people about the country's history of racism. When did you find out about segregation, the Lithuanian asks, about the Jim Crow laws? One American might answer, "I always knew." The next might say, "Not until my high school history class." A third might look blank: "Jim Crow? Who or what is Jim Crow?" Another: "Yes, I know there used to be race discrimination, but only in the South. Today it's white people who are discriminated against."

Layers of memory, gradations of memory, ways to know and simultaneously not to know.

When Matoniene first began teaching about the Holocaust in a high school classroom, she thought it would be best to start with the oldest students, those in the senior class. But she found that by the age of seventeen or eighteen, the students' views were already formed. Now she believed it was better to begin with younger children. "The earlier the better," she said.

In the town of Ukmerge, for example, middle school students carried out a project called "Butterflies Don't Fly in the Ghetto." A final presentation brought to life the cultural richness of the ghetto — the concerts, drama performances, and other means of "spiritual resistance" created by imprisoned Jews. The student audience was open-mouthed, silent, Matoniene said. Everyone cried.

The participation of Lithuanians in the killing of the Jews was the most sensitive topic of all, she continued. "It wasn't just a handful," but it wasn't everyone, either. Most people were bystanders.

Should we judge the bystanders? I asked.

She didn't answer directly. The commission's goal, she said, was to foster dialogue between the generations, to encourage students to ask their grandparents, "What were your moral choices?"

I pushed. "But do we judge?"

Matoniene paused. "My mission," she said finally, "is to ask this question, not to answer it."

Indre nodded. Nurturing the wish to communicate was a very slow process, she said, but there was no shortcut. Studying the Holocaust, she hoped, would help students develop a new view of the moral choices they encountered in their own lives and see themselves as actors rather than passive onlookers.

To my surprise, the two of them did not believe in *requiring* educators to teach about the Holocaust. It was important not to create a backlash, they said. Instead, teachers were *invited* to sign up for training programs. They were *invited* to use the curricula designed by the commission. They were *invited* to establish "tolerance centers" within their schools.

As for the commission's dual agenda — addressing the Soviet and Nazi eras together — the two women thought it was sensible. To shape their future, Lithuanians needed to examine what had happened in both eras. And if people felt that their own grievances were being given short shrift, they would find it difficult to listen to the grievances of others. Bringing non-Jewish suffering to the table alongside the Jewish tragedy could help to open minds and hearts.

"It is not for the Jews that we are doing this," Indre said suddenly.

I sat back in my seat. Was this a hostile statement? Should I take offense?

It was not for international relations, either, she was saying. Not for admission to NATO or the European Union. It was not simply altruism, not simply guilt. No, "this is for all of us."

I understood. It was not a hostile statement. And her next words were so simple and clear that over the next weeks I would remember them often and repeat them to myself:

"Our goal," she said, "is to transform ourselves from a society of bystanders into an active civil society."

ON my way home I stepped into the nave of St. Casimir's. The four-hundred-year-old church with its ornate pink facade was named for Lithuania's patron saint. It had been founded by the Jesuits, the scholarly order that occupied something of the same cerebral position within Catholicism that Vilna's learned Litvaks once held within Jewish culture. The church was located just outside the confines of the former ghetto. In 1942, said the brochure I picked up in the entryway, the crown of the lofty cupola had been restored. A curious moment for a repair job, I thought. I imagined workers high inside the spire looking down into the ghetto and seeing the ragged throngs of ghetto Jews with their yellow patches.

During part of the Soviet era the church had been turned into a "Museum of Atheism" that displayed artifacts from various religious faiths. "It was very stupid," a curator at the Jewish museum told me.

In 1988 the church was returned to the Catholic community for reconsecration. In 2000, Lithuania's bishops issued two statements. They apologized for those clergy whose "human weakness" had led them to collaborate with the KGB or the Nazis. "It pains us," they wrote, "that a part of the Church's children lacked love for persecuted Jews during World War II and did not use all possible means to defend them." Whether as a result of weakness, fear, or greed, clergy and laypeople alike had "not only submitted to criminal occupation regimes, abandoning their religious, moral and civic duties, but also helped the oppressors." Not everyone participated in the Holocaust or conspired with the KGB. "But some did, and this must be admitted as a lesson for the future."

LITHUANIA'S Jewish newspaper claimed to be the only such publication in the world that appeared in four languages — Yiddish,

Russian, Lithuanian, and English. The eight tabloid pages seemed to me to contain equal parts of joy and pain. The latest issue reported that the Sholem Aleichem Jewish secondary school in Vilnius was celebrating its fifteenth year — and also that gravestones in the city's Jewish cemetery had recently been defaced with swastikas.

The editor, Milan Chersonskij, met me in his office at the Jewish community center. Trim and energetic, with close-cut gray hair and an expressive face, he greeted me with a firm handshake. Before posing my questions about the newspaper, I asked him to tell me a little about his own background. What he said turned out to be so surprising that we never did get around to discussing the newspaper itself.

He and his mother had survived the war in a remote corner of Siberia, he said, and after the war he had studied drama in Moscow. It was his drama training, I guessed, that explained his forceful, physical delivery and made his blend of English and Yiddish so easy for me to understand.

In 1979, he went on, he came to Vilnius to work as the stage director of the Jewish Amateur Folk Theater.

The *Jewish* Amateur Folk Theater? In 1979? During the Soviet era?

Yes, he said, the theater was founded in 1956 and lasted until 1999. "*Alts af yidish*, all in Yiddish."

I looked at him in astonishment. Hadn't Yiddish been banned during the Soviet era? As I understood it, all expressions of Jewish culture were prohibited after 1949. Yiddish presses were smashed and Yiddish schools closed.

Yes, he said, Yiddish was banned. *Farbotn, ummeglekh* — forbidden, impossible. But — he held up a triumphant finger — "we called our language 'theatrical Jewish speech.' The party functionaries didn't understand what it meant" — or perhaps pretended not to.

Other people, I said tentatively, had told me that there had been no Jewish culture in Lithuania until the late 1980s . . .

He leapt out of his swivel chair. "This is a lie! This is a lie!" he

cried. During the Soviet times, there had been a Jewish folk theater, a Jewish dance troupe, a Jewish symphony orchestra, a Jewish
band, a Jewish chorus. He had *piles* of archives about Jewish life in
Vilnius during the Soviet times.

Out of a cardboard box in the corner came programs and yellowed newspaper reviews and colorful posters that he unfolded and
displayed with outstretched arms. Here was a poster for Sholem
Aleichem's play about Tevye the Dairyman, whose adventures
inspired the Broadway musical *Fiddler on the Roof.* Here was another
announcing a commemoration of the Warsaw Ghetto Uprising.
Here were others for *The Singers of Brody, The Night before Babi
Yar, The Jewish Divorce, Tales of Chelm, Mirele Efros.*

I was right about the crackdown in 1949, Chersonskij said. In that
year, all Jewish professional theaters throughout the Soviet Union
were closed down, including GOSET, the renowned Moscow State
Yiddish Theater in Moscow. But after Stalin's death in 1953, the tide
turned. Jewish theaters opened again, not only in Vilnius but in
Kaunas, Riga, Tallinn, Kishinev — a dozen Soviet cities.

Rehearsals took place three times a week, after work. Tailors
sewed costumes and carpenters built sets for free. Composers,
musicians, singers, graphic artists, all worked without pay. It was
a labor of love.

Who, I asked, was the audience? Maybe the performances had
been tiny efforts known to only a few. That would explain why
neither Irena Veisaite nor the directors of the Jewish museum had
mentioned them to me.

But no. "Every show had an audience of a thousand," Chersonskij
said. For every performance, the hall of the Palace of Trade Unions,
atop Tauras Hill, was packed to capacity.

For a time, he went on, his troupe had the opportunity to tour
other Soviet republics, including the Baltics, Moldova, and Belarus.
Then, between 1971 and 1988, restrictions were imposed. The troupe
was forbidden to travel outside of Lithuania. But Jewish vacationers

from all over the Soviet Union flocked to performances in the Lithuanian resort towns.

He stopped speaking and looked at me, his eyes bright.

Why had no one else told me about this?

He frowned. "Some of our leaders in the Jewish community today," he said, "act as if Jewish history after the war began only when *they* came forward." Uninvolved in Jewish culture during the Soviet years, "they became Jews only when it was no longer dangerous to be a Jew." He leaned forward, hands on knees. "I was a Jew all my life," he said. "I grew up in the Soviet times, but I was a Jew in school, in the academy, in the army, in the Russian theater, and as director of the Jewish Folk Theater. I don't run and cry that I had to give up my life as a Jew. I live as I live."

In 1988, he said, new opportunities opened up. Now his account converged with that of other Jewish leaders I'd spoken with. In that year, he said, for the first time he was able to write and mount a *purimshpil*, a dramatic production of the sort that Jews traditionally present during the spring festival of Purim, recounting the historic tale of how the Jewish Queen Esther saved her people from annihilation by the Persian king. In Chersonskij's version, the Soviet premier Brezhnev stood in for the king. Chersonskij himself played the part of Brezhnev. In the final scene, characters with suitcases filled the stage — a multitude of Soviet Jews bound for Israel. The hall was packed to the rafters. A thousand audience members stood and sang "Hatikvah," the Israeli anthem. It was the first time the song had been sung in a public place in Vilnius since before the war, he said.

But the theater that had thrived through all the permutations of Soviet policy — serving variously as a preserver of Jewish memory, a showcase for Soviet multiculturalism, and an outlet for antigovernment expression — did not survive the fall of the Iron Curtain. As the Soviet ban on emigration loosened, thousands of Jews departed. In 1988, twelve thousand Jews had lived in Lithuania. Now their ranks were down by two-thirds.

The troupe disbanded in 1999.

Was there no museum that could display Chersonskij's archives? I asked. Didn't this facet of Soviet Jewish life belong in the historical record?

He sighed. "Who would label it all? Maybe when I'm a pensioner—but me, I expect I will have such a pension that I must keep working after I die."

He rummaged on a shelf and popped a disc into his computer. I watched over his shoulder as little doll-like figures in colorful costumes began to dance. Scarves flew and flowed in complex patterns. He pointed a finger at the diminutive players, now frozen in place on the screen. This one was now in America, that one in Canada, this one in Israel. Today there were no Yiddish-speaking actors and few audience members left.

He pushed back his chair. "Every person," he said, "is of great value. When he goes away or dies, it is like teeth: it grows not up again in this place."

I left in tears.

ON a warm, cloudy afternoon, I consulted my map, which had grown soft and creased, and started out toward the winding river known to speakers of Lithuanian as the Neris and to speakers of Yiddish as the Vilye. I was on my way to meet a certain Yudl, an elderly Jewish man who was a friend of Regina, my Rokiskis guide. In our marathon translation session with the documents we'd photocopied in Rokiskis, Regina and I hadn't quite reached the bottom of the pile. To finish the job, I would need someone special, someone familiar with the Soviet vocabulary. Yudl had had a long career with *Tiesa*, the Lithuanian Communist Party newspaper. He was exactly the right person, Regina said.

As I crossed the courtyard in front of the Presidential Palace, where Czar Nikolai's ambassadors met with Napoleon during the War of 1812, I thought of a legend I'd heard. While the French

9. European Union banner in Vilnius.

emperor was in Vilnius, it is said, he came across a Jew on his knees in the street, shouting imprecations to the heavens.

"Who insulted you?" Napoleon asked.

"Today is Tisha B'Av," the Jew replied, "the day our temple was destroyed."

"And when was that?" Napoleon asked.

"Two thousand years ago," came the reply.

"Two thousand years — and today you weep?" Napoleon marveled. "Such a people will live forever." According to tradition, it was Napoleon himself who dubbed Vilnius "the Jerusalem of Lithuania."

By now, the elegant expanse of Gedimino Prospect, the city's grandest boulevard, was familiar to me. I passed the building that flew the flag of the European Union, which Lithuania had just joined, with its circle of gold stars on a blue background. *Mes Europoje*, the banner said, and then, upside down, an iffy English translation: "We in Europe." I passed the McDonald's fast-food restaurant with its English-language slogan, "I'm lovin' it," and then what seemed like a hundred shoe stores, each displaying outrageous footwear in rainbow colors with stiletto heels and needle toes. In my sensible lace-up oxfords, I'd nearly twisted my ankle many times on the city's ubiquitous cobblestones. I couldn't imagine how the stylish women of Vilnius managed to get around in high heels. At our dinner early in my visit, Violeta had told me a gruesome story, complete with a diagram on a napkin, about her daughter-in-law falling in stilettos, a bone poking through her groin. I passed a jewelry shop whose windows glowed with amber. The polished bits of petrified resin, mined from Lithuanian peat bogs, looked like caramel candy or solid blocks of honey. Amber was a national treasure. Especially prized were the rare pieces that contained a fly or another bit of trapped detritus, a silent fragment of the past.

Reminders of more recent history were not hard to find on the avenue. Near the former Lenin Park, I paused before a stone cairn with a figure of Jesus on the cross, and a plaque:

Sovietines okupacijos
aukoms atminti

In memory of the martyrs
of the Soviet occupation

And near the bridge, not far from the Seimas, the dazzling white Parliament building, I copied down the words engraved on a stone marker:

Cia 1991–1992 stovejo
gynybine barikada

Here on this spot, the marker said, Lithuanians had constructed barricades and faced down Soviet tanks.

Halfway down a quiet, tree-lined street on the other side of the river, I rang the bell at a first-floor flat. Yudl opened the door clad in shorts, his shirt straining over his belly, and led me into the parlor.

He was eighty-three, he told me in English, which made him a contemporary of Uncle Will and Steponas, the old man in Rokiskis. Old enough to have clear memories of Jewish life before the destruction, he'd grown up in the town the Lithuanians called Ukmerge and the Jews Vilkomir — the town, I remembered, where middle school students had recently mounted the dramatic production called "Butterflies Don't Fly in the Ghetto." His father, his grandfather, and his great-grandfather had all been craftsmen. In the summer they made umbrellas, and in the winter, spinning wheels. But this was not enough to make a living, so all three were also *klezmorim*, musicians who played violin and clarinet at Jewish weddings. "And so we lived before the war."

When the German army invaded, Yudl escaped to the east and joined the Red Army. He laid mines and blew up bridges and was wounded twice. "We pushed the Fascists through Germany," he said. "It was the happiest day in my life, to remain alive to see them surrender." His sparse gold-capped teeth gleamed as he smiled.

When he returned home to Lithuania, he found not a single relative alive. His parents and every other member of his family had been shot in the forest.

He shuffled through the newspaper articles I'd brought with me from the Rokiskis archives. "Hmmph," he said. He would do the job provided he could work on his own, at home, in longhand. He was an old man, he reminded me, who needed his rest.

He showed me to the door. I was to call him in a week.

He was one of the "teeth that grow not up again," I thought as I made my way back across the river, the irreplaceable ones whom Chersonskij, the theater director, had lamented. On Pilies gatve, I joined some of my fellow students for dinner. Under the cottony sky, we ate tender rolls of stuffed cabbage and *blini*, little buckwheat pancakes, crisp and brown around the edges, topped with dollops of sour cream and bright orange beads of caviar that popped sumptuously on the roofs of our mouths.

Walking home in the dark, we talked about a poem we'd read in class by Mani Leyb, a Ukrainian Jew who'd immigrated to New York:

Bay di vayse tishn
bin ikh lang gezesn,
un gekukt in oygn,
un geredt, geredt . . .

For a long time,
I sat at the white tables,
talking and talking,
and looking into the eyes of others
I forgot myself —
until the old waiter came
to whisper in my ear:
It's late.

Good night
and out into the street,
where those eyes
glittering with tears
came swimming out of the mist
like stars
to guide me home.

Near City Hall plaza, an old man appeared out of nowhere and attached himself to our group. He spoke Yiddish, saying something about *Daytshe gas,* German Street. Maybe he could tell that some of us were Jewish, or simply that we were foreigners, or maybe he just liked to talk to women — any women. For some reason, I had an inkling that he wouldn't leave without attempting to embrace at least one of us. Sure enough, before turning away down *Rudnitsker gas,* Rudninku gatve, he brought his face toward mine and his grizzled whiskers scraped my cheek. It was a *kush,* a kiss, from another one of the irreplaceable "teeth" that would not grow back again.

An Indelible Memory and
an Unhealing Scar

AT the midpoint of the summer program, I felt mute and withdrawn. I was tired of the labor of learning, beaten down by the complexities of language and history alike. My fellow students looked the same: irritated and worn out.

My essay about the feud in the Chor Shul came back at last, sprinkled with Niborski's red marks. My sentence about the old men who sat with their hands *oysgepreste bay di oyren* — pressed against their ears — had a circle around it. "I was not in *shul* Friday night," my teacher had written in the margin, "so I didn't see the men, but I do know that *oysgepreste* means 'pressed' in the sense of 'well-ironed.'" Who knew? "Try *tsugepreste* instead."

"When you select words from your dictionaries," Niborski admonished us all, "you must not simply grab the first ones you see. Turn them over and inspect them from every angle, as if you were buying a new pair of shoes."

We tackled some words imported from Hebrew, the language known in Yiddish as *loshn-koydesh*, the holy tongue. Most of Yiddish is phonetic, but many *loshn-koydesh* words are written with no vowels. Imagine: *n vwls!* Sometimes these Hebrew words are used to refer to an aspect of religious observance, such as a blessing or a holiday candelabra. But sometimes they describe a perfectly ordinary aspect of daily life — a landlord, a cow, or the moon (though not the sun). Others tug on the reins of discourse, creating a twist here and a turn there: *perhaps, anyway, on the contrary, for example, in truth.*

Most interestingly, when *loshn-koydesh* words show up in a sentence otherwise composed of "regular" words, they sometimes impart a lightning-fast switch of register — from the down-home to the high-flown and back again in a flash. Our teacher's case in point was a pun involving the word involving *kashe*, which had two Yiddish identities. On the one hand, it was a Hebrew-origin word meaning a religious question (for example, *di fir kashes*, the Four Questions at the heart of the Passover service). On the other hand, it denoted the humble buckwheat porridge that is, or was, a staple of the Eastern European diet. Niborski devoted a large part of this day's session to explicating the richly comic confusion that could result. Such matters, he stressed, were key to the very essence of Yiddish — indeed, to the essence of *yidishkayt* itself.

Unable to grasp the nuances he was so lovingly enumerating, I stopped listening. The tasks ahead seemed endless, impossible: barely understanding, really understanding; speaking to get a point across, speaking well; reading for basic understanding, reading with a feel for literary style; writing, writing with style. So far, it seemed to me, I had made little progress. All that was happening was that my English had continued to deteriorate. I was no longer able to complete the crossword puzzles my husband was sending me from the *New York Times.*

Grammar class was equally tedious. We spent an hour on the word *zol*, or "should," which showed up so often in the "Yinglish" of my elderly relatives. "Close the door, you shouldn't catch cold." "You should live and be well." "You shouldn't know from it."

All the while, my eye kept snagging on the little swastika that had been scratched onto my desk with a ballpoint pen, no doubt during the regular school year when the seats were filled by local students. The challenges facing Lithuania seemed as endless and insoluble as my struggles with Yiddish.

AT the break, one of my fellow students buttonholed me to complain about the apartment he was living in. Too depressing, no grocery store nearby, too far from the university. Would I mind if he moved in with Minette and me and slept on the couch?

I said no right away. Minette would hate the idea. I didn't particularly like this student. I didn't want to share a bathroom with him. Too crowded.

In the days of the Small Ghetto, probably fifty people lived in our apartment.

THE elderly woman in the flowered dress who had welcomed us to Vilna on our first evening returned to the institute. Back then, through the pattering of raindrops in the damp university courtyard, she'd told us how happy she was to see people returning to the city to study Yiddish. Now, clad in an elegant white blouse, she was escorted to a chair of honor in the lecture hall, in front of a sign in lavish Yiddish script spelling out "Welcome, Bluma!" Another irreplaceable "tooth."

I took a seat as far away from everyone else as possible. Other students were doing the same, I noticed. In our midterm blues, we all wanted to be left alone.

Just before the war, Bluma began, she was sent into exile. She and her Jewish activist friends, along with many others, were considered a threat to Soviet power. The prison camp she was assigned to was a particularly remote one in the northeastern corner of Siberia, all the way on the Pacific coast, more than four thousand miles away from home.

Mendy Cahan, the program director, who was sitting next to Bluma on the dais, had announced that he would translate into English as she went along. But as soon as the quavering Yiddish sentences began, he seemed to forget all about his promise. We were on our own.

Upon her release from the prison camp after the war, Bluma said, she returned to the place where she grew up, her childhood *shtetl*, a town some forty-five miles north of Vilnius that the Jews called Svintsyan (Svencionys in Lithuanian). Before the war, as in virtually all Lithuanian towns, about half of the residents of Svencionys were Jewish. But now nearly all the Jewish houses were in ruins. The Jewish high school, Jewish college, Jewish libraries, Jewish theaters, and three synagogues were gone.

The dimly lit hall seemed to grow darker and gloomier as Bluma continued. Soon after returning home, she made her way to the mass-murder site in the nearby forest. There, beneath a thin covering of earth, lay the bodies of some eight thousand Jews who had been rounded up from all over the region. Over the years the place had been left untouched, with tattered psalm books and children's toys scattered on the ground. The only indication that anyone had paid notice to the site was the pockmarked surface: holes where local people had dug for gold.

"Sometimes," Bluma said, "I wished to be back in Siberia."

This was what I thought she said, anyway. As the words streamed by, I felt I was understanding very little. I could feel my throat closing up, tears lurking behind my eyes.

Suddenly I was very angry — at my thick head, at the Yiddish language, and at the program director who was failing to translate what Bluma was saying. What a shame, what a waste, to be in the presence of this rare envoy from the vanished world and to be unable to understand most of what she was saying. I ripped a sheet of paper out of my notebook. My pen dug into the page as I wrote Cahan a furious letter: "I'm missing at least half of this! Why aren't you translating???" I creased the paper sharply and shoved it into my bag.

Afterwards in the courtyard I stood with a fellow student from London. I asked her how she'd found the talk.

"Really hard," she said.

I agreed. "She talked so fast."

Frowning, she looked down at the ground. That wasn't what she meant, she said.

I saw that her eyes were rimmed with red. Very few of the victims were actually shot, she said in a choked voice. Most were simply pushed into the pit, where quicklime burned their skin. The women would jump in on top of their children, to suffocate them, to spare them the agony. Afterwards, it was said, the ground moved for days.

My eyes began to sting, too, as I understood: Yes, it had been frustrating to miss some of Bluma's words. But the real source of my anger was — this. What my fellow student was saying. The enormity of the crime. For all the worthy projects I was hearing about, there was no getting around the sheer gruesomeness of Lithuanian history.

I reached into my bag and crumpled up the letter to Cahan.

OUR reading assignment for the week, a piquant tale by Avrom Karpinovitch about Vilna's prewar Jewish underworld, was studded with references to places we'd become familiar with over the past few weeks. On Friday night, for example, the hero arranges to meet his date under the clock behind City Hall. Today the clock was gone, but we all knew the corner of *Rudnitsker gas* and *Daytshe gas*.

We would address the text, our teacher said, in a more advanced fashion than usual. Instead of taking turns reading the story aloud, we'd jump right into a discussion of the work as a whole. But first he pointed to each of us in turn and asked whether we'd read the piece all the way through at home, as assigned. Many of us looked down at our notebooks and muttered "almost" or "some of it."

He sighed. He looked as tired as the rest of us. We weren't working hard enough, he said. We were lazy. Our essays were sloppy.

He went to the blackboard and scrawled a long list of errors that speakers of English were especially prone to commit. For example, in English you said "he spoke *for* an hour," but in Yiddish you left out the "for" and said simply "er hot geredt a sho" — "he spoke an hour." Never, ever did you say "er hot geredt *far* a sho." In English you said "*on* the Sabbath we eat challah," but in Yiddish you never said "af shabes" — "on the Sabbath." Instead, it was simply "shabes est men khale," "Sabbath we eat challah."

On and on he went, offering example after example, while we sat fidgeting, wishing he would talk about something else. He wouldn't. Over the course of his career he'd probably corrected such mistakes hundreds of times, maybe even thousands. Clearly, encountering the same blunders year in and year out made his *kishkes*, his guts, burn.

That night, at the *shabes tish*, once again the candles threw their flickering light over the white tablecloths as we clapped our hands and swayed to the sounds of age-old melodies. One of my fellow students tossed back her long hair and raised her glass. "Zingen af shabes iz a mekhaye," she said, her voice full of feeling. "Singing on the Sabbath is a joy."

Several of us froze. We didn't dare look at our teacher. Here was the misdemeanor — or was it a felony? — he'd spent much of class railing against. Hadn't he made himself crystal clear? We were not to say "af shabes." Just "shabes."

Our teacher turned to me, his face red. "Should I shoot her?" he asked.

I scrambled for an answer. One false move and I, too, could find myself in the line of fire.

"Me shist shabes?" I said very carefully. Three words, not four. Not "af shabes." Just "shabes." "Does one shoot on the Sabbath?"

IT seemed fitting, a form of Sabbath observance, for me to spend Saturday morning painstakingly making my way through "The Woman in the Panama Hat," a short story by Avrom Sutzkever, who had been a resident of the Vilna ghetto. As a member of the Paper Brigade, he had been forced to sort through mountains of looted Jewish books, selecting which should be preserved and which destroyed. At the turn of the twenty-first century, Sutzkever was still alive in Tel Aviv. He was considered the greatest living Yiddish writer. Set in the Vilna ghetto, his story began:

In eynem a tog fun der shkhite-tsayt, bin ikh gezesn in a tunkl kheyderl un geshribn . . . .

One day during the time of the massacres, I sat in a dark room, writing. . . . I felt like the quivering tongue of a bell. With the slightest breath of air, the bell would ring.

As the writer's words shatter the silence of the black ghetto night, the story itself becomes the tolling of the bell. How privileged I felt to be able to hear those somber tones. Bent over my work at the kitchen table, here in the very place where Sutzkever had been confined, I followed the encounter between the narrator and the bizarrely dressed woman in the Panama hat, the fellow ghetto resident to whom he offers his last crust of bread.

In the early afternoon, I went out and walked through the same streets into which the woman in the Panama hat had disappeared. Yiddish words flowed in my head — words of Hebrew origin, words of qualification and transition that I'd heard over and over again in class without always being certain of their meaning:

mistome — probably
ledugme — for example
mamesh — truly
avade — of course

Unlike the fictional woman in the Panama hat, and unlike the writer who had created her, I was free to leave the narrow lanes of the old ghetto quarter, to cross Pylimo gatve and continue up the hill to a broad, tree-lined avenue where the elegant buildings were surrounded by spacious grounds. Here, encircled by a giant parking lot, sat the Maxima, Vilnius's new hypermarket, the successor to the market square of old. Inside, the aisles were crammed with products of all kinds — cartons of milk and jars of herring, bins of potatoes and bottles of vodka, pots and pans, computers, televisions, boots and basketballs. A public address system touted the latest bargains to crowds of cart-pushing customers, and a long row of cash registers beeped insistently.

In short order I located what I was looking for: the apron that my guide Regina had suggested I send to Steponas and his wife in their Rokiskis home. Bib, sash, and full skirt were sprinkled with a whimsical pattern of flowers and a message, in English, in quaint cross-stitch: "American as Apple Pie." The label made clear that it had been made in China. I bought a card, too. I would ask someone in the institute office, I decided, to help me pen a few sentences in Lithuanian, starting with "Aciu," thank you. Then I would send it off to the cottage with the steep tin roof, not far from Sinagogu gatve. A token, an offering to a fellow wanderer in the haunts of the past.

THE next afternoon I sat on a stoop in the university courtyard with Giedrius Kiaulakis, a stocky gentile man with a heavy brow who was a leader of an organization called The House of Memory.

"If you ask people about the silver spoons in their parlor — where are they from," he said, " — they will say they don't know. And in fact, some of them really *don't* know. They really *have* forgotten."

Multiple shocks to Eastern European society explained some of the not-knowing, Kiaulakis said. He picked up a stick and scratched at the stones under our feet. Imagine, he suggested, a Lithuanian man born in 1920. In 1940, with the Soviet occupation, he faces the threat of deportation. In 1941 comes the German occupation. In 1944, the Soviets again: guerrilla warfare, more deportations, collectivization. "Such a man is always expecting a hit."

An essay published by his organization underscored his point. During the Soviet era, it said, Lithuanians' "psychological dissociation was reinforced by a lengthy post-war period" in which "the Holocaust was not totally silenced, but Soviet ideology distorted its essence."

Moreover, the Jewish and the gentile worlds had always been entirely separate communities, Kiaulakis said. People didn't know each other, and they didn't really care. How deeply did the disappearance of the Jews affect the lives of those who remained? He shrugged. "They thought, 'in the forests we used to have bears and wolves; now we don't. We used to have Jews; now we don't.'" For many, the tragedy of the Jews was "like a movie, like King Arthur or Troy. Even intelligent people say, 'Okay, okay, we're very sorry, but that's a Jewish problem. Let's remember *our* problem.'" Another shrug. Suppose, he said, the Lithuanians had disappeared. Maybe this would not have been a big tragedy for the Jews.

I found it hard to listen to these blunt words. Kiaulakis's sentences felt like blows. Perhaps it was the very harshness of his pronouncements that led me to think of my own country, where Native American culture had been all but obliterated by white settlers. As a child, I remembered, on occasion I had put on a fake buckskin vest and brandished a toy pistol in a game of "cowboys and Indians." Sometimes I fashioned a headband with a feather sticking up and fastened it around my forehead, or strapped a doll to my back like a papoose and padded silently through our backyard. Nowadays, as I wait at the *Takoma* Metro station, drive across the *Potomac* River, or plan a trip to the *Chesapeake* Bay, I pay scant attention to the names of native tribes. Half of all American states have Indian names, and so do many of our lakes, rivers, mountain ranges, cities, towns, streets. The vestiges of a vanished culture are all around me. I do know. But how aware am I? How fully do I acknowledge the reality? In a way, I *don't* know.

Was it really so strange for Lithuanians to walk casually down Zydu gatve, Jewish Street, or Sinagogu gatve, Synagogue Street?

The House of Memory ran an annual essay contest, Kiaulakis was saying, called "Jews: Neighbors of My Grandparents and Great-Grandparents." Students in towns and villages across Lithuania participated by interviewing old-timers — sometimes their own relatives — about the lost Jewish world. Especially in the tight-knit communities of the rural areas, Kiaulakis said, there was always someone who knew who once lived in a particular house or who used to own a certain store. The students sat down with their elders and drew maps. They combed through old newspapers and telephone books. They took photographs of the cinema that was once a synagogue, the warehouse that used to be a Jewish school.

I pictured Steponas talking in Rokiskis with Tatiana-now-Miriam, the young woman who'd learned about the Jewish history of the town from her aged pen pal in South Africa. Both would embrace the opportunity to join the program, I imagined.

Participation in the essay contest was voluntary, not compulsory. And the organization's touch was light. Rather than, say, attending a lecture by an expert, people talked to one another. Questions posed by the young were answered by the old. Kiaulakis and his colleagues trusted that when the generations were brought together in a spirit of respectful remembrance, something good would emerge.

Indeed, Kiaulakis said, it often did. As the students listened to their elders' reminiscences and charted the vanished Jewish community, they began to "look at their surroundings, the houses, streets, and squares that they see every day in a different light." After weeks of "traveling the paths these people once took, touching the walls of their buildings, brushing up against real lives," they found the Jewish world becoming vivid and personal, and "the mysterious silence becomes a terrible silence."

The best essays had been published in several volumes, in Lithuanian, for Lithuanians. Kiaulakis showed me some heart-rending passages:

> The old woman remembers very well that black terrifying road on which innocent people were herded to their deaths. The road wallowed in moans and tears.

One passage in particular stood out:

[The killers were] those who so recently had been in no way different from everyone living in the village.

Often during my time in Lithuania, I'd heard the killers stigmatized as unusual people. But this essay took a different and more difficult approach. Surely it was harder to hold the killers close, as this young writer did, than to brand them as rare exceptions.

A final passage encapsulated the organization's key tenet, the driving force behind the work of Kiaulakis and his colleagues:

The events became embedded in [people's] lives like an indelible memory and an unhealing scar.
The past cannot be forgotten. It is alive in future generations.

Kiaulakis shifted his heavy shoes on the stones. Shadows had crept over our feet, and the stoop where we were sitting had grown chilly.

It would be naive, he said, to believe that in the space of only two or three generations Lithuanian society would become a model of tolerance. After all, "for forty thousand years, since Cro-Magnon man, human beings have been xenophobic." But the country was moving in the right direction.

In 2000, he said, a poll had been conducted throughout Europe. People were asked whether they would want to live next door to a Jew. In Lithuania, 23 percent of the people had said no, they would not — compared to Germany, where only 5 percent had responded that way. Yet a few years later, when the poll was repeated, "this time we were the same as Western Europe. So at least now we don't say publicly whom we hate." He flashed a rather gloomy smile. "That's quite a good result, don't you think?"

Was it? It was a step forward, I agreed. Even if some of today's gains were lost, even if there was farther to go, it was a step. An important step.

Kiaulakis stretched and stood up. "Very slowly," he said, "things are changing for the good."

10. Vilnius graffiti: "Up with white Lithuania" replaced by "Up with a world without racism."

On my way home, I passed a wall that had been defaced with black spray-painted graffiti:

Uz balta Lietuva!

Up with white Lithuania!

It was an anti-Semitic message, an anti-Roma (gypsy) message, and also, probably, a protest against the influx of Muslim refugees from the recent conflict in Chechnya. Preserve Lithuania for the ethnic Lithuanians, it cried.

But someone had crossed out the original slogan with a big blue X. And so, next to the original plea was a second call to arms:

Uz pasauli be rasizmo!

Up with a world without racism!

BACK at my apartment, my roommate Minette came in from a field trip to the former Kovno ghetto — the cramped corner of the city of Kaunas where some thirty thousand Jews had once been confined. The ghetto itself was long since gone. In July 1944, as the Red Army was approaching, the Nazi command had conducted a final roundup of the remaining ghetto residents — those who had survived hunger, cold, forced labor, and murderous *aktsyes* — and packed them into barges and freight trains bound for concentration camps in Poland and Germany. Then the wooden buildings of the ghetto were set ablaze. Two thousand Jews who had hidden themselves in sheds, attics, and holes died in the flames. By the end of the war, piles of rubble and forlorn rows of chimneys were all that remained. But in the years since, a new crop of wooden houses had been built atop the ruins, and people — gentile Lithuanians — had moved in.

Minette plunked her bag onto the kitchen table. The trip had been hard, she said. As the bus lumbered up and down the narrow dusty lanes, shutters began to close. "The people were so hostile, so anti-Semitic," she said. "Maybe they deserve to live in those shabby houses."

"They're just poor, powerless people," I said. During my weeks in the Old World, I found, I had become sure of this.

She frowned.

A sharp note crept into my voice. "How would you feel if a tour bus pulled up in front of your house and everyone was staring at you?"

She turned aside. Now *her* shutters were closing.

Without looking at each other, we sat down with our homework. My assignment looked easy at first — eight pages of poetry, with plenty of white space. It turned out I had to look up several words per line, though, and it didn't help that the poet's ideas were as complicated as the vocabulary:

un mit tifer opgrunt-faykhtkayt otemt zeyer vesh

and with deep abyss-dampness their laundry breathes

But we worked on, Minette and I, underlining phrases and flipping the pages of our dictionaries. As we went deeper into this realm where each word had a fixed definition and every task had a beginning and an end, a sense of calm overtook us both.

At 11:00 p.m., when our neighborhood cat, the voice of the Small Ghetto, began its nightly yowling right on schedule, we looked up at each other and smiled.

WITH the notable exception of the International Commission, whose work addressed both the Nazi and the Soviet eras, so far I had seen Lithuania's twentieth-century history served up in pieces. On one side of town, the Jewish museum told the story of the Nazi years. On the other side, the Museum of Genocide Victims told the story of the Soviet years. Then I heard about a curious memorial under construction near the banks of the Neris River — a place where the two epochs were inextricably intermingled.

In 1994, some seven hundred bodies had been discovered under the green lawn of an old Vilnius manor house. Forensic analysis showed that the victims had been executed by the KGB just after World War II, then secretly buried on the grounds of the old estate, which was called Tuskulenai, right in the middle of town.

In the newly independent republic, the hunger to grieve for these dead, these martyrs of the anti-Soviet resistance, was enormous. Plans for a memorial immediately got under way. But then a painful truth emerged. When KGB records were examined, they showed that many of those executed and buried had been not only anti-Soviet patriots but active pro-Nazi partisans. Hundreds had helped to massacre Jews during the war.

What does a country do when the martyrs dear to one part of the population are implicated in the annihilation of another part of the population? It wasn't possible to separate the bones into two neat piles — patriots here, murderers there. For a while, construction came to a halt. A stormy debate began over what to do with the bodies and with the site itself. The leaders of the Jewish community issued a statement protesting "the erection of a common memorial to those who are considered to be freedom fighters and those who, based on all moral norms, are war criminals and indictable offenders."

After ten years of discussion and delay, a new plan emerged. The place would not be designed as a shrine or a pantheon of heroes. Instead it would be a place of reflection. Its official name would be "The Park of Quiet."

Shimon, a Jewish museum director with a mop of curly hair, arrived in his battered Volkswagen to take me to the site. We crossed the Green Bridge, and after a few false turns we spotted a tall wooden fence and a sign. When we got out of the car, we could see the half-built structure, which had an unmistakably Christian appearance, with a massive stone entrance formed by twin crosses. As we picked our way around heaps of dirt and stacks of logs, a guard wearing a cap with the logo "Hollywood Chewing Gum" came out of a shed and agreed to lead us into the sunken domed interior. His flashlight played over earthen walls and supports made of tree trunks with the bark still on. The high-ceilinged room was as black as a cave and smelled like a damp cellar. Unsteady planks made a path on packed dirt. Urns containing the remains of the dead would be embedded in the walls, he said. The site was set to open in four months.

I turned to Shimon and started to pose a question for him to translate.

"No questions," he muttered. Sniffing around this complicated place of pain, it seemed, made him profoundly uncomfortable. Hastily, he thanked the guard and led the way out into the chilly light.

A blustery wind had sprung up. In the car we didn't say anything for a while.

What did he think? I asked finally. Would this place accomplish what it intended to? Could "The Park of Quiet" achieve its goal of remembering the dead, with their bones full of meaning—yet without sanctifying their actions? Could it succeed in addressing both the Nazi and the Soviet eras simultaneously? Would it indeed become a place for Lithuanians to reflect on difficult truths?

Shimon sighed heavily. "I have no idea," he said.

11. The Tuskulenai "Park of Quiet" under construction in Vilnius, 2004.

Jewish Ways of Learning

THE next afternoon I walked over to the Jewish community building, where Mendy Cahan was to speak on "Jewish Ways of Learning." His topic was the religious teachings that the Jews of the Old World had been expected to master back in the days when Vilnius had been the Jerusalem of the North. As I made my way through the streets, I remembered something I'd heard during my visit to the Jewish museum. "Vilna was our kingdom," Rokhl Kostanian had said. For the Jewish families who lived in the *geselekh*, the lanes, with their ten or fifteen children, "the only property they had was knowledge."

Standing at an oaken lectern in his white linen shirt and black jacket, Cahan looked, as always, as if he'd stepped right out of the prewar era he was talking about. It all started in *kheyder*, he began, referring to the tiny room — often located in the home of the *melamed*, the teacher — where Jewish boys began their schooling at the age of three. First came *khumesh* (the Five Books of Moses, known to Christians as the first five books of the Old Testament), then *rashe* (commentary by the eleventh-century rabbi Rashi) and *siddur* (prayers). These three elements made up the basic body of learning that the *proste yidn*, the ordinary people, were expected to acquire. (Ordinary *men*, he meant. Most women learned only the rudiments of reading and writing, and the daily prayers.)

The volume of knowledge required of even the simplest souls was staggering. If you knew all of this today, Cahan said, you would be considered a professor.

On top of these fundamentals, a *sheyner yid*, a refined person, was expected to study *mishnayes*, the collection of oral teachings that began to be written down in Hebrew about two millennia ago. If you could learn a *blat gemore* — a page of interpretive commentary written in Aramaic, an ancient Semitic language related to Hebrew — by yourself, you were considered a master. Those men, like my great-grandfather Dovid-Mikhl, who reached the goal of *hobn smikhes af rabones*, being ordained as a rabbi, knew much more.

How did people gain and maintain this knowledge? Boys sat in *kheyder* from dawn to dusk for ten years. Then, some, including my great-grandfather and my grandfather, were sent away, often to a distant city, for further education at a *yeshive*. After that, for the rest of their lives, men attended adult study groups that met constantly. Often they relied on a work called *Khok LeYisroel*, a five-tome anthology published in Cairo in the Middle Ages. Every week, a *parshe*, a selection from the scriptures, was assigned; each day, the study group took up one portion of that *parshe*. The men learned in pairs, studying psalms, proverbs, the oral teachings, the interpretive commentary, and some mystical writing on the side.

Cahan handed out a fat packet of photocopied pages — a single day's worth of such material. I'd never seen anything like it, nor was I familiar with any of the terms he was using. All of this was new to me.

Each day's study was a mosaic, he said, a little bit of everything: some Hebrew and Aramaic text, then some Yiddish exegesis. Footnotes upon footnotes. Only the most dedicated scholars studied every word. But the lifelong task of analyzing, questioning, conceptualizing, and understanding belonged to everyone, without exception.

My eyes closed. Was drowsiness also a long tradition? My brain recoiled from this journey into the dusty back rooms of piety, rooms packed to the rafters with ancient words and beliefs and customs I knew nothing about.

It was all too much. I handed my packet to another student and walked out. In a daze, I staggered to Pilies gatve and collapsed into a chair at an outdoor café. I was unnerved when the waiter, for the first time, handed me the Lithuanian-language menu instead of the English one. I ordered pink borsht with boiled potatoes and latkes with mushroom sauce.

Slurping my soup, I remembered that my grandfather Yankl had complained till the end of his days about the hunger he'd experienced as a *yeshive* student. Far away from home, he was dependent on the local Jewish community for his meals. In keeping with custom, the responsibility of feeding young scholars like him was rotated among several families — a tradition known as *esn teg*, or "eating days." His belly was never full. After *yeshive*, he abandoned the whole enterprise — *khumesh* and *rashe* and *siddur*, *mishnayes*, *gemore*, *parshe*, *haftoyre* and all — to become a lifelong secularist and socialist.

Now here I was, back in the land my grandfather had fled, devoting myself to mastering the old alphabet, soaking up the sounds and syntax of the Old World. Yet this afternoon, like him, I was on the run from the religious wisdom that had been carefully tended and passed down through the millennia. I hadn't been able to sit still for even an hour with this part of my heritage.

My great-grandfather Dovid-Mikhl had immersed himself in his holy books with *groys kheyshek*, great enthusiasm. His scholarship was a part of my *yikhes*, my pedigree — as was his wife Asne's *beryeshaft*, her expertise in taking care of the household, raising the children, and making a living on the dairy farm, without which my great-grandfather's life of scholarly devotion would not have been possible. Whether by choice or by chance, the children and grandchildren of Asne and Dovid-Mikhl had scattered to the four winds and put down roots on new continents, in the United States,

South Africa, Siberia. *Their* children, too, had put down roots all over the world — in Tel Aviv, Capetown, Vancouver, London, San Diego, New Jersey, and many other places. Some of us adhered to the old religious ways. Others adhered to the secular path charted by our rebellious parents. Some rebelled against the rebellion by reverting to the old ways. So many variations.

I ate my latkes and recalled the text we were studying in class — a story by Sholem Aleichem, the renowned *eynikl*, or grandson, of modern Yiddish literature. "Mir iz gut: ikh bin a yosem," it was called — "Lucky Me: I'm an Orphan." When young Motl's father dies, he's allowed to skip school.

Ikh bin fray. A gantsn tog gefin ikh mikh baym taykh.

I am free. I spend all day down by the river . . .

Alone on the riverbank, Motl entertains himself with a net he has fashioned from a knotted shirtsleeve. As he whiles away the hours, his thoughts dart about like little fish. Something about this story made me feel as if it had been written just for me. With my clumsy lack of fluency, I struggled to catch hold of the writer's meaning. Every sentence seemed slippery, elusive, and utterly alluring. As I reflected on the story, my thoughts, too, began to dart about.

I remembered a dream about my mother I'd had the night before. They were rare, such dreams; each one was precious. I'd flown home from the Yiddish program to be with her, but after just one day it was time for me to return to Vilnius. "Of course I want to go back," I said matter-of-factly. "You *do*?" she said, as if she knew better.

I once read a description of Yiddish as "a window which permits us to retrieve the world of our mothers." I spoke English with my own mother, but there was another "language" in the mix as well, a private "mother tongue" that belonged only to the two of us. As a child, I honed my fluency in this special idiom. I attuned myself to my mother's keen take on the nuances of human behavior, her love of language, her sly humor. I learned to read her face and the set of her shoulders. I mastered when to laugh and when not to, what could be brushed off as trivial and what needed my full attention. When my mother died, I had no one with whom to speak this *mame-loshn* that I knew so well. Now, studying Yiddish was helping to salve the loss.

A Yiddish folksong:

Hob ikh mir a mantl fun fartsaytikn shtof...

I've got me a coat made of ancient cloth...

When the coat frays, the song says, I make it into a jacket. When the jacket rips, I turn it into a vest. When the vest falls apart, I make a purse. Then only a button remains. And when even the button is no more, I make a song.

My sojourn here in Yiddishland was part of my own idiosyncratic "way of Jewish learning." Just as my daughter had put together her own distinctive bat mitzvah out of elements of Yiddish and Hebrew and English, I was shaping my Jewish identity on my own — shaping and reshaping it, over and over. Because of many historic events, I hadn't received my heritage as an intact, shining whole. Instead, I'd had to do the sewing on my own — stitching together a new garment out of scraps, like the inventive songwriter. In some ways this was sad. But maybe, I thought, remembering Sholem Aleichem's orphan boy with his homemade net — maybe I should also be glad. Just as Motl takes a dreamy pleasure in his freedom even in the face of his father's death, so I, too, perhaps, should value the opportunity I'd been granted. Maybe it was a privilege — that I *got* to do that sewing.

IN the spirit of "sewing the garment" of my Jewish identity, I asked Niborski, my teacher, to talk with me about how I could contribute to the cause of preserving the Yiddish language. What would be the best way for me to carry forward the legacy? Between classes, we sat down near the coffee urn under a yellow umbrella. My teacher's ginger beard glowed in the sunlight as I stumbled through a clumsy *reyd*, a discourse, *af yidish*, in Yiddish.

It was Yiddish that had drawn me to the Old World, I told him, and Yiddish that was serving as my lifeline as I explored my uncle Will's actions during the war, as well as the larger story of Lithuania's engagement with the past. Now I wanted to give something back. How could I help build the future of this language I loved? I didn't think I'd ever be much good at speaking Yiddish, I said, but I loved translating, loved coaxing the treasures of Yiddish literature to cross over into English. To make this rich cultural heritage available to readers of English — that was a vital task, was it not? Maybe he could give me some suggestions as to which texts I should work on.

My teacher's response was indignant. "Redn iz ober zeyer vikhtik!" he exclaimed — but speaking is very important! Suppose two people were speaking Yiddish, he said, and a third person happened to pass by and overhear them. In his opinion, such an encounter would be worth ten conferences in some other language about the status of *mame-loshn*. He swirled his coffee in its paper cup. Unless Yiddish was spoken at home, in the community, and at work, he said, the language would die.

But —

He drained his coffee and stood up. Time for class.

A lump formed in my throat. Was that the last word? How could it be? Niborski himself was living his philosophy. He had brought up his children in Yiddish, and now they were bringing up *their* children in Yiddish. He worked at a language center in Paris where all transactions were conducted in *mame-loshn*. But was this the only path? The only path for me?

Before setting out for the Old World, I'd pored over a small collection of family documents — a ship's manifest, a marriage certificate, the postcard with my grandfather's picture, and a letter that my uncle

Shaya had written in 1979. Shaya was one of my great-grandfather's ten children. He was the brother of my grandfather and Uncle Aaron and Uncle Will. When he wrote the letter, in response to questions posed by one of my cousins, he was eighty-five and living in Johannesburg, South Africa. His handwriting — in what had to be his third alphabet, after Hebrew and Russian — was halting, the letters joined together like beginner's stitches, and his English was primitive, studded with Yiddish and Hebrew words. Uncle Will had passed on the letter to my mother, and with his help she had penciled into the margins the meaning of words she was unfamiliar with. Like the tape recording I'd made of Uncle Will and Aunt Manya at their dining room table, Shaya's nearly unpunctuated sentences, along with my mother's bracketed translations, seemed to me to form themselves into a poem:

I will try to tell as much as I know.

My father was the oldest son by Welwe Levin
lived all his life on a little hill
crossing 4 large way to other places
Rakishki was the largest.

My father *o"h* [peace be upon him]
was the oldest
and send him in Bobroisker *yeshive.*
He finished there,
he got *smikhes* [ordained as a rabbi]
and he came back.

They were looking for *shidukh* [a match]
and that had to be to the top of the cream,
till they find
Shneyer Zalman Rubin from Shenburg,
well known from the first Hasidim
in the Baltic States.
That suited my *Bubbe o"h*
and they got married.

And *mekhutonim* [the bride's parents]
desired to get a *Pacht* [a dairy franchise]
from a *Poretz* [a landowner]
they used to have very big Estates,
and the *Pachter* [the franchise-holder]
used to get the fresh milk,
and we used to make Butter and cheese.

They used to give us a house to live in
also a garden for vegetables
wood for winter
and food for our 2 Cows some sheep,
and a horse,
and we had to pay him every month for the milk
& that was the hardest thing.

I treasured the letter and the picture it offered of late-nineteenth-century Jewish life. Once, when I went to visit my son in his college dormitory in New York, I brought along a copy for him. Why I chose that particular moment to pass on this beloved fragment, I don't remember. Maybe it was one of those times when, sensing him growing away, I wanted to attach a thread between the past and the future, between him and me.

My son squinted at the letter for a few minutes. Then he shook his head and handed it back. "What is this?" he asked. He couldn't make head or tail of it.

What was wrong with him? I wondered as I sat on the edge of his bed in his scholarly cell. Why didn't he share my excitement over this gem from our common past? His bookshelf groaned under the burden of Plato, Shakespeare, Walt Whitman, Virginia Woolf. How could the life and language of his own forebears seem more remote, less worthy of his attention, than these classics from other times and places?

Maybe the unfamiliar words were an obstacle. After all, an entire generation had passed since the letter had been written. For all I knew, Uncle Will had been amazed when he had to explain to my mother what a *pacht* was, and what was a *poretz*, and what did *smikhes* mean. Quickly, I scribbled a new layer of translation onto Uncle Shaya's letter. A *bubbe* was a grandmother, a *yeshive* was a Jewish school of higher learning, Hasidim were members of a Jewish religious sect. To me, these words had barely registered as foreign, but maybe my son didn't know them. Or maybe he did.

I handed the letter back to him. Maybe he would put it in a safe place and pass it on to his children. Or maybe he wouldn't.

Maybe Niborski was right about the future of Yiddish. Or maybe he wasn't.

Sholem Aleichem himself, in his last will and testament, stipulated that after his death, his son and sons-in-law should say kaddish, the prayer for the dead, for him — if they wanted to. "But," he wrote, "if they don't feel like it, or if time won't permit, or if it should be against their religious convictions, then they should gather with my daughters and the grandchildren and with good friends, and pick a story from among my stories, and read it aloud — in whatever language will be most understandable to them."

"Di yidishe shprakh shtarbt shoyn toyznt yor," a renowned Yiddish linguist has been quoted as saying — the Yiddish language has been dying for a thousand years. "Lomir hofn az zi vet shtarbn nokh toyznt yor" — let's hope it will die for a thousand more.

IN class, something opened up for me: all at once it was easier to follow what was going on. I was not yet taking notes in Yiddish — although I could write fairly quickly, I still had trouble deciphering what I'd written after the fact — but writing in English no longer felt entirely comfortable, either. My notebook filled up with bizarre hybrids — two alphabets within a single word. And like all the other English speakers, I sounded more and more like a beginner in my own native tongue: "You have had already coffee? At the break?"

Our teacher Bordin, who loved stories, told us that in 1978, when

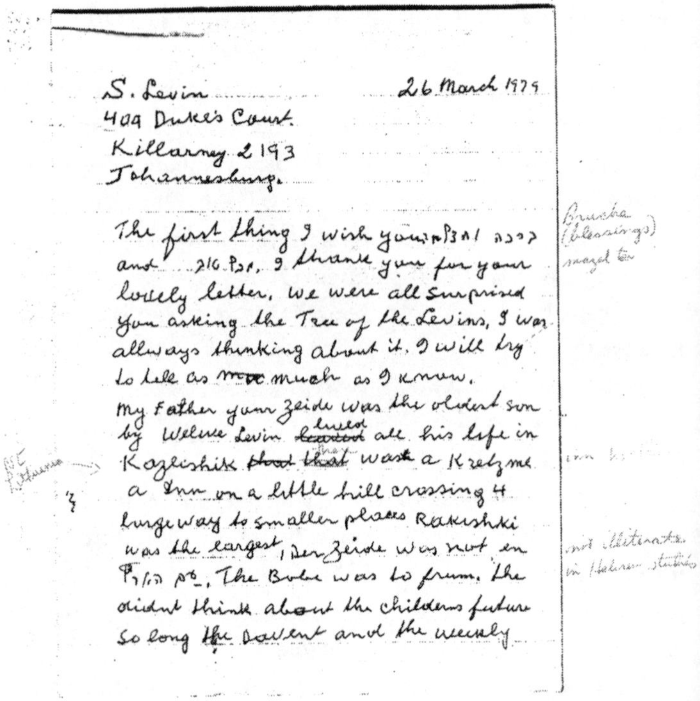

The handwritten letter reads:

> S. Levin   26 March 1979
> 409 Duke's Court
> Killarney 2193
> Johannesburg.
>
> The first thing I wish you, ברכה מזל טוב
> and ... 216 צ״ע, I thank you for your
> lovely letter. We were all surprised
> you asking the Tree of the Levins, I was
> allways thinking about it. I will try
> to tell as [much] much as I know.
> My Father your Zeide was the oldest son
> by Welwe Levin lived all his life in
> Kozloshik [that] was a Kretzme
> a Inn on a little hill crossing 4
> large way to smaller places Rakishki
> was the largest, Der Zeide was not an
> צ״ע, The Bobe was so frum. The
> didn't think about the childerns future
> so long the davent and the weekly

12. Letter from Uncle Shaya about family history in Lithuania in the nineteenth century.

Isaac Bashevis Singer was awarded the Nobel Prize for Literature, he was asked why he chose to write in Yiddish. "Because," Singer said, "when the Messiah comes" — and here Bordin's shoulders lifted and his voice ascended into the characteristic Yiddish inflection, the old singsongy Jewish trope — "when the Messiah co-omes, and all those people come back to li-ife . . . they're going to need something to read."

Two years later, when the poet Czeslaw Milosz, the son of Polish Vilnius, accepted *his* Nobel Prize, he described Polish literature in words that seemed eerily applicable to Yiddish as well: "It is a kind of secret brotherhood with its own rites of communion with the dead, where weeping and laughter, pathos and irony coexist on an equal footing."

After class, my fellow student Vivi and I stood in the courtyard arguing about a poem called "Pastorale," in which the poet, Aron Tsaytlin, quotes the Talmudic teaching that making love is a holy act because the Messiah might thereby be conceived.

Vivi, a self-described former *"frummie"* — a nickname for an ultra-orthodox Jew derived from the Yiddish word *frum*, meaning pious or observant — maintained that making love had nothing whatsoever to do with the Messiah. To claim that an obviously profane act was somehow sacred was ridiculous. Leave it alone!

I, raised in a secular family, countered that it was good to invest ordinary things with a sacred spirit. Why maintain that only the unattainable can be holy? Should we not honor the everyday?

If we'd had beards, they would have been wagging vigorously.

Landsman

AT the breakfast table, I rattled the vitamins in the bottle I'd brought from home. Only a few left: it was my last week here.

In class, Niborski spoke about the writer Moyshe Nadir. "He was born in 1885 in Galicia," he said, "a part of the Austro-Hungarian Empire that today lies within southeastern Poland. In those days, Galicia was not a bad place to be a Jew, but even so, Nadir immigrated to America as a young man. He was a bohemian, a freethinker."

I realized with a start that I had followed every sentence without even trying. "Nadir had an elegant European demeanor," our teacher continued. "At one point he ran a café frequented by artists. His work was sometimes condemned as pornographic, but in fact, though erotic, it was rather chaste."

No tuning out for entire paragraphs, no panicked grasping for a familiar word.

"In the 1920s, he joined the Communist movement and wrote for the New York Yiddish newspaper *Morgn frayhayt* . . ."

When my fellow students began to read aloud, to my amazement I no longer had to follow along line by line with one finger. Instead, I found it easier simply to listen.

The English-language *Baltic Times* reported that Czeslaw Milosz had died. He had been born near Kedainiai, the obituary said — the town I would soon be visiting with my friend Violeta, where her mother, she promised, would tell me how her family had rescued Jews during the war. Milosz had attended Vilnius University, where the Yiddish Institute was now housed, then spent the war years in Warsaw. Over his long career he became a leader in encouraging Poles to reflect on the Holocaust.

In the institute office, crowded as always with students and teachers chatting in many languages, Niborski and I sat down at one of the heavy wooden tables to read through one of Milosz's best-known poems, "A Poor Christian Looks at the Ghetto" (1943), which appeared, in his own English translation, in the newspaper alongside his obituary. In a reversal of roles, I led my teacher haltingly through the text in my native tongue.

> Slowly, boring a tunnel, a guardian mole makes his way,
> With a small red lamp fastened to his forehead.
> He touches buried bodies, counts them, pushes on . . .

My teacher put a finger on the word "mole."

"Es iz vi a moyz," I told him — it's like a mouse. I knew better than to address him in any language other than Yiddish.

"A rats?" he asked. A rat?

"Neyn, a *blind* moys."

"Aha! A krot."

We inched forward together:

> I am afraid, so afraid of the guardian mole.
> He has swollen eyelids, like a Patriarch
> Who has sat much in the light of candles
> Reading the great book of the species.

It is said that when Milosz was asked to explain who or what the mole signified, he would not answer. What could it be, this creature that creeps forward, observing, tallying, pressing ahead? A Talmudic scholar? A historian? A judge?

MY roommate Minette, who had come to Vilnius unable to read or write in Yiddish, left me a note in *mame-loshn*: "Oyb du host lib a gut shtikl hering . . ." "If you like a good piece of herring, we have in the fridge such a tasty herring — maybe as good as Mother used to make!"

With the summer program almost over, Minette had begun to relax over her books at the kitchen table. She dreamed of her swing under the orange tree back in Los Angeles. I continued full-steam, wrestling with every line of every assigned text, looking up every unfamiliar word in the dictionary. Our final assignment was to write a new ending for the text we were reading in class, the story about small-time Jewish thieves in prewar Vilna. This time, instead of writing out everything in English first and then translating into Yiddish, the way I'd done at the beginning of the course, I was able to start right off in *mame-loshn*, with only occasional trips to the dictionary:

crumpled — *tsekneytsht*
swagger — *tshaken*

ONCE again I made my way down the length of Gedimino Prospect and across the river to call on Yudl, the elderly translator who was working on the Soviet-era newspaper articles from the Rokiskis archives that I'd left with him. As before, he came to the door in shorts, then shuffled to the table in the parlor. He handed me several pages of scratchy longhand.

"Read this *itst*, now," he said. I read:

EYEWITNESSES TESTIFY:

I was born and still live in Rokiskis. Before the war, several Jewish families lived in our neighborhood. We got along well. . . .

During the war, the women from the ghetto were made to sweep the streets and weed the pavements. They would give us money and ask us to buy milk, butter, and cheese for their children.

Once, the B. family saw me handing over the food. They dragged me into their yard and beat me up. I was brought home all bloody.

What was this? There was no date, no byline. Hands clasped across his belly, Yudl exhaled audibly but said nothing. I took out my glasses and read on:

It is not true that it was only the Germans and not Lithuanians who did the shooting. It wasn't like that.

The White Bandits took the Jews in groups of fifty and lined them up at the edge of the trench. . . . The shots could clearly be heard from the town.

A few days later, officials brought the belongings of the dead people to sell in the market square. Very soon there were line-ups of buyers.

What did these pages have to do with the articles I'd left with him?

"What you gave me," Yudl said at last, "was only Soviet material. I decided you didn't need that." His gold teeth flashed. "I went to the library and looked for something better."

At the library, he'd found a recent issue of the Rokiskis paper, in which local residents had been asked to submit their memories of the Holocaust. These he had carefully translated for me.

I read another page:

Our neighbors . . . were driven to the woods and shot. It is shameful that young Lithuanians whom we had known were the ones who carried out this act.

It was a slaughter, it was base.

How easy it was to do while hundreds of people watched and kept quiet!!!

What had he done with the articles I'd given him from the Soviet era?

He had cut them up and thrown them away, he said.

So. This old warrior, a longtime Communist whom Regina had recommended because of his familiarity with the Soviet vocabulary, hadn't been willing to translate the old accounts of "bourgeois nationalists" and "innocent Soviet activists." He didn't want me reading them, couldn't bear to pass along that old way of ordering the past. *It wasn't like that.* Only the true story, as he saw it, would do.

I'd hired Yudl to do one thing, and he'd chosen to do something else entirely — something that was a revelation in itself. The articles he'd found showed that the town of Rokiskis was moving on. The local newspaper was providing a public platform for eyewitnesses to the Holocaust — people like Steponas. The way these writers described the wartime events was similar to the way Steponas had spoken when we drove through the town together. Maybe the day was coming when Steponas would not need to reach out all the way across the ocean to share his story. Maybe, in towns like Rokiskis, the silence was beginning to melt.

I paid Yudl for his help, and he kissed my hand, and I went off across the river.

The white of the sky was just beginning to shade into gray when I rang the bell at an apartment building across from the former Lenin Park to pay a call on Ida, an eighty-three-year-old woman whom Regina, my Rokiskis guide, had urged me to visit. Ida was one of the very few surviving Jews from the Rokiskis region still alive in Vilnius. She had grown up not far from my great-grandfather's yellow study house and the green cottage of Steponas's youth.

"Kumt arayn" — come in, she said as she accepted the damp, floppy bouquet of sweet peas I'd bought on Gedimino Prospect. A small table was elaborately set for two, with cream cakes dotted with red currants and a silver bowl brimming with plump sour cherries. (Just the night before, doing my homework, I'd learned the Yiddish word for the fruit: *vaynshl.*) For her no less than for me, a visit with a Rokiskis *landsman,* a fellow countryman or descendant, was a special occasion.

Ida and her sister had happened to be away from Rokiskis when the massacre took place, and so the two of them were the only members of their entire family to have survived the war, she told me in Yiddish — she knew not a word of English — as we sipped tea from delicate china cups. Every September she traveled to the forest in Bajorai, the same green glade where I'd stood with Regina and Steponas's wife, to honor the memory of her loved ones.

She fixed her penetrating eyes on my face. There was something she wanted from me, something I couldn't figure out. *Umgekumen*, she kept saying. *Umgekumen*. What could this mean?

Again she explained, and again I strained to understand. Finally, seemingly through sheer force of will, I grasped what she was asking. *Umgekumen*: "killed." She wanted to know if she was visiting the right place. Were the bones of her mother and father, her brothers and her aunts and uncles and cousins and grandparents, truly buried beneath the grassy tufts of this particular clearing, the one in Bajorai? Or were they in fact lying in another killing field, in Obeliai, a few miles up the road? Was there a *reshime*, a list, somewhere?

I shook my head. *Neyn*, I said, I didn't believe there was such a list. And no, I couldn't answer her question. All I could do, as her attempt to tend to the dead touched my heart, was hold her hand. I could listen to her words, and I could respond, however haltingly, in soft syllables of our mother tongue.

Walking back up Gedimino in the dark, I recalled a poem by Mani Leyb titled "Zey" ("They"), which we'd read in class:

Zey zenen dort, oy, got, geven a sakh, a sakh . . .
itst . . .
a tsvey-dray beymer fun an oysgehaktn vald.

Once, oh God, there were so many of them, so many . . .
Now . . .
Lone trees standing in a chopped-down wood.

I let myself into my apartment and sat down with my homework, a story called "Mentshn un geter" ("People and Gods") by Sholem Asch (1888–1957), a Polish-born writer whose plays and novels had been much discussed in Yiddish circles. Two poor women, one Jewish and the other Christian, are neighbors in a tiny *shtetl*. Side by side they cook their meals, wash their clothes, and observe the rituals of their separate faiths. One lights the candles on Friday night, while the other keeps a lamp burning before an image of the Virgin Mary. Relations between the women are prickly. Their respective gods, the Jewish and the Christian one, "could not live together in peace and created great quarrels between the two."

Outside my window, I began to hear marching feet, singing, chanting. *Lie-tu-va! Lie-tu-va!* Lithuania! Lithuania! The Lithuanian Olympic basketball team was playing the Americans tonight. Basketball was this country's national pastime, so intensely beloved that President Adamkus called it "the second religion." Apparently the Lithuanians had just won the game. I heard the rat-a-tat of firecrackers and the gunning of engines. Brakes screeched, horns blared, and a thunderous drumbeat boomed out, accompanied by a shrill series of whistles and a blast of trumpets.

Just before my visit, the Simon Wiesenthal Center, an international organization committed to hunting down former Nazis, had kicked up a storm that had to do with basketball. In July 1941, the center alleged, members of a Lithuanian basketball team in the city of Kaunas had murdered Jews. Not long after the German invasion, according to the grisly story told by Holocaust survivors, the local team had played against a German army team and won the game. As a reward, the Lithuanians were taken to the Seventh Fort on the outskirts of town. There they were handed rifles and invited to shoot Jewish prisoners. Without hesitating, they took aim and killed more than two dozen Jews.

Was the story true? The Wiesenthal Center tracked down a pair of eighty-three-year-old Lithuanian twin brothers living in Connecticut and accused them of having taken part in the shooting. ESPN, an American TV sports network, interviewed one of the brothers. The old man acknowledged that he had indeed been a member of a Kaunas basketball team in 1941. And yes, a few weeks after the German invasion, while thousands of Jews were being killed at the Seventh Fort, basketball games were being played in the city. But there had been no game against the German team, he said, and no shooting.

The words with which the old man phrased his plea of innocence, however, were chilling: "We had to work, go to college, teach, and date girls," he told the network. "We didn't have time to kill the Jews."

The Wiesenthal Center demanded that Lithuanian prosecutors conduct an investigation. Prosecutors did look into the matter, but soon closed the case. Nothing but rumor, they declared.

The center launched a project called "Operation: Last Chance," which offered rewards for tips about Nazi collaborators in the Baltics. Some information emerged. Western governments extradited several alleged collaborators. Lithuanian prosecutors put about a dozen defendants on trial. Several were convicted but deemed too frail for prison.

A spokesman for the center voiced his ire that "to date . . . not a single Lithuanian Nazi war criminal has been punished for his crimes in independent Lithuania" — that is, after the fall of the Soviet Union — "nor has a single such criminal ever sat a single minute in a Lithuanian jail."

The Wiesenthal Center was not alone in its criticism. Lithuania's failure to take significant legal action against Nazi collaborators drew censure from many in the West and Israel.

Some in Lithuania responded by pointing out that the West itself had hardly been exemplary in its own handling of former Nazis. By some estimates, ten thousand Nazi criminals had been admitted into the United States immediately after World War II. The U.S. government's effort to bring such people to justice had not begun until 1979, when an Office of Special Investigations was established at the Department of Justice. By the start of the twenty-first century, that office had succeeded in tracking down only about a hundred alleged former Nazis. About sixty had been deported to their countries of origin.

Close to midnight, Minette came back from a noodle-making session at the institute. Everyone had been allowed to roll out the dough, she said, and the results were delicious. On the way home, heart pounding, she'd threaded her way through convoys of convertibles jammed with drunk, screaming basketball fans.

Two separate worlds.

I remembered what Irena Veisaite had told me at the very beginning of my trip about the challenges facing members of a multicultural society. The ideal, she said, was not assimilation — everybody becoming like everyone else. Rather, the goal was tolerance, which she defined as "a permissive or liberal attitude toward beliefs or practices different from or conflicting with one's own." To that definition, however, she appended a codicil: "I would add the non-acceptance of intolerance."

The intolerance of intolerance. A tricky concept.

I went back to the Asch story about the two old women. Old age brings the two neighbors closer. Their husbands die, their children leave for America, and they decide to move in together. On Friday nights, they share a meal of fish and challah. The Jew's candles gutter on the dinner table, and the Christian's lamp shines on the portrait of the Virgin. As the two women lie down to sleep, "two gods flickered — the little Sabbath candles on the table and the little lamp in front of the holy picture." "Un zey zaynen in der shtil, in der shtil oysgegangen . . ." — and quietly, quietly, they went out.

MY survey of Lithuania's efforts to engage with its past was almost at its end. I'd met the leaders I'd set out to meet — except for one. Vytautas Toleikis, a gentile man in his forties, was the director of an organization called the Foundation for Educational Change, which had designed innovative curricula about the Holocaust. When I showed up in his office late one afternoon, however, I found

I wasn't eager to discuss the particulars of his work. Instead, all I wanted was to be with someone who cared about all of this. To sit with him. To breathe.

Just back from vacation and clad in a red T-shirt, Toleikis seemed glad to oblige. He pushed his chair back from his cluttered desk and clasped his hands behind his head as if the two of us were seated on a porch somewhere in the countryside, shooting the breeze.

"I can touch the Holocaust with my own skin," he said, "because my mother told very freely about the murders." He rummaged in his desk and held out a black-and-white photograph for me to see. His mother, Elizabieta.

For a long moment I peered at the weathered, smiling face. Hair parted in the middle in a plain, old-fashioned style. Shoulders framed by a lacy white blouse and cardigan sweater. She had finished only three years of school, "but she understood the evil and the goodness," Toleikis said. And so, "when the Holocaust issue began here, in my mind it was all absolutely clear."

When Soviet power collapsed, Toleikis was among the first to push for public discussion of the Holocaust. As a teacher, he worked with his students to refurbish overgrown Jewish cemeteries. But when "my old friend Emanuel Zingeris" — now the ebullient head of the Tolerance Center at the Jewish museum — wanted to *require* all schools to teach a course on the Holocaust, Toleikis had opposed the plan.

Holocaust education was so sensitive, he felt, that it needed teachers who were truly committed to the task. Without them, it would fail. This was his view as a teacher.

For four years, he said, he had taught high school seniors about the Holocaust. The point, he told the students, was not how many local people pulled the triggers. The point was that many Lithuanians *agreed* that the Jews should be killed, and that there had been those who didn't agree but didn't feel that they could do anything, and those who clearly could have done something but had not. "No, we must not feel guilt," he told the students, "but yes, we must remember that we have a very, very black mark in our history."

After his lecture, he would ask his students to write down their thoughts. In an average class of twenty-five students, only two or three would be negative. "Only two or three — that's pretty good."

He looked out the window into a tiny courtyard. "I know that our culture — our Lithuanian and our Jewish Litvak culture — is among the richest in Europe," he said softly. "I also know my country's dark history. I don't separate the two."

He brought his chair back down on all four legs. "I am open to all of our history, the good and the bad," he said. "For me, it is all Lithuania. And I am very proud of being Lithuanian."

ON the steps of the Presidential Palace opposite the university, we students posed for a class picture. Afterwards I sat down for a few minutes with Mendy Cahan, the program director. I told him about the angry note I'd scribbled to him on the gloomy day midway through the course, when I struggled to understand Bluma as she spoke in Yiddish about the mass-murder site in the forest. I told him that instead of giving him the note I'd crumpled it up and buried it in my bag.

He nodded. In listening to Bluma, he said in English in a voice laden with *gefil*, feeling, it wasn't necessary to absorb everything she was saying. It didn't really matter how many words I had understood. What was important was the osmosis that took place. The program opened up the sounds, he said, enabling us to begin to listen; then we could go on discovering.

The encounter with Bluma was important not only for us students but also for Bluma herself, he said, and for other elderly Jews who had contact with the institute. In a land that had not always wanted to hear their stories, "we bring a listening ear to part of their identity."

I told Cahan what I'd been up to, described some of my meetings. In addition to serving the elderly Jewish community, I asked, did the institute aim to have an impact on Lithuania as a whole?

It did, Cahan said, and in a particular way, one that had been carefully thought through. Before, he said, the meeting ground between Jews and non-Jews here had tended to be *only* about the Holocaust. "Did you commit the crime? Are you a good Lithuanian or a bad Lithuanian? Will you say you're sorry?" Now the institute was bent on creating a new kind of connection. Like the summer program, the classes offered to Lithuanian students during the regular term focused mostly on the Jewish culture that had flourished before the war — not on the destruction of that culture.

"Obviously, the Holocaust is very important," Cahan said, "but we tackle the Holocaust by teaching what came before. We move away a little bit from the destruction."

Lithuanian students were introduced to the theology of the Vilna Gaon, the political fervor of the Jewish Labor Bund and the Zionist movement, the literary work of Zalman Shneour and Avrom Karpinovitch and Moyshe Kulbak, the silver ornaments that once adorned the Great Synagogue, the folk art of the *shtetl*. As they came to know the glories of the nearly vanished Jewish world, it was hoped, they would find their way to a moral encounter with the past. And that, in turn, would lead them to a new vision of the future.

An end run, I thought. Rather than rubbing people's noses in the bad deeds of the war years, Cahan was saying, the key was to invite them to join in treasuring what had been lost. From there, they could begin to take steps — their own steps — toward reflecting on the destruction. "We emphasize common interests, shared values, the richness of the culture," Cahan said. "In this way, seeds are sown."

How did he see those seeds sprouting? What did he think this country needed to do?

For a long moment he didn't answer. I considered asking a different question, changing the subject. But my time here had helped to develop my own "listening ear." I waited.

"I hope," he said at last, "that this country will open up and answer the challenge of engaging with Jewish history in a proud and responsible way."

Another silence. Again I waited.

"I hope this . . . this basketball joy will be transformed," he said, referring to the wild celebration that had surged through the city streets after the Olympic game the other night. "It may not be easy for this country to become a society that is proud and joyful and respecting of others. But that is my dream."

I parted from Cahan and began walking slowly toward my apartment, where my homework assignments were waiting. I thought of the people I'd met who were striving to make Cahan's dream a reality. Their various programs were not formally connected, but it seemed to me that their efforts formed a cohesive whole.

First, they *celebrated*, rather than simply condemning. They connected people not only with the tragedy of destruction but with the magnificence of the Jewish past.

Second, they *invited*, rather than requiring. The people I'd met believed that Lithuanians should not be *forced* to accept responsibility for the misdeeds of the terrible years. They had surprised me by insisting that teachers not be *compelled* to teach about the Holocaust. Instead, they wanted to *encourage* people to feel their way into the darkness.

Third, the initiatives I'd seen posed *questions*, rather than supplying answers. In this, they reminded me of the "Jewish Ways of Learning" lecture I'd walked out on, where Cahan had described the age-old Jewish scholarly tradition. Rather than receiving answers from a member of the clergy, Jews from every walk of life were encouraged to become scholars. *Everyone* was expected to join in the search for understanding.

Here are the facts, these programs said. Here are the questions. Now it's your job — everyone's job — to reflect on them. Giving people the opportunity to take matters into their own hearts and design their own vehicles of remorse, it was hoped, would foster a transformative empathy and an open-minded vision of the future.

Finally, these efforts called on people to *join together*. Jews were not the only victims in the tumult of the twentieth century. But acknowledging that non-Jews also suffered — "Yes, you, too, were victims" — was not exactly the point. In fact, by and large these programs did not address themselves directly to gentile martyrdom. It was not as *fellow victims* that non-Jews were called to participate in a moral exploration of the past. Nor was it simply as people who needed to be *taught a lesson*. Instead, Lithuanians were asked to participate in these initiatives because their finest selves were respected, their presence actively desired. The Jewish tragedy was not only a tragedy for the Jews. It mattered to everyone, and all hands were needed in the project of understanding and repair.

It was a less aggressive approach than I had expected to find. Perhaps, in a land riddled with resentment and resistance, there was no choice but to proceed gently. Whatever the rationale, the Lithuanian approach had opened my eyes and shown me a new way to carry the past.

I took out my old-fashioned key and opened the door into the courtyard that led to my apartment on the site of the Small Ghetto. None of the people I'd met, I reflected, had used the word "forgiveness." Nor had I heard the word "reconciliation." A country did not "overcome" a bloody past, I had seen. We could never truly leave the past behind. Yet there were ways to help people expect the best from themselves and others.

Were these initiatives gaining ground in Lithuania? It was hard for me to say. The people I'd met felt sanguine enough to keep on with what they were doing. No doubt there would be ups and downs. At times anti-Semitism and intolerance would gain the ascendancy. At times hatred would trump goodwill. But these brave people were showing a way forward — for Lithuania and for other places grappling with complex histories. I felt grateful to be able to learn from them. And I wished them well.

I Helped What I Can

SUNDAY morning, I waited on the curb outside my apartment building, inhaling the sharp, earthy smell of freshly washed Stikliu gatve and listening to the sounds of organ music and the bell-like voices that floated from the open doorway of a nearby church. Today was the day Violeta was to take me to her hometown of Kedainiai, a couple of hours northwest of Vilnius, where she'd promised that her mother would tell me about how the family had saved Jews during the war. When she pulled up, I got into the front seat and turned around to greet Natasha, Violeta's English teacher, who'd come along to help with the translating. She had bleached blond hair like Violeta's and was dressed like her, too, in tight-fitting slacks and a snug matching jacket. She was not Lithuanian but Russian, she said, and had grown up in Vilnius as the daughter of a Russian military engineer. Now, at forty, fifteen years younger than Violeta, she was the widowed mother of a teenage son.

The capital was soon behind us. On either side of the nearly empty highway, flat fields stretched to the horizon. Here a clump of black-green trees rose up, there a group of turkeys scratched in the dirt. Here a cow strained on its chain, there an abandoned collective farm building stood exposed to the elements, its windows smashed. On the roofs of the farmhouses, Lithuania's national birds with their long bills were roosting on wagon-wheel nests.

"Strokes?" Violeta asked.

"Storks," Natasha corrected.

Today, August 15, Violeta said, Lithuania was celebrating a holiday called Zolines, or Meadow Grass Day, when people brought bouquets of rye, barley, oats, herbs, thistles, and garden flowers to church. After being blessed by the priests, "all year these plants will be in our homes," Violeta said contentedly. "They will protect us." Today was also the Feast of the Assumption, honoring the Virgin Mary's ascent to heaven.

And, I remembered suddenly, it was the date of the massacre of the Rokiskis Jews in the forest of Bajorai.

"Please excuse me," Violeta was saying. She needed to talk for a few minutes about her marriage. A *mabl*, a flood, of rage and betrayal poured out, at first in English. Her son, she said, had advised her to separate from her husband, to let go.

"He is right," Natasha said forcefully, upon which Violeta let loose another torrent of words, this time in Russian.

Natasha made suggestions, then soothing noises. Finally she sighed. "So," she asked me, "what are American men like?"

Violeta chimed in. Did they respect women? More than Lithuanian men did?

Throughout my time here I'd been the one firing questions. Now that it was my turn to supply the answers, I was at a loss. I scrambled to call up memories of the American men I knew. My father. Uncle Will. Who else? My brain fogged over. My husband. The two of us had a highly textured relationship, I remembered dimly, full of negotiations and renegotiations. How to begin? "Well," I said, "we needed a women's movement . . ."

"Oh, the Soviet Union had that, too," Natasha interrupted. She stared out the window. It had been easier for women to adapt to the post-Soviet times, she said. Women were willing to take the lower-paying jobs that followed Lithuania's independence. Men, on the other hand, "lie on sofa and complain and not move their butt."

Violeta pounded the steering wheel. "I am free woman!" she hollered.

We rode in silence for a while. Then I asked them what they remembered of the Cold War. When I was growing up, I told them, children were terrified that nuclear war was about to break out. To prepare for an attack by the Soviet Union, we were taught to crouch under our desks to protect ourselves when the bomb fell, and to cover our eyes so they wouldn't melt.

"We did this, too!" they cried. "'The Americans are coming!'"

The two of them had divergent views of the Soviet era, however. Natasha believed that it had been necessary for the Red Army to march into Lithuania in 1940. The goal was not to oppress Lithuanians. It was to prevent, or at least postpone, the German invasion. But foremost in Violeta's mind were the tens of thousands of her people who had been sent to Siberia, and the many who had died there. Only hard work had saved those who made it through. "Our Lithuanian people in Siberia were *famous* for doing everything they could to survive," she said.

"And the Russian people *helped* them to survive!" Natasha interjected. Russians themselves had been repressed under Stalin. In fact, "Russians suffered the most."

To this, Violeta responded with several loud paragraphs in Russian. In the Soviet times, Natasha translated, the Soviets wanted the Baltic countries to be very dependent. The decision was made in Moscow that in Panevezys there would be a TV factory and in Kedainiai a leather factory. "I translate her words exactly," Natasha said. "This is not *my* opinion." In her opinion, life in the Baltics had been much better than in Russia. Of course there was centralized control of the economy, but Lithuanians should be grateful for all that Russia had given them. Houses for all, for example. Maybe not beautiful houses, but just the same. . . . Yes, in the Soviet times, there had been scarcity. Salaries were small. But education was free, medicine was free, and you paid not a penny for your flat, for water. People were not able to travel abroad, a car was a luxury, everyone was poor — "but we were rather happy." Growing up, she could never have imagined desperate people hunting through the garbage bins for food, the way they did today.

We arrived on the outskirts of Kedainiai. Natasha pointed out a Maxima hypermarket. "All we needed back then was more stuff," she said. "The rest was not so bad." Today the shops were full, but not everyone could afford to buy. The disparity in people's means distressed her greatly. She taught some students for free because they had no money. "Some teenagers don't have what others do, and it makes them very unhappy."

Violeta pulled up on a narrow street in the center of town and parked the car. She pointed to the unusual gabled roofs. In the seventeenth and eighteenth centuries, she said, this street had been home to a Scottish community. *Another* lost people. This one had not been murdered, yet it had vanished just the same.

Not far away was the market square. For four hundred years it had been the heart of the Jewish community. Now the cobblestoned expanse was empty. Two large synagogues were still standing side by side, both handsomely restored. One, which Violeta described as the "summer synagogue," was being used as an art school; the other, the "winter synagogue," had been turned into a community center.

"I asked my friend why these synagogues are no longer working," Violeta said. "She explained it is because we have no Jewish people."

I knew, I said.

Growing up, she continued as we stood looking up at the great roofs pitched against the blue sky, she and her friends hadn't made a big deal out of who was Jewish — or Russian. They didn't even *know* who was Russian and who was Jewish, she said, in part because the Jews hid their nationality, adding Lithuanian endings to their surnames.

Perhaps mistakenly, I sensed a whiff of accusation in her words. Hiding one's Jewishness couldn't have been easy, I imagined. Did

Violeta think it was a sneaky or cowardly thing for people to do? Did she understand how enormous the annihilation had been, how few the survivors, how traumatized the remnants of the Jewish community had been after the war?

Did she get it?

"My son's music teacher was a Jew," she said. "She was a fantastic woman." She had told me the same thing the first time we'd met, at the café on Pilies gatve.

We got back in the car, and a few minutes later we arrived at a cluster of five-story apartment buildings, which were called *khrush-chevki*, Natasha said: thousands of them had been erected in the Khrushchev era. We started up the stairs. Once carefully painted and stenciled in green, yellow, and red (the colors of the Lithuanian flag), the walls of the stairwell were now scuffed and peeling.

This was the typical Soviet building, Natasha said, puffing. "But at least people had a flat to live in. It was free, and no one could take it away from you." When her mother and father first moved into their apartment, they were so happy to have hot and cold water that they kept the faucets running all night long.

Violeta's mother greeted us in a housedress, her white hair gathered into a soft bun. After I presented my gift, a box of tea, she led the way into the sunny parlor, where a heavy armoire laden with knickknacks extended along one whole wall.

Before the war, she said as Natasha translated, relations between Lithuanians and Jews were "normal." She and her family were friendly with Jews and called one another by their first names. In fact, "I had so many Jewish friends, I was considered Jewish myself!"

When the Germans came, at first nothing bad happened to the Jews. All was calm. Lithuanians remained on friendly terms with Jews, as before. But later, everyone grew afraid. She drew her thin sweater tighter. "Then no one could help the Jewish people."

One day, after all the Jews had been forced to move into the ghetto, she got permission to go in and see a childhood friend, who asked her to take some valuables from one house and store them in another.

"I promised to help her," the old woman said. She thumped a hand against her breast. "I helped what I can." But as with Steponas and his mother in Rokiskis, what she had done had not been enough. She hadn't been able to do what her friend asked, or to save her life.

She shook her head. Her family had aided a family of Russians, she continued. When the war began, a Russian military officer had gone to the aerodrome and fled the country, leaving behind his wife and three small children, who had nothing to eat and nowhere to live. They tried going to the railway station to run away, but the Germans bombed the train. The wife got off with two of the children, but one of her sons was still on the train, and the train went away with him on it. "The wife and two children came back to us. They lived with us for three years."

Were these people Jews? Was this the story Violeta wanted me to hear?

It wasn't clear, Natasha murmured to me. The story was confusing.

One day, the old woman went on, a German came looking for the Russian family, and her family saved their lives by saying they knew nothing about them. The Germans threatened that if they failed to turn in the Russians they themselves would be taken. Even then, they hadn't given the Russians away. In the end, her family was not taken, "but they did take everything from our garden and our orchard."

The Russian woman and her two children survived. After the war, the boy who had gone away on the train was found in an orphanage and the husband returned. "But of course, like all men, he had another woman already."

There was a burst of loud talking — shouting, really — from Violeta, her mother, and Natasha.

When the hubbub subsided, the old woman said that everybody — Russians, Lithuanians, and Poles — had suffered during the war, but the Jews had suffered the most. "It was very difficult to help the Jews."

There was more.

"Tell the story," Violeta prompted.

Her mother sat up straighter and folded her hands in her lap. "My husband brought a little baby girl over the bridge out of the Kovno ghetto," she said. He delivered her to a famous tenor named Kipras Petrauskas.

I knew about this incident. I'd read about it in several books. The baby was Dana Pomerants, the daughter of the Jewish founder of Lithuanian jazz. She had been smuggled out of the Kovno ghetto in a potato sack. Petrauskas, the famous tenor, had hidden her for the duration of the war. Afterwards, she had been reunited with her family. She grew up to become a professional violinist.

Was it possible that Violeta's father had played a role in the rescue? I looked at Natasha.

"I'm sorry," she said. "The translation is hard for me."

When the Jewish survivors returned after the war, the old woman said, they went from house to house looking for their property. Her own family hadn't taken anything, she said.

"It is a nation's tragedy," she said. "I ask God, don't give birth to another Hitler."

She fell silent.

Violeta had moved to the window and was staring out. "Time for a break," she said.

So these, as promised, were the stories about saving Jews — a collection of fragments that had been fiercely tended through the decades. If the facts were sometimes confusing, the overall import was clear. It was a tale of fits and starts, fear and compassion, brave impulses and insurmountable obstacles, successes and failures.

In the dining room, the table had been laid in my honor with buckwheat pancakes sprinkled with slivers of bacon, potato pancakes swimming in lard, and ham sandwiches with butter and dill. A feast of pork for a Jewish visitor, I smiled to myself as I picked up my fork.

After we ate, the three of us got back in the car and Violeta took us to see her childhood home on a street not far from the market square. During the Soviet era, she said, the house had been nationalized. Later, it was returned to the family, then sold. Today, adorned with a shabby sign, it was home to a secondhand clothing store.

We stepped into the garden, a weedy expanse bordered by a row of hedges. Violeta picked her way among thick tufts of grass. She remembered this rosebush, she said softly, this chestnut tree, this well. Here — she pointed — was a forest of plum trees.

Vaisiu sodas was Lithuanian for "orchard," she said.

The Yiddish, I told her, was *sod*.

In front of a row of tall pink blooms swaying in the sun, she reached for my notebook. *Piliarozes*, she wrote carefully: hollyhocks. Here in the Eden of her youth, she seemed stilled, her heart brimming.

Through the trees she pointed to an old church with dark wooden walls. Geographically, she said, Lithuania was the center of Europe, Kedainiai was the center of Lithuania, and this church was the center of Kedainiai. (Later, I learned that numerous other spots in Lithuania also claimed this honor.)

As we watched, the great double door of the church swung open. A bride in white and a groom in black emerged. Beside them an old man stood erect, a veteran's sash across his chest.

Loss, love, war.

AFTER that we drove into the countryside, bumping along an unpaved road. In August 1941 the Jews of the Kedainiai region had been transported along this same route. They would have seen the same flowers lining the ditches — dandelions and ragweed, Queen Anne's lace and sky-blue chicory. The branches of the apple trees would have sagged with fruit, just as they did now.

A thick stand of pines appeared, then a black sign: *masiniu zudyniu vieta* — mass-murder site — *1 km.*

When a dusty clearing appeared, we got out. Birches, the Russian national tree, had been planted around an iron railing that encircled a sandy area about three feet deep. A small plaque, placed in 1957, said:

Here are buried 2076 people

Beside this, a larger, later plaque said:

Here the Hitlerists
and their local helpers
on VIII 28 1941
killed 2076 Jews

Violeta opened the trunk of the car and brought out candles and white hydrangeas from her garden. My eyes filled with tears. The melted remains of several votive candles lay scattered nearby in glass cups. It was her mother who had placed them there, Violeta said. She handed me two white candles and a stick she picked up off the ground. "Dig some holes," she said. She gestured over the railing.

As the two women stood watching, I did what she asked. I climbed over the railing into the pit and stooped to scratch in the dirt. Waves of reverence and nausea passed over me. I used the stick to make holes in the sand, propped up the candles, struck matches, and cupped my hands around the fragile flames. Yiddish words rushed into my head, a cacophony and a consolation:

in dem ort ale yidn — in this place all the Jews
mener, froyen, kinder, alte mentshn — men, women, children, old people
hobn zikh oysgeton — undressed
nakete — naked
froyen, geblibn lebn — women, still alive
hobn zikh gevorfn af di kinder — threw themselves on top of their
  children

me hot geshosn — they shot
me hot geshosn — they shot
me hot geshosn — they shot

"They say the ground moved for days afterwards," Violeta said. "I cannot imagine."

The two of them stretched out their hands and helped me up. I dusted the sand from my hands.

"As a Lithuanian," Violeta said, "I want to apologize."

Over our heads, the birch leaves sighed to one another:

shushken — to whisper
shorkhn — to rustle

"But," she added, "we must remember that every nationality has both good and bad people."

We got back into the car and drove away up the dirt road. After a few miles, we stopped at a roadside stand to buy small yellow apples, Violeta's favorite kind.

Farther on, the road cut straight through a pine forest. The black trunks pressed close on either side.

"My father had a baby in a bag," Violeta said dreamily. "A man brought the baby to the factory and said, 'Someone needs to take this baby. Take her to the tenor.'" If the Germans had intercepted her father, it would have been the end for him.

We emerged from the woods. The sun was golden on the fields.

"My son's music teacher was Jewish," Violeta said. It was the third time I'd heard her mention the music teacher. "She was a fantastic woman."

"You have told us this already," Natasha said sharply.

After that, for a while no one spoke.

Finally, Natasha rolled down her window and threw out her apple core. She was remembering the 1970s, she said, when the first wave of Jews left Lithuania for Israel. Their luggage stood in the street in big wooden boxes. "They thanked us that they had lived here with us," and went off into the unknown. They had not been seen again. Cheek in hand, she gazed out the window at the waning light. "Just now I am wondering about their feelings."

We had reached the suburbs of Vilnius. Violeta turned to me with a mischievous grin.

"Do you know an American widower for me?" she asked.

PART THREE

We Are *All* Here

The process of becoming is history. . . . It grows out of ourselves, out of even our smallest deeds. . . . Woe . . . to those who deceive themselves by their obedience to an unchanging moral claim.

CZESLAW MILOSZ, IN *NATIVE REALM*

From the Archives

EMIL came to my apartment with the pages he'd copied at the Special Archives. At the kitchen table, he declined a cup of tea. I clutched my own steaming cup with tense fingers. Within the file of Efroyim Gens, the chief of the Jewish police in the Shavl ghetto, I hoped, lay answers to questions that had begun to simmer inside me when Uncle Will had revealed his hidden past — questions about the police, about victims, collaborators, and bystanders.

Gens had been sent to Dachau along with Uncle Will and Uncle Aaron and other Shavl prisoners, and after the liberation he made his way back to Lithuania. He settled in Klaipeda, a city on the Baltic Sea, where in 1948 he received a visit from the MGB, the precursor to the KGB. The authorities questioned him about his wartime activities, and an official transcript of the interview appeared in his file. Emil had copied the transcript, and here it was.

According to this document, "GENS Efroyim Vulfovicius" had begun serving as police chief in the zone of the Shavl ghetto known as "Traku" in September 1941, shortly after the ghetto was sealed. (The adjoining zone was called "Kavkaz.") He supervised "eleven or twelve" policemen, he said, and when asked for their names, he came up with nine — my uncle's not among them.

The policemen's duties, Gens said, were to oversee housing, prevent stealing and speculation, and enforce sanitary measures.

They had no arms or ammunition. People who violated ghetto rules were subject to three kinds of penalties — fines, confiscation of goods, and suspension from work — which were imposed by a ghetto court presided over by two or three Jewish judges.

It was a benign account with no mention of violence. I wondered if Gens was telling the whole truth. But his questioners did not probe. His answers were deemed satisfactory, and he was asked to become a secret agent — an invitation that was not uncommon in those days. "He signed on to save his life," Emil said. Refusing would have meant risking arrest.

Not long afterwards, however, in June 1949, Gens ran afoul of the organization he was secretly serving. He had not performed well as an agent. Having learned that a group of his friends were planning to emigrate illegally to the West, he had failed to turn them in. Now he was arrested and put on trial on charges of betraying the Soviet Union. As pages from the trial record showed, once again he was questioned about his behavior in the ghetto, this time more closely.

Gens insisted that as chief of the Jewish police, he had been a force for good. He had helped people escape. He had smuggled in medicine. And during the *kinder-aktsye*, he said, he had helped to hide two children.

Gens called several witnesses. Among them, as Emil had told me, were Uncle Will's brother, my uncle Aaron, and his wife, my aunt Sonya. But the two of them did not testify in quite the way Gens had hoped. It was they, not Gens, they said, who had hidden the two children. No one had helped them, least of all Gens. In fact, they had feared that Gens might punish them for what they'd done:

A: In November 1943 I was afraid [Gens] might turn me in to the German authorities because I [hid] two children and two old ladies [in a storage area behind a heavy cabinet]. But everything went well.
Q: Who was in the apartment at that time?
A: Only my wife.
Q: Where were Gens and his wife at that time?

A: Gens and his wife were not in the apartment. I cannot tell where they were exactly.

I had no doubt that these were the two girls whom Uncle Will had always proudly talked about hiding. Here Gens was claiming credit for the rescue, and so were Uncle Aaron and Aunt Sonya. As I followed Emil's finger down the lines of text, I shook my head. How elusive the facts were!

Aaron was not an entirely hostile witness, as this exchange makes clear:

Q: What do you know about Gens Efroyim's traitorous criminal activities during the period when he was chief of the ghetto police? A: I do not recall any such activities.

When Aunt Sonya was asked about Gens's "mistreatment of Jews in the ghetto," she, too, replied in the negative: "I cannot tell you anything about that. I know nothing about it."

Emil turned the page. Those were the witnesses, he said. That was the trial.

How could that be? "Didn't anyone testify against Gens?" I asked.

"Yes, of course," Emil said. "Many witnesses testified, 'Gens was brutal, he beat me, he confiscated our food.'"

But he hadn't brought me any of their testimony, hadn't had any of it copied. Why not?

Emil's mouth tightened. "Gens had no choice!" he burst out. "He was simply a victim of the Nazis, just like all other Jews." The prosecutors had tried to portray Gens's behavior in the worst possible light, but it all added up to "Soviet nonsense."

"But —"

Emil reached for the next page in the pile. "Here we have the findings of the tribunal," he said. The verdict.

On a single page, three points had been typed:

1. During the war Gens worked voluntarily as chief of police of the ghetto.

2. He supervised twelve to sixteen policemen. He subjected the residents of the ghetto — "Soviet citizens of Jewish nationality" — to searches, confiscated their food, arrested and beat them.
3. After the war, as an agent of the MGB, he knew of the traitorous intentions of several citizens seeking to flee the Soviet Union, but withheld this information from authorities.

The sentence: twenty-five years of corrective labor.

Gens served three years at Vorkuta, the grim camp near the Arctic Circle. In 1953, when Stalin died, the camps began to empty out and Gens began to pen eloquent letters pleading for release. These Emil had copied — letters of five, six, seven pages each, addressed to various authorities, all the way up to Premier Nikita Khrushchev. In a firm, confident hand with spiky black downstrokes, Gens defended himself and his Jewish policemen with increasing fervor.

"I do not plead guilty and I never will," he wrote. If he had actually committed the crimes he'd been convicted of, the Soviet Union would not have had to prosecute him. "The Jews of the ghetto would have taken care of me. They didn't touch me." He went on:

> We had no guns. We reported only to the Jewish people. I had nothing in common with the Germans and did not speak with them.
> Order and work were our weapons in fighting for the survival of the Jewish people. Refusal to work meant death.
> Yet today I suffer for saving the majority of the ghetto residents, for their being able to enjoy life.

These last words were painful to read. Yes, more than five thousand Jews had survived in the ghetto until July 1944. And yes, perhaps Gens's efforts had helped to keep them alive up to that point. But as Gens most certainly knew, most of the five thousand were not able to enjoy life. They had not been saved. They had perished in the camps.

Gens continued:

> The Germans dirtied their hands with rivers of blood. Today they are at home with their families, and I, their victim, am made to suffer.

The question was to be or not to be. To be meant to survive being continually downtrodden and detested and hope that one day justice would prevail. It was pointless to rebel without guns. . . . The only weapon we had was hope and faith that the Nazis would be defeated.

A little later, however, Gens hinted at the presence of weapons other than hope and faith, and made clear that the police had turned those weapons (if nothing more than fists and truncheons) against Jews who didn't obey orders:

Of course, as everywhere, there were some people who didn't understand. We had problems because of them.

We looked death in the eye every day. We could not be too sentimental and pander to individuals who could bring misfortune to our nation.

Those "poor victims" who allegedly suffered from my actions should be thankful to me for saving their lives. To whom do you think they should be thankful? To the Germans — killers? Or to me, who saved them using force?

In June 1956, having served five and a half years, Gens was released. He lived for the rest of his life in the Moldavian Soviet Socialist Republic (now known as Moldova), near Ukraine, where he worked as a senior economist. In 1971, at the age of sixty, he died.

Gens's words, Emil said, reminded him of those that his grandfather, the Jewish police chief in the Kovno ghetto, had spoken at *his* postwar trial:

We were left with only one choice: whether to refuse to work in the police and thus surrender the Jewish population of Lithuania to the Germans to be torn to pieces, or to take this population under our own protection and thus to reduce to a minimum the number of innocent victims. My conscience regarding the Jewish inhabitants is pure.

This statement, in turn, echoed the words of Jacob Gens, Efroyim's brother, who had commanded the Jewish police in the Vilna ghetto:

When they ask me for a thousand Jews, I hand them over, for if we Jews will not give them on our own, the Germans will come and take them by force. Then they will take not one thousand, but thousands. With the thousands that I hand over, I save ten thousand. I did everything in order to . . . ensure that at least a remnant of Jews survive.

My aunt Manya had said the same thing in the New York apartment: "It was much better to have the Jewish police do it. Otherwise the Germans would have."

Emil stacked up the pages and slid them over to me.

That was all.

Nothing in the Gens file connected my uncle to any violent or corrupt actions, Emil said. In fact, my uncle's name did not show up at all — even in connection with the saving of the two little girls. What was I to make of that? Possibly, Uncle Aaron and Aunt Sonya had acted alone and deserved full credit for hiding the girls. Or maybe Will had indeed lent a hand before reporting to his post at the gate, but Aaron had decided it would be best not to mention his brother during the trial. Maybe Will hadn't personally hidden the girls but had helped to spirit them out of the ghetto after the roundup. Maybe simply keeping the secret had made him feel, with reason, that he'd played a role in saving them. Or maybe . . .

The picture of the Shavl ghetto police as a whole remained cloudy, too. I did not dismiss Gens's positive slant on his behavior. But I could not dismiss the tribunal's findings out of hand, even if Emil rejected them as "nonsense."

Frustrated, I was tempted to feel angry at Emil for bringing me only part of the story. But Emil wasn't out to deceive me. He wasn't trying to distort the truth. He wasn't "using" me, as my fellow student had warned. He was genuinely trying to help me — and he *had* helped. He'd brought me Gens's words and even, to my amazement, those of Uncle Aaron. But there was no denying that his mission was different from mine. A generation before Emil was born, his grandfather had been driven to his death by the Soviets.

Emil had grown up in the Soviet era. For him, as for many others in today's Lithuania, the injustices of those times were more vivid than the moral quandaries of the Nazi era.

It was not the same for me. Uncle Will had not been punished by the Soviet Union (though if he'd returned to Lithuania after the war, he might well have been). I'd come of age in the United States, where the Holocaust had long been the subject of public discourse. That era was what gripped me.

But now my time in Lithuania was almost up. It was too late to send Emil back to the Special Archives to copy more pages that might tell me more about how Gens and his men, including my uncle, had interacted with their fellow ghetto residents.

Over Emil's protests, I paid him for his work. After we parted, I stood at the kitchen window looking down into the street.

It was time for me to visit Siauliai. Not that I could expect to find any official documents there. None had survived, it appeared. Most of the city had been destroyed by bombs during the war, so even old landmarks would be few. But I had to go. I had to put myself there, to sense the scale of things, to breathe the air. Following my teacher Niborski's advice about approaching a Yiddish text, I needed to explore *oykh mit der noz*, with my nose.

At the Gate

USING my nose in Siauliai was not a pleasant experience. That much was clear the moment I got off the train and tried to breathe while waiting at the curb for my guide. Heavy trucks roared past, their tailpipes spewing exhaust and their tires churning up dirt from the road. Home to a major military airbase, Siauliai was a far cry from Vilnius with its carefully restored Old Town, Kedainiai with its cobblestones and gables, Rokiskis with its sleepy market square. Here all was noisy, gritty, unforgiving. Or maybe my frame of mind was to blame for how unfriendly the place seemed. Far from the Yiddish Institute that had come to feel like a home of sorts, I was stepping directly into the territory where forces of hatred had been unleashed against my uncle, and where his own actions were open to question — by me, if no one else. I felt ill at ease.

Boris Stein, the director of the Siauliai Jewish community, arrived to greet me. A robust seventy-one-year-old former economist, he boasted a barrel chest and big cheery features. He strolled comfortably through the city center, making his way calmly across the lanes of speeding traffic. He had grown up here, he told me in Yiddish as we walked. When the war began, he and his parents escaped across the Russian border into Tatarstan, some five hundred miles east of Moscow. In 1945, like nine hundred other Jews (including my uncle

Aaron and his wife and daughter), they had returned — "*ontsuheybn fun dos nay*, to start over again."

He paused to greet two young mothers wearing Jewish stars on delicate gold chains. So Violeta was right, I realized with a start. When we met for dinner at the beginning of my visit, she acted confused when I told her I'd had relatives in Siauliai. "You do?" she asked. "No, I *did*," I said. I had to say it twice before she understood. Of *course* they weren't still there, I thought at the time. How could they possibly be? Now my reaction seemed harsh, ignorant. There were Jews in twenty-first-century Siauliai after all. A few, anyway. Before the war, they had numbered about 8,500 out of a total population of 32,000. Now, according to Stein, they were 230 out of 130,000.

It seemed fitting that on my last weekend in the Old World I was handling this encounter entirely in Yiddish. Stein spoke no English. He had a strong Litvak accent with a Russian tinge, different from the standard pronunciation we were taught in class. For *mentshn*, people, he said *mentsn* or *myentsn*, with an "s" sound in place of the standard "sh." He said *Ros hasana* instead of Rosh Hashanah, the Jewish New Year. "*Farsteyt?*" he kept asking me — do you understand? To my amazement, I did understand. To make sense of what he was saying and find the words for my replies, I had to strain with all my might. But to a far greater extent than I would have thought possible, I managed.

We got into his car, a Russian Lada.

"The best car in the world?" I asked. I remembered how Regina had praised the Soviet stove in my Vilnius kitchen when she came to translate the documents from the Rokiskis archives.

He looked at me as if I had lost my mind.

"So," I said, "it was not a tragedy when the Soviet Union" — I groped for a verb — "*iz aroys*, went out."

"Nah!" he said forcefully. "*Materielish*, materially, yes, we lived better back then. In the Soviet times we had work; now we have no work."

"But?"

"*Ober in yener tsayt*, but in those days, we had big problems. Now we have a Jewish community; then we had none." He spun the wheel onto a larger street and gave me a frank, warm look. "Today some things are better and some are worse."

We stopped at an empty green field, coarse grass dotted with clover. This was the site of the old Jewish cemetery, founded in 1701. In 1967, victim of the ravages of Soviet policy, it had been bulldozed, the bodies dug up and moved to other burial grounds. The Jewish community had had a plaque installed.

Stein knew why I had come. I had written to him about Uncle Will and the Jewish ghetto police. Now I showed him the spot Uncle Will had pointed to on the map I'd downloaded from the Internet. The house where Will and his mother had lived with Uncle Aaron before the war was gone; an apartment building stood in its place. But the high school, a tall, imposing building, was still standing on Dvaro gatve. Today it served as a government office, with a paneled lobby where people waited in line to speak to clerks behind glass.

Stein drove me past the site of the old ghetto, but at my request we didn't go in. I told him I wanted to go by myself the next morning. For most of this visit, I realized, I wanted to be alone.

Before leaving me, he gripped my hand and held my gaze. "*Di politsey zaynen geven bay di yidn gut*, the ghetto police were good to the Jews," he said. Then, without words, using only his eyes: Don't worry, he told me — your uncle was a good man.

Touched, I thanked him for his kindness. But I was not yet finished with my search.

After Stein drove off in the less-than-superlative car, I walked to the street where Aaron's beauty salon once stood. Before the war, Vilniaus gatve was "the Fifth Avenue of Siauliai," as elegant as New York's famous shopping street, lined with the finest establishments. Recently, as part of the House of Memory essay contest that Giedrius Kiaulakis helped to administer, a group of Siauliai students had interviewed an elderly resident of the city, who remembered:

> When *shabes* came, all the Jewish stores would be closed, and candles shone in all the windows. On *Vilner gas* and also other streets, Jewish families would go out walking, calm and proud and dressed in fine clothing. The old rabbi could be seen, too, with his long white sidelocks and black head covering, and the old Jewish women with their wigs.

In the evening light, *Vilner gas*, Vilniaus gatve, was elegant still, a pedestrian walkway closed to traffic that offered a rare haven from the roaring trucks. Balconies spilled over with flowers. I located the place where the beauty salon had been, now a trendy clothing shop, and pressed my nose to the glass. Every afternoon, Uncle Will had told me, an employee of the Victoria Hotel used to make his way across the street to Uncle Aaron carrying two cups of espresso on a tray covered with a white linen napkin. Inside the salon had been rows of private cubicles where women could have their hair dyed in secret.

Even back then, the orthodox ways were beginning to yield. In spite of the rabbi's disapproval, the salon was open on the Sabbath. Otherwise Aaron could not have made a living, he insisted.

Now, just a few yards away from the old shop, a public address system was piping Beach Boys music from 1960s America into the plaza. I sat down at an outdoor table and ordered pizza.

Later, back at my hotel, I got into bed under the green coverlet and curled up into a ball.

I missed my mother.

I remembered her arm. As a girl in New York City, she'd broken her arm three times in roller-skating accidents. The last time it had been set wrong and had never properly healed. Her awkward gestures — she couldn't turn her palm up all the way — seemed emblematic of a larger lack of ease. The child of the immigrant from Rokiskis was uncomfortable in the world. Shy in a crowd, she tended to lurk on the sidelines, collecting observations to share later at home.

Here under the Baltic sky, we could have been observers together, she and I. In all the years I knew her, she had shown little curiosity about the great trauma of twentieth-century Jewry. But if she were here tonight, maybe she could have helped me imagine the thousands of ghetto residents who had been confined under the rule of a murderous regime, so close to where I now cowered under my blanket. Together we could have tried to absorb the reality of these souls, including our own family members, who were at one and the same time so great and so small — each of them simultaneously a being of infinite complexity and a speck in the stream of humanity.

IN the morning, I lay for a while in bed and contemplated a change of plans. Instead of visiting the ghetto, I could sneak off to a beauty salon and get my hair cut in honor of Uncle Aaron, then catch the bus back to Vilnius. I was tempted. But instead I forced myself to pull out the glossy tourist map the reception clerk had given me and to locate the tiny ghetto streets — Ginkunu, Padirsiu, Traku, Zilviciu — that were tucked into the lower right-hand corner. After coffee and a roll, I started up Vilniaus gatve. Less than a mile separated the site of Aaron's stylish salon from the place where he and my other relatives had been confined for three years. Back then, they had trundled their belongings along this very street.

Uncle Will had told me what happened during the summer of 1941. In July, during the first weeks of the German occupation, members of the Lithuanian Activist Front, the so-called White Armbands, went from house to house seizing property and arresting Jewish men. When they came to Dvaro gatve 74, my aunt Sonya fell at their feet and promised to give them anything if they would spare my uncles. The intruders snatched a camera, a silver cigarette box, and a watch and agreed to leave Uncle Will and Uncle Aaron behind. "But you must hide them," they said.

The two men climbed into a cistern in the attic. There they stayed until an employee of Aaron's beauty salon came and escorted them to the home of a woman pediatrician and her husband, a judge. For a week, until the door-to-door roundups came to an end, they crouched in a shed in the yard; then they returned home. No money changed hands, Uncle Will said. The judge was sent to Siberia after the war.

The city's vice-mayor, a Jew, fled to Vilnius and was arrested and killed. The mayor was removed from office and replaced by the German command. Regulations were promulgated that required Jews to surrender their property and forbade them from walking on the sidewalks, sitting in public parks, or using any form of transportation. At last came the order to move to the ghetto. September 1, the ghetto was sealed.

I turned off Vilniaus gatve onto Ezero gatve (Lake Street), and now I could see it: within a small grove of birch trees sat a plaque half-choked by weeds. This was the site of the ghetto gate: the spot where Uncle Will had stood on the day of the *kinder-aktsye*, the roundup of the children. With insistent cheer, the postwar Soviet regime had sought to transform a place from which children had been sent to their deaths into a place where children would play. A rusty slide ended in a muddy hole, and several benches peeked out of tall grass. As I got closer, I could see wild roses blooming beside a crab apple tree, the hard green fruit warming in the sun.

I didn't want to go in. A stiff, cold wind bit through my jacket. The sunshine was blinding—far too bright for a trip into these black years, it seemed to me. I sat down on a crumbling wall not far from the former gate. After a few minutes I became aware of a long brick building not far from my seat. It was surrounded by a high wall topped by concertina wire. A flag flapped next to the entrance, an old-fashioned archway with tall pillars whose graceful curving span had been fitted with a steel electronic door, behind which a dog was barking. It was a prison.

This had to be the former Red Jail, I realized. The high wall I was looking at had formed the western border of the ghetto. During the Nazi years, thousands of Jews had been executed here. At the bottom of the steep hill, beyond where I could see, would be Lake Talsos, the ghetto's northern boundary. And shading my eyes against the brilliant sunshine, I spotted what had once been the eastern boundary: the huge Frenkel leather factory, now row upon row of ghostly shuttered warehouses and garages and a single tall smokestack. Under the arrangement worked out between the Jewish ghetto leaders and the German command, nearly a thousand ghetto residents had worked in the factory, producing boots and other supplies for the Wehrmacht. They and their families had constituted the bulk of the ghetto population. As with the Kovno Jews who toiled to build the airfield, the Jews here had believed that it was their work in the factory that kept the German command from putting them all to death.

The prison, the lake, the factory, and, to the south, the former cemetery. These had formed the boundaries of the two ghetto zones, each a warren of narrow lanes. Uncle Will and Uncle Aaron and their family members had lived in the Traku zone, separated by "only a *shmate*," a ragged curtain, from the police chief, Efroyim Gens. The second zone, known as Kavkaz, was named for its hills, like the Caucasus Mountains.

The dog yapped on. Somewhere a car engine turned over and over. I still didn't want to go in.

The memorial plaque, when I got up from my seat and crossed the road at last, read in Lithuanian:

Sioje Vietoje
1941 VII 18–1944 VII 24
Buvo Siauliu
Geto Traku —
Ezero Rajono
Vartai

On this spot
July 18, 1941–July 24, 1944
stood the gates
of the Siauliai
Ghetto Traku —
Ezero district

At the base of the stone, entangled with a bright-red candy wrapper and a species of tiny yellow and orange wildflower I knew by the quaint name of "butter-and-eggs," lay a black memorial ribbon. Here, right here, Uncle Will had stood and chased away the Lithuanians who came in violation of the rules to trade with the imprisoned Jews — "a mink coat for a stick of butter." I wondered whether anyone had been disposed, as Steponas had in Rokiskis, to throw food over the fence. Here, when the Germans had shown up for surprise inspections, Uncle Will had warned the returning work brigades to drop their illegally acquired parcels. Here, on the day of the *kinder-aktsye,* Uncle Will had stood at his post as the trucks idled, filling up with their human cargo. Here Efroyim Gens had handed over his daughter to the Germans. Here Dr. Pace had implored the commander, Forster, to release two girls he claimed were his children.

And what else? How little I knew! What else had happened here, on this very spot and within the then-teeming streets beyond the gate?

Finally I took a deep breath and stepped in, into the territory of the ghetto. I started down the steep lane, picking my way among the ruts and gullies. From a distance came the roar of traffic, but here all was quiet, save for the twittering of birds and the growling dogs that pushed their noses out from under the fences. The ghetto had been bombed in July 1944, and so the original houses were gone. But they must have looked much like these — short, solid cottages with corrugated roofs and thick wooden walls painted bright green or ochre. The small outbuildings that now served as storage sheds for garden tools would have served as dwellings back then.

More than two thousand people had been crowded into these four small blocks, and more than twenty-five hundred others into the Kavkaz zone. Somewhere on Zilviciu gatve, Uncle Will had lived in an attic with the others. It was there that the two girls and the two old women had been hidden behind the heavy cabinet under the eaves — hidden by Will? by Aaron and Sonya? by Efroyim Gens?

Now lace curtains hung in the windows and washing stirred on the clotheslines, but no one was about. In vain I sniffed at the air. I could sense nothing, no one — neither the lost Jewish souls nor the Lithuanians who had moved in later. I peered at the leaning trees and the bushes that sprawled over the cracked pavement. I took in the woodpiles, the gardens full of petunias and raspberries, the rustic well, the small apple orchard, the spray-painted scrawl — FUCK OFF — in English on a garage wall.

At the end of the lane, a solitary figure appeared, a white-haired woman wearing a sweater and carrying a shopping bag. "*Labas, laba diena*, good day," I greeted her in Lithuanian when she came near, but as if I were as insubstantial as the vanished ghetto Jews, she showed no sign that she had seen or heard.

When she had passed, I listened to the birdsong and the dogs and felt the sun on my face in this blank, still spot. There was nothing more to see, and nothing, it seemed, to feel. A heavy weight had settled in my chest, but my mind was as empty as the deserted lanes.

I walked out through the gate that was no more and started back up Vilniaus gatve toward an apartment building that bore a giant exhortation worked into the brickwork:

*Amzina slove
didvyriams!*

Eternal glory
to the heroes!

An all-purpose slogan, I thought, eternal indeed. With the identity of the heroes left unspecified, there was no need to change a word when the political winds shifted.

On the way to the bus station, I noted more English-language graffiti: EAT THE RICH! FUCK AMERIKKKA! Equally all-purpose. I remembered such slogans from the 1960s back in the United States. They would have served during the Soviet times, and apparently they suited the post-Soviet era just as well. Inside the waiting room, "Guantanamera," the Cuban ballad made world-famous by Pete Seeger, the iconic American folksinger, emanated from the ceiling. Out on the platform, buses of all makes and colors were pulling up, on their way to and from Vilnius, Kaunas, Kaliningrad, Moscow, St. Petersburg.

When the bus to Vilnius arrived, I got on and took a seat. I opened my Yiddish textbook, but the lines of print wouldn't come into focus. When the bus began to move, I stopped trying to study and instead stared out the window at the yellow-green fields dotted with sheaves of wheat.

Nearly sixty years ago, it had all happened here. On this ground. Under this sky, this blazing sun. I had touched the spot.

We reached the small city of Panevezys, a place where I suspected that my grandfather might have been a *yeshive* student nearly a hundred years ago. A young woman boarded and sat down next to me. After a long, curious glance at the homework in my lap, she held out her hand. She was an English teacher, she said; her boyfriend was Jewish, a student of Hebrew.

Slowly I wrested myself out of the realm of the past. I introduced myself and pointed out the window. By the side of the highway, every few miles, groups of people dressed in folk costumes could be seen bearing bouquets of flowers and waving flags. A holiday?

"Ah!" my seatmate exclaimed. Today was the anniversary of Baltic Way Day.

Fifteen years ago today, on August 23, 1989, more than one million people had formed a human chain in an all-Baltic protest against Soviet rule. The joined hands extended from Tallinn in Estonia through Latvia all the way south to Vilnius. The date marked the fiftieth anniversary of the hated Molotov-Ribbentrop Pact, the treaty I'd heard about so often, the agreement between Germany and the USSR that had ceded the Baltics to the Soviet Union on the eve of World War II.

The day of the human chain was a Wednesday, my seatmate said, a workday. At 7:00 p.m. everyone joined hands. Small planes dropped flowers and pamphlets. "Everybody took part," she said, her face aglow. Seven months later, Lithuania declared independence, and Estonia and Latvia followed suit. In September 1991, Moscow recognized the new nations.

I was glad to listen, not at all eager for the trip to end. But now the spires of Vilnius appeared and the bus began its descent into the city. At a red light we paused at Paneriu gatve, Ponar Street, which led, no doubt, to the forest where tens of thousands of Jews had met their end. The dark trees and the pits crowded into view in my mind's eye, and along with them, the black memorial ribbon that someone had left near the ghetto gate where Uncle Will had been standing on the day of the *kinder-aktsye*. Among the wildflowers and the discarded candy wrapper, the sinuous reminder slithered like a snake.

13. The former "Red Jail," which formed a border of the Shavl ghetto during World War II.

Leaving the Jerusalem of the North

ON our last day at the Yiddish Institute, we students sat together one last time in the university courtyard. We breathed in the scent of the sun-warmed petunias in the window boxes that brightened the ancient walls and traced with our eyes the graceful lines of the tree that cast its shade over the neatly swept cobblestones. I thought back to our first evening in this spot, when I shivered under my umbrella as white-haired Bluma welcomed us to Vilnius in her flowered dress. The land of my ancestors, once distant and unknowable, had become near and real to me.

I took my time climbing the stairs to the classroom under the eaves. In my head I could see the red tile roofs of the former ghetto quarter and the sooty hulk of the old KGB headquarters. I saw the mounds of raw earth at the Tuskulenai "Park of Quiet," and farther afield, in Rokiskis, the ragged borders of Sinagogu gatve and the steep tin roof of Steponas's cottage. I remembered the tall grass in the overgrown garden of Violeta's childhood home in Kedainiai and the sandy pit in the forest where she handed me the memorial candles. I recalled the narrow rutted lanes in the former Shavl ghetto. Full of meaning, these places jostled together, forming an image of a land that was now mine in a way it had not been before. Propelled initially by my mother's death, I had indeed forged a connection,

233

in ways I had not anticipated, both with the old Yiddishland and also with the Lithuania of today.

On this final day in Niborski's class, once again a breeze floated in through the window, bringing the clatter of silverware and the bustle of pedestrians from Pilies gatve down below.

We were tackling a piece called "A mayse on a sof" ("A Story without an End"), by Mordechai Strigler, a Polish Holocaust survivor who ended up in New York as the editor of the *Forverts*, a venerable Yiddish newspaper. It was the very first text we'd studied that dealt with the Holocaust, I realized, and the narrative was horrendous, otherworldly. Could it be — yes, the narrator was describing himself pulling a wagon piled high with dead bodies. An apt metaphor indeed, I thought, for the burden of a horrific past.

It was our hardest story yet, a thicket of obscure words and fiendishly complex constructions, but I found I didn't mind. Like multitudes of readers before me in the heartland of Litvak learning, I pressed a finger to the text and bent myself to the task. When it was my turn to read aloud, I stumbled as always, and when I asked a question Niborski had to correct my syntax, but I wasn't embarrassed. In this place of love and pain, I'd come to believe, it was the effort itself that was important. What mattered was simply trying — to understand, to speak.

Our time was up before we finished the story without an end. We simply stopped, in the middle of a paragraph.

We filed into grammar class, where Bordin went over a few last essential points about noun genders.

After that, our teachers and my roommate Minette and all our fellow students gathered in the lecture hall, where there were flowers and herring and vodka. Alas, Bluma was ill, too sick to attend, but Rokhl, another of the last Yiddish speakers, was there to send us on our way. When Mendy Cahan stepped to the podium to deliver his closing remarks, this time he spoke in Yiddish. I didn't understand every word, or even every sentence, but by now I had learned to do what Cahan had urged in the beginning: to listen.

Finally we began to bid one another "zayt gezunt," good-bye, be well. *Mir hobn getut a kush,* we kissed one another. *Mir hobn gekusht,* we kept on kissing. And crying.

AFTER returning home from Lithuania, I made my way to the New York apartment, where my aunt and uncle stood waiting for me in the doorway. Carefully I embraced the fragile shoulders that had carried such an extraordinary load. As Aunt Manya bustled in and out of the kitchen, I knelt on the floor next to Uncle Will's chair and unpacked my bag.

One by one, my uncle held up my photographs to his good eye. He examined the wooden houses in Rokiskis with their coats of ochre and green. The woodpiles, the outhouses. The spacious town square, the church with its spire, the old palace on whose grounds thousands of Jews had been confined before being driven into the forest. He inspected Steponas's cottage with its steep tin roof, and Steponas himself, and his wife in her sleeveless blue dress. He peered at Vilniaus gatve in Siauliai, and the storefront that had been Uncle Aaron's hairdressing salon, and the rutted ghetto lanes, and the plaque marking the site of the ghetto gate where he had stood wearing his policeman's armband.

He put the pictures on the tablecloth. "Beautiful," he said. His lips formed the mild, sweet smile I loved.

I sat back on my heels and waited for him to say more. He didn't.

What would happen if I pushed him to tell me more? What would he say if I told him about the trial of Efroyim Gens, the accusations of beatings that appeared in the file, Uncle Aaron's testimony that *he* had been the one to hide the two girls who were now grandmothers in Israel? How would he feel about Steponas's wracking sobs, and about the Holocaust curricula that were being developed by the International Commission in Vilnius, and about the House of Memory essay contest and the Park of Quiet with its mingled bones?

I felt my various identities — niece, researcher, writer, member of a successor generation after the Holocaust, moral being — clashing and rubbing against one another. Once again I could hear Irena Veisaite's words: "As long as you are hiding the truth, as long as you fail to come to terms with your past, you can't build your future." I knew that for Lithuanians, too, opening up the past meant upsetting delicate psychological and social balances. Still, forcing my uncle to confront the past seemed like a kind of aggression I didn't want to engage in. Unlike Steponas, he wasn't seeking an opportunity to unburden himself. He had told what he wanted to tell.

I wouldn't do it, I decided. I wouldn't press him for more. If leaving my uncle in peace meant I didn't learn everything there was to learn, so be it.

After lunch, Aunt Manya drove me to the subway. Beside her in the passenger seat, Uncle Will lifted his face to catch the sun. The two old people murmured to each other in Yiddish until we came to *Fir-un-zibitsik gas*, Seventy-fourth Street.

"So," I said to my uncle as I got out of the car, "look through the pictures and let me know what you think."

"I already told you," he said.

I kissed my aunt and uncle and went into the station. My moral questions about the past were *my* questions, I reflected as I hurried down the stairs. It was my responsibility, not his, to answer them.

Voices of the Shavl Ghetto

AND SO I went back to the library of the U.S. Holocaust Memorial Museum to see what more I could learn about the Jewish police in my uncle's ghetto. Right away, a strange thing happened. In a manila folder with a nondescript title, I found a list of people who had been tried by the Soviet tribunals after the war, each one described with gruesome concision:

Guarded Jews in Vilna ghetto and at Ponar killing site. Sentenced to
twenty-five years in Siberia.
Escorted Jews to pits, covered bodies with lime. Sentenced to twenty
years.
Participated in massacre of six thousand Jews, wrote anti-Semitic
book. Sentenced to death.

I took the folder to the librarian, who told me that after the fall of the Soviet Union, the Special Archives in Vilnius had presented the museum with microfilm copies of thousands of KGB files. Efroyim Gens's file, she said, was among them. Unlike in Lithuania, where access to such material was restricted, here anyone could look at it. The thick volume from which Emil had selected forty pages was available here in its entirety. I now had access to everything Emil had decided I didn't need to see. Of course, I still faced the obstacle that the records were all in Russian. But a museum volunteer — a retired CIA agent, as it happened, who knew the language from years of spying in the Soviet Union — agreed to help me. The two of us closeted ourselves in an airless cell off the main reading room, and as he translated the handwritten pages, I wrote down his words.

More than a dozen ghetto survivors, it turned out, had testified against Gens at his trial. They had a lot to say.

Gita B. testified:

In the summer of 1943, I was arrested in my house by three ghetto policemen and delivered to police headquarters, where Gens began to ask why I wanted to escape and beat me with a rubber truncheon.

Nison F. testified:

I was called into the police office, where there were about ten police officers, including Gens and the head of the Kavkaz district, Zavel Gotz.

Gotz asked me whether I would in the future bring food into the ghetto. I answered, "I will!" Then Gotz began to beat me in the face with his fist and one of the policemen hit me in the head with a rubber truncheon. I lost consciousness and fell to the floor.

As I read the statements of those who had suffered under the blows of the truncheons, I understood that Gens and his fellow policemen had beaten their fellow prisoners not once or twice but many, many times. Clearly, Gens's statement, in the part of the file that Emil had brought me, that wrongdoers in the ghetto were punished with fines, confiscation of goods, and suspension from work was far from the whole truth. Nor did Uncle Will's description of his duties — chasing Lithuanians away from the gate, keeping order in the food lines, warning people, hiding children — do justice to the tactics that the Jewish police, possibly including Will himself, had employed in the course of their work. Like the police in other ghettos, Gens and his men had used violence to keep order.

Of course, all of this was not news to me — or at any rate, it shouldn't have been. Emil had told me more than once, in so many words, that ghetto survivors had described Gens as violent. Beatings were explicitly mentioned in the trial verdict. In Gens's pleading letters from Siberia, he himself referred to the blows he'd administered: survivors should be grateful, he wrote, "to me, who saved them using force."

It was all spelled out in black and white. Nonetheless, as I went through the hostile testimony line by line, the picture of brutality that emerged *felt* new to me. I was surprised, even shocked. And that in itself was a revelation.

During my time in Lithuania, I'd had a hard time grasping how facts about the Holocaust that had been in plain view for decades were nonetheless said to have astonished the nation when they came to light after the collapse of the Soviet Union. No matter how many times this phenomenon of not knowing, this surprise, was explained to me, I couldn't quite absorb it. Now I understood better.

With the help of my spy-turned-translator, I read on. The hostile witnesses, I learned, had accused Gens of more than beatings.

On the day of the *kinder-aktsye*, Nakhum Kh. said, Gens had helped to round up children and had urged his fellow Jews to help the Nazis win the war:

Gens took his baby to the lorry and later he gave a speech [saying] it was for the best to help the German army in the fight against the Soviet Union. After that he was checking, with his rubber stick, that all the people gave up their children.

Abe M. confirmed this testimony and added another serious charge. After beating ghetto residents for illegally bringing food into the ghetto, he said, Gens had on some occasions delivered the guilty parties into the murderous hands of the German command.

Gens denied these charges. His child had been taken from him, he said. He had not gone from house to house forcing parents to give up their children. He had not delivered Jews to the German command.

Abe M. stood by his statement: "I reaffirm that Gens delivered Jews to the ss," he said.

But what was this? In 1966, the file showed, ten years after his release from Siberia, Gens had mounted an ultimately unsuccessful bid for rehabilitation. His case was reopened, and several of the original witnesses were called in for a new round of questioning.

Again, Abe M. took the stand. Now, in a possibly courageous act, he recanted part of his earlier testimony:

> As far as Gens's handing over of Jews to the organs of the Gestapo, I cannot remember any concrete facts. If I gave such testimony during the previous investigation, my testimony was not correct — it was at the requirement of the investigator.

For me, these words threw everything up in the air. Was the trial just a sham? Had Emil been right after all when he insisted that the hostile testimony was nothing but "Soviet nonsense"?

I didn't know what to think, nor did my translator. He shook my hand and took his leave. In the airless cell, I sat looking at my notes and wondering how to proceed.

THE next day I pulled up a chair at one of the long tables in the reading room of the museum library, switched on a green-shaded lamp, and began a systematic examination of what survivors of the Shavl ghetto had had to say *outside* the context of the Soviet judicial system.

Although the record of the Shavl ghetto was not extensive, I found materials from Germany, Israel, Canada, and the United States — memoirs that had been published in book form, personal accounts that had simply been typed by their authors and bound between cardboard covers, transcripts of oral interviews. Some of the materials were in English. Those in Hebrew I farmed out to a cousin here, a friend there. And as for those in Yiddish, all that I had learned in the classroom under the eaves at Vilnius University, and all the homework I'd struggled through with Minette at the kitchen table, now came to my aid. As I pored over the pages written in *mame-loshn*, the shapes of the letters and the sounds of the syllables in my head enfolded and consoled me just as they had in Lithuania, helping me to make my way through a fearsome terrain. On the day when I had walked through the Shavl ghetto, the tiny rutted lanes had been empty. Now they filled up with the people whose presence I had tried in vain to sense on that chilly, sun-splashed day. As Mendy Cahan had put it, I "lent a listening ear"—first to one voice, then to the next. As I allowed the sounds to swirl around me, the role of the Jewish leaders of the Shavl ghetto, and of the police, grew clearer.

The moral quandary of the "gray zone" in Shavl, as I came to see it, began to take shape even before the Jewish police force was formally created—in fact, before the ghetto was sealed. In June 1941, when the Germans invaded, Siauliai's Jewish community was bursting at the seams. On top of the prewar Jewish population of 8,500, more than 6,000 Jewish refugees had streamed into the city from Poland and other places after the war began in 1939. Shortly after taking control of the city, the German command appointed a "vice-mayor in charge of Jewish affairs," a Lithuanian, who in turn appointed committees to go from door to door, ordering Jews to vacate their houses and move to the ghetto. Operating under official German orders, these committees were different from the wild White Armband squads that had rampaged through the city a month earlier, seizing Jewish property and arresting Jewish men. During that "liminal" time, a revolutionary anarchy had prevailed. The work of these committees, in contrast, was a systematic effort—but a no less deadly one.

The twenty or thirty most revered members of the Jewish community—rabbis, intellectuals, and businessmen whose names, it appeared, were provided to the Germans by Lithuanians—had been arrested and executed. But new Jewish leaders arose in their place, and as the committees made their rounds, these leaders negotiated with the authorities for an expansion of the space initially allocated for the ghetto. Thanks to their efforts, the number of city blocks was doubled. But even this larger area was far too small for 14,500 Jews. With characteristic precision, Nazi regulations specified two square meters (about six square feet) for each ghetto resident. Officially, there was room for no more than 4,000.

Thus, throughout the summer and into September, thousands of "excess" Jews were separated from the rest of the community. They were packed into designated holding places, including synagogues and the Jewish home for the elderly, then loaded onto trucks bound either for Zagare, a town less than thirty miles to the north with a short-lived ghetto of its own, or directly for the forests. All of those sent away — more than 8,000 — were murdered.

Who decided which Jews received the green passes permitting them to move into the ghetto and which Jews were sent away to be shot? In an interview conducted in Yiddish in Israel in the 1970s, I found an exchange with Khayim Zh., who became a policeman in the ghetto. Here is what he said about how the selection was made:

> KHAYIM ZH.: *Dos iz litviner geven, vos zenen gegangen* . . . It was Lithuanians, with a representative from — in every committee there was one representative.
> Q.: A Jew?
> KHAYIM ZH.: A Jew, yes.
> We were there, I and R., he was at the table, and he knew the Lithuanians, and he would bribe them, the four or five on the committee would be bribed. . . .
> As for the old people, if they were with someone, a son or a daughter, they stayed in the ghetto, but otherwise they were sent away. Wagons were standing by to take them to the synagogue, and from there they were driven to somewhere not good.

So R., a Jew, served on the committee, and Khayim Zh., also a Jew, assisted him. R. used a pot of money to bribe the Lithuanians on the committee. In this way, certain Jews received passes that guaranteed them room in the ghetto, while others were denied passes and taken away to their doom.

In a frank and detailed memoir published in Yiddish in Germany after the war, a survivor named Levi Shalit made searing observations about Jewish involvement in the selection process:

Di komisyes zaynen bashtanen fun litvishe politsistn ...

The commissions consisted of Lithuanian police, assisted by one Jew.... [Jews] did not hold back from serving on the commissions, though no one forced them to do it. They acted out of purely selfish motives, to save themselves, their families and friends.

It could be that the Jews themselves, if they did not actually invent the passes, at least facilitated their use. Jews wanted to be secure. Thus one began to concern oneself with little papers, a form ...

Shalit wrote about the oppressors' psychological manipulation of the ghetto inhabitants:

Eyne fun di psikhishe aynvirkungen oyfn geto-mentshn iz fun ershtn tog geven dos lozn yidn aleyn administrirn zeyer lebn ...

One of the psychological tactics imposed on the people of the ghetto from the start was to allow the Jews themselves to administer their lives. Possibly this policy was specially devised to appeal to the Jews of the diaspora, with their yearning for a place to call their own. It was also a calculation that the Jews in the ghetto, hungry and overcrowded, would devour one another.

Shalit's tone was bitter as he described the emergence of Jewish ghetto leadership, including the police:

In di ershte teg, ven s'hobn bavizn di yidishe eltste ...

In the first days, when the Jewish leaders appeared, nicely dressed with big files under their arms, and the Jewish police with yellow or blue Stars of David on their armbands, resplendent in their smart boots (attractive policemen had been recruited), the whole devils' dance — the ghetto — looked like some kind of Jewish autonomous region. People were pleased. "Here we will be able to live freely, among ourselves, in our own corner, with a Jewish administration and our own police."

The Jewish leaders of the Shavl ghetto were practical sorts, mostly small businessmen. To a greater extent than the leaders of other Lithuanian ghettos, they appear to have been considered "of the people." One survivor said, "they were very honest, very devoted. They really did quite a lot." Another agreed: "Very fine, very fine people. They were very devoted to the Jews, very devoted." Uncle Will, too, viewed them favorably, especially compared to Efroyim Gens's brother Jacob, the most powerful Jew in the Vilna ghetto. "Shavl was a smaller ghetto," Will said; "it was easier to be a good head."

For all his bitterness, Shalit concurred:

Dos lebn in shavler geto un di firung fun di geto-manhigim . . .

Life in the Shavl ghetto, and the leadership of the ghetto, existed on a much higher moral plane than in the other two ghettos in Lithuania, Kovno and Vilna, and also higher than in most ghettos in Poland.

Supporting these positive assessments was a strange and moving incident recounted by Khayim Zh., in which the Jewish leaders, including the police, behaved heroically. One evening at the end of August 1942, as the work brigades were returning to the ghetto, German soldiers showed up without warning at the gate. They searched the brigade members and threw their contraband on the ground, littering the street with food. Twenty-seven people were seized and held in the Red Jail. Then the district commissar, the German official who ruled over the ghetto, came to the Jewish Council and announced that in exchange for these twenty-seven random hostages, the council was to select fifty ghetto residents of its own choosing and deliver them to be executed.

In response to this cruel order — guaranteed to cause the

maximum agony among the ghetto population — the Jewish Council called a meeting of all ghetto officials. The police came, and the administrators of the labor and food departments, and even the ghetto bill-collectors. They sat up all night. By morning, they had arrived at a plan. Instead of selecting fifty ghetto residents and providing their names to the command, they would offer *themselves* for execution. Two representatives went to the head of the German command and announced their decision. Astounded, the commissar refused to accept it. "Your leaders cannot be killed," he said — "who would oversee the ghetto?"

Amazingly, the ploy worked:

Keyn andere gebn zey nisht . . .

They would provide no other names. His only option was to go in and find fifty men himself. And so the demand was changed to a fine of 20,000 marks, to be paid within two months.

And when the representatives came back, everyone was waiting for them, and we all kissed, and we all ran home.

Like the Jewish Council, the Jewish police were viewed in a generally positive light by survivors. "Some of them were nice people," one said mildly, "and did not harm the Jews." Another, asked if ghetto residents were afraid of the police, expressed a similarly benign opinion: "No, not afraid. They themselves were *betndike* — beggars, needy people." A third wrote, "Residents of the ghetto respected the Jewish ghetto police. We believed the Jewish Council and the Jewish ghetto police were trying to ease our lives and protect us."

Even the most negative statements I could find were couched in a moderate, "on the one hand, but on the other hand" tone. Eliezer Yerushalmi, the secretary of the Jewish Council, kept a diary that was published in Jerusalem in Hebrew after the war. He wrote:

The policemen's duties made them unloved among the people of the ghetto, but they didn't mistreat people, as their friends in other ghettos did. They didn't exploit them or hand them over to the authorities.

In times of danger, they would run far distances to the outlying workplaces to warn people. At the gates, the police acted as middlemen between the Lithuanian guards and those who fell into their hands. In times of need, they would help people bring objects into the ghetto and even escort them to Lithuanians in the city who were holding their property.

This work was done without a reward.

Yerushalmi did write these critical words, however:

Oct 2, 1942. Some people resent the Jewish policemen who beat Jews when they attempt to bring in potatoes. They are harsher than the Lithuanian police. Many ask why Jews would be worse than non-Jews.

Along the same lines, a young ghetto resident composed a song addressed to the police:

Derfar, liber bruder,
Dayn khaver farshtey
Un helf im vi meglekh,
Ven es tut im vos vey. . . .

So, dear brother
understand your comrade
and help him as much as possible
when he is in pain,

Because a blow from an enemy
hurts terribly,
but a blow from a friend
is ten times worse.

After translating the words of this song, I put down my pencil and pushed aside my dictionary. The business of confiscating food at the gate and beating the smugglers puzzled me. For one thing, the policy was inconsistent. Uncle Will told me he had stood guard to prevent Lithuanians from trading with the imprisoned Jews. Yet when he had the chance, he himself smuggled food through the gate, including the live chicken he concealed in his pants for his mother. Besides, the whole situation made no sense. The rations supplied by the German command — meager amounts of bread, potatoes, and horse meat — were insufficient to feed the ghetto population. What good did it do to forbid the Jews to barter for more? Wouldn't better-fed Jews have made better workers?

The more I thought about it, though, the more the system, inconsistency and all, seemed to suit the needs of the German command. An enormous amount of smuggling was allowed to proceed unimpeded. Day in and day out, Jews who were sent to work outside the ghetto would barter or buy food from Lithuanians and carry it back into the ghetto. I read about a nighttime operation in which entire live cattle were smuggled into the ghetto. Food *was* allowed to get through — but only under conditions of terror. The Jews had to steal and cheat, conceal and cringe. They lived in constant fear that the Germans would show up, that the Lithuanian guards who usually looked the other way or accepted bribes would suddenly decide to crack down, or that the Jewish police would administer beatings. Chronic fear and uncertainty made the Jews easier to control.

Were the Shavl Jewish police truly more brutal than the Lithuanian guards? If so, why? Maybe they needed to appear tough in front of the German and Lithuanian guards. Maybe they felt a deeper motivation to enforce the rules because the survival of their own community was at stake. Or maybe they confiscated food because they wanted it for themselves and their hungry families. Maybe all of these factors were in play. Pulled this way and that by the impossibly conflicting demands of their positions, maybe the police did what they could to help their fellow Jews in one instance — and in the next instance swung out at them with fists and sticks.

When I scoured the memoirs for mention of Efroyim Gens

himself, I found that survivors who spoke mildly of the police in general were less kind toward the chief. Uncle Will had called Gens "very stupid." Shalit characterized him thus:

A hoykher, shtark geboyter man in di draysiker yorn....

A tall, strongly built man in his thirties. A fool and an arrogant person. He took his position dead seriously and conducted himself like a true functionary. He demanded a military salute from his policemen and would return the greeting in kind. He would have caused a lot of trouble if the [Jewish Council] had not restrained him every step of the way.

Another survivor penned an even more caustic portrait:

Mr. Ganz, the commander of the Jewish police, was a giant of a man, tall and wide shouldered. His dream, dreamt on from his very youth, was to be a policeman: to dress up in a shining uniform, to enforce order under threat of bodily harm, and to absorb the fearful looks which a policeman's appearance arouses among many citizens....

True, he was not given a beautiful uniform, just a miserable band on the arm, and instead of a pistol he had only a stick. Still, where is the man who has been able to fulfill his dream to the last detail?

Finally I turned to accounts of the *kinder-aktsye*. The diarist Yerushalmi called it "the darkest day of our unhappy life in the ghetto." A number of survivors recalled that ghetto residents were aware ahead of time that a roundup would occur that morning. Shalit, with his customary acuity, wrote that as the work brigades filed out, people were eager to escape, even knowing that they were leaving loved ones behind to be seized:

Beyde geto-toyern zaynen balagert geven....

Both ghetto gates were besieged. Jews pushed and shoved in their haste to leave the ghetto.

No, no, nowhere is the psychologist who will explain to us what psychological complex was at work, or not at work, among the people at that moment. Why did they hurry through the gate, leaving the children and old people alone? Were the mothers and fathers not thinking clearly — was it the blind impulse to live?

After the brigades left, the gates were closed. All children up to the age of thirteen and all adults without jobs were ordered to assemble in the courtyard. Uncle Will told me that this was when he was standing at the gate.

Did the Jewish police obey the German order to go door to door? Some accounts said yes, others no. One account referred by name to two individual policemen who participated "zealously" in the roundup. One survivor wrote:

> The German commandant went to [the Jewish Council] and demanded that the Jewish ghetto police . . . go to one house after the other and notify the people who were staying there that the children have to be brought to the gates. . . .
> [But] the Germans and Ukrainians did not trust the Jewish policemen. They proceeded to search one house after the other, took children and old men and marched them to the trucks. . . . One hand carried a bottle of vodka, and the other held a baby like one holds a puppy.

As for what Efroyim Gens did that day, everyone remembered his surrender of his daughter. Some thought he had been forced to give her up. Others believed he could have hidden her but chose not to. Shalit wrote:

> *Ver ken farbay geyn, nit farshraybndik lezikorn, tempe pakhdones un narishkeyt . . .*

> Who could fail to record the memory of dull cowardice and stupidity: the police chief, Efroyim Gens, with his own hands, *as an example,* bringing forward his own child! Forster smiled as he took the victim from her father's hands. Gens saluted.
> Neither that day nor the next did he hang himself in self-disgust.

Another survivor acerbically spelled out what he imagined to be Gens's moral code:

(a) If a conflict exists between one's role and one's private life, duty takes precedence, and
(b) A commander must set an example for his orderlies.

Still another lamented, of Gens's surrender of his child: "We were so naive and obedient until the bitter end."

Had Gens delivered a speech urging ghetto residents to surrender their children, as the hostile trial witnesses had charged? Nowhere in the survivor memoirs could I find corroboration of this claim. Regardless, Gens's surrender of his daughter undoubtedly encouraged some ghetto residents to follow his example amid the snarling of dogs and the brandishing of machine guns.

How many ghetto residents were seized that day? One source said 725 children and 92 unemployed and sick people. Another said 823 children. A third said 570 children and 260 elderly. To this day, it is not known where they were taken.

After the action, according to Shalit,

Fintster iz geven in geto . . .

That night . . . it was dark in the ghetto, and wild, desperate voices sliced the darkness like knives.

[The next] night, at the end of the *shabes*, the ghetto leaders went from house to house, recording the names of those who were gone and who no longer had to be fed.

Another survivor wrote:

After the tragedy . . . we stopped talking. The Jewish Council and the police helped the children and old people who had been hidden to leave the ghetto. . . . My grandmother would not leave. Better to die than to eat pork.

At this time, a Ouija board became popular in the ghetto. The magic table provided grief-stricken residents with answers to the questions that were tormenting them. A survivor who lost a child in the *kinder-aktsye* described this phenomenon:

Hunderter mentshn zenen gelofn dos zen . . .

Hundreds of people went running to see that table. . . . The crowd was so thick, you couldn't even see what was happening. People believed in it.

"Where are the children?" — and the table would rise into the air. "Who took them? Are they alive? Are they in Germany?" Those who were in pain asked many questions, and the table answered. It helped, it calmed people down.

Heartbreakingly, this woman and others blamed themselves:

We couldn't forgive ourselves. Some children were saved . . . but at such a moment not all parents were able to — how do you say it . . . to pull themselves together and figure out how to hide a child.

In July 1944, as the Red Army drew near, the German command liquidated the ghetto. The Jews were deported in four large groups. Here is Shalit's account, in my abridged translation:

Dray likhtike vareme yuli teg hot gedoyert di rayze. . . .

The journey from Shavl to Stutthof lasted three bright, warm July days. The cattle cars were crowded, but not unbearably so. Through the half-open doors we could see the lush Lithuanian countryside, the golden-yellow sheaves of rye standing in the fields. The aromas of field and forest were intoxicating.

All the way to the German border, people pressed toward the doors. Everyone wanted to gaze out, to catch one last glimpse of the landscape, even while hoping against hope that we would soon be on our way back.

The train sped through stations, past the very towns where we had been born and raised. With wistful eyes we looked out into the Lithuanian provinces where we had had friends and family, places that had long since become *judenrein*, cleared of Jews. The train sped through *Lite* as if offering us a final farewell tour — one last look at all the years we had dwelled in this country — before hurling us into purgatory.

When Shalit and his fellow prisoners reached German-occupied Poland, they were transferred onto flatcars, 150 men to a car:

Shteyendikerheyt iz men geforn....

We rode standing up. The sick were fainting. We embraced one another so as not to fall off as the train puffed along. The guards sat silently on the roof of the locomotive, aiming at us with their machine guns.

In the middle of a wood, the train slowed. Suddenly: *oy*: a single *oy* escaped from hundreds of hearts. Our blood froze. From behind a barbed wire fence, a gruesome picture came into view: skulls jutting out of the ground, bodies half buried in earth.

Then, from a distance, long columns appeared: prisoners dressed in striped clothing, marching in straight rows that extended for kilometers. The clatter of wooden shoes announced their coming and their going away.

Among us a deathly silence took hold. Each man was mute, absorbed into himself.

When the columns had disappeared, the train began to move forward.

After ten minutes, or maybe longer, the dark woods came to an end.

A sign: Camp Stutthof.

Stutthof, located in northern Poland, was the first Nazi concentration camp established outside of Germany. It opened in September 1939. Over the course of the war an estimated 100,000 people were deported there; more than 60,000 are estimated to have died. When the transports from the Shavl ghetto pulled in, the older women (including Uncle Will's mother, Soreh) and the women with children were sent on to their deaths. Women who were deemed able-bodied (including Uncle Aaron's wife, my aunt Sonya, and their daughter, Asya) were put to work digging ditches and constructing military fortifications. Beginning seven months later, in January 1945, 50,000 prisoners were evacuated from the camp and driven in a death march toward Germany. Of these, more than 25,000 died. Sonya and Asya survived.

The men of the Shavl ghetto were held at Stutthof for a few weeks before being sent on to Dachau, ten miles outside of Munich, in southern Germany. Of the more than 188,000 people deported to Dachau, tens of thousands died; the exact count is not known. Although Dachau, like Stutthof, was officially not a death camp but a forced labor camp, many prisoners were shot or experimented on, then cremated. In April 1945 a death march of 7,000 began out of Dachau toward the Tyrol. Those who could not keep up were shot. Many died of hunger, cold, or exhaustion. Uncle Will carried his brother Aaron. They survived.

Of all the Jews of Shavl—the 8,500 from before the war, plus the 6,000 refugees who had fled into the city from elsewhere—it is estimated that between 350 and 500 survived the war.

The Bystander and the
Jewish Policeman

THE librarians at the Holocaust Museum were switching off the lights as I packed up my dictionary, my notebooks, and my pencils and took a last look around the reading room with its green lampshades and its shelves crammed with records of uncountable acts of cruelty and kindness, callousness and caring. In the lobby, I joined a long line of schoolchildren and out-of-towners laden with cameras and backpacks. One by one we passed by the guards at the glass doors and emerged into the chilly Washington evening.

Horns blared and exhaust fumes mingled with the smell of burned grease rising from the hotdog stand on the corner, but my mind was far away. I could see Uncle Will — young Uncle Will — standing at the ghetto gate with his policeman's armband, and young Steponas driving his wagon loaded with carrots past the doomed Jews who would soon to be marched into the forest. My investigation was finished, for now at least. It was time for me to draw conclusions about the questions I had taken with me to the Old World.

I had gone to Lithuania wanting to get to the heart of the matter of the bystander and the Jewish policeman. Should people like Steponas be condemned or forgiven by people like me? Did Jewish policemen like my uncle act as collaborators, or were they victims? My goal had been to make up my mind, once and for all.

But my journey did not turn out the way I expected. Instead, as

255

I observed how Lithuanians were being encouraged to question their assumptions, I felt challenged to rethink the very notion of reaching a judgment. For people who live through terrible times, it may be difficult or impossible — or even inappropriate — to move on beyond hatred. But for people like me, members of the later generations after the Holocaust, I came to see a different role and different responsibilities. My journey changed me.

By the end of my investigation, Uncle Will's personal past still hovered out of sight. He was not named in any of the documents I examined. He had not been interviewed by an oral historian or written a memoir. I had chosen not to violate my own sense of ethics by questioning him aggressively. Instead, I had listened to what he was willing to say and had gone on to gather the words of people who had lived in the ghetto with him, presuming that the truth of his individual experience could be found within the collective history these others described.

The actions of the police in my uncle's ghetto turned out to have been more brutal than I'd imagined — and also, at times, more heroic. I learned, to my horror, that the police had beaten their fellow Jews to the point of unconsciousness. They had punished mothers who were desperately seeking to feed their children. Jewish leaders had helped to decide who lived and who died. But I also learned that these leaders had selflessly put their own names on a list of those to be executed, rather than hand over others to the Nazi command. I read Efroyim Gens's contention that if the Jewish police had not enforced the rules, the German command would have done so even more brutally. I learned that survivors of my uncle's ghetto tended to remember the Jewish leaders as "fine people."

I noted that the ghetto voices I was able to listen to were those of the very few who had survived. Those who died might have viewed the police in a far less positive light. Nonetheless, it mattered very much to me that none of the survivors whose words I read outside of the Soviet trial setting had condemned the police. Some of my questions about the harsh punishments meted out by the police, I came to feel, could be directed at any police force. Didn't every civil "peacekeeping" body employ at least the threat of force in doing its job? And there was the matter of scale: the Jewish police used truncheons to keep the ghetto residents in line, but their oppressors used machine guns.

No longer was I inclined to see the question of the Jewish police as a matter of pure principle. Details mattered. In the face of a regime that sought to erase the uniqueness of its victims, I came to feel, it was important to pay close attention to distinctions among individuals, to insist on remembering that this one was kind while that one was cruel.

The particularities of places carried weight, too. Every ghetto had its own characteristics that helped to determine the actions of the Jewish leadership, from the imperious "King Chaim" Rumkowski in Lodz to the anguished Adam Czerniakow in Warsaw, from the ruthless Jacob Gens in Vilna to the aloof Elkhanon Elkes in Kovno. The practical businessmen who led the Jewish Council in Shavl put their stamp on how my uncle's police behaved. Each ghetto was different, and the differences were not trivial.

Circumstances counted. If the Red Army had arrived with less warning, for example, the Nazi command might not have had time to liquidate the Shavl ghetto, and its residents might have survived. The calculations made by Efroyim Gens and the other Jewish leaders would have turned out to be correct. The question of their collaboration and moral turpitude might never have arisen. They might have been hailed as saviors.

Just as the story of my uncle's wartime actions had not come fully into view, Steponas, too, remained a shadowy figure in my eyes. But although my encounter with him was brief, it taught me a great deal. As a result of my contact with him and other Lithuanians who could be characterized as bystanders, I came to see that here, too, the particularities of individuals and places and circumstances mattered deeply. In those tumultuous years, most Lithuanians failed to help their Jewish neighbors. Some committed heinous acts. Others took action on behalf of the Jews. Of these, some succeeded in saving lives, and others tried but failed. Steponas and his mother would never be inducted into the famous pantheon of "righteous gentiles" at Yad Vashem, Israel's Holocaust museum, with its stringent criteria. Neither would Violeta's mother or Aldona's mother. Despite their efforts, the Jews they sought to help had died. Yet even if their actions were ineffectual, I came to feel they deserved our notice. To understand the truth of a terrible and murderous time, we needed to look closely enough to pay attention to individuals like them.

Did Uncle Will and Steponas belong in the column called bystander? Or collaborator? Rescuer? Or victim? Or would we perhaps do better to put these columns aside and dig for a deeper truth?

When Primo Levi, the renowned survivor of Auschwitz, writes about the "gray zone" between oppressor and oppressed, he directs our attention to the Jews who occupy this shadowy realm, "the space which separates . . . the victims from the persecutors." The Jewish police are members of this category, "the hybrid class of the prisoner-functionary." They are both masters and servants.

"The harsher the oppression," Levi goes on, "the more widespread among the oppressed is the willingness to collaborate." Of those Jewish prisoners who became part of the death machine at Auschwitz, the so-called "crematorium ravens," he writes, "I ask that we meditate on [their] story . . . with pity and rigor, but that judgment of them be suspended."

If we turn away from pronouncing a verdict, however, Levi does not mean us to abandon the act of moral questioning itself. We *must* wrestle with what is right and what is wrong, what is better and what is worse. I thought back to the sunny morning in the university courtyard, when my fellow students sat on the steps talking about what they would have done if they'd been confined in the Vilna ghetto. "I would have joined the underground," said one. "I would have been too scared," said another. At the time, these hypotheses offended me. They sounded irreverent and shallow. But now I'd come to a different view. Now I believed that however impossible it was to know, it was important to ask such questions. Imagining ourselves into unimaginable situations, putting ourselves in other people's shoes, was at the very heart of moral behavior.

As a ghetto inhabitant, would I have pushed to the front of the bread line? Would I have descended into madness like the woman in the Panama hat in Sutzkever's short story? Would I have kept my head down and cooperated with the authorities, or tried to escape, or become a resistance fighter?

And if I had found myself on the other side of the fence — if half the residents of my hometown, but not my own family, had been assembled at gunpoint — what kind of "bystander" would I have been? Would I have tried to organize a public protest, or helped in secret? Would I have endangered my family to try to save my neighbors? Would I have helped people I barely knew? Or would I have been too afraid to do anything at all?

Given how limited people's choices were during the Holocaust years, the matter of "resistance" was complicated. Picking up a gun or making a bomb was one form of resistance, but so was smuggling a loaf of bread through the ghetto gate. It may not be possible to draw a clear moral line between those who joined the underground and those who didn't. (In the Shavl ghetto, a small group of men organized what they called an underground, but although they amassed a small stockpile of weapons, they never used them.) There were many kinds of heroism, many varieties of moral behavior. Abandoning one's mother to join the partisans could be a moral and heroic act — but *refusing* to abandon one's mother could be moral and heroic as well. And while heroism is good, and honoring it is a good thing, is it realistic to demand that everyone be a hero?

In Levi's words, "the greatest responsibility lies with the system, the very structure of the totalitarian state." As we examine the conduct of individuals, we must consider the context in which they decide to "stand up" or "stand by" (or worse). It is one thing to act ethically if your society supports such a choice, and a very different thing to stick your neck out alone. I remembered the words of the two educators I spoke with at the International Commission, the women who were designing Holocaust curricula; their objective — "to transform ourselves from a society of bystanders into an active civil society" — was a social and political goal, not a personal one.

For me, the point was no longer to reach a final verdict about the bystanders or the Jewish police. Instead, the idea was to try to *know* them. Whatever happened in the Shavl ghetto, I did not need to push my uncle away. I could hold him close — and Steponas as well. I would never cease to wonder about Uncle Will's actions in the ghetto or Steponas's role in the annihilation of my people. To try to open my mind and my heart, to listen and to comprehend: this, I came to feel, was my role and my responsibility. In this way, I could seek to honor my heritage without perpetuating the hatreds of the past. To ask, without ever expecting to be done with the asking — that would be the work of a lifetime.

AT the graduation ceremony at the Yiddish Institute, Fanya, the former partisan with the steel-gray hair, went to the front of the room to lead the traditional Partisan Hymn. We all rose.

Earlier, the song's bold refrain — "Mir zaynen do!" ("We are here!") — had struck me as unbearably sad, even pathetic. The ghetto singers of old were not here. They were gone, perished, murdered. But as I stood up to sing, the song sounded different to me. Now, alongside the tragedy, I sensed something else as well. Spinning through my head were the faces of the people I had met here in the land of my ancestors. They were brave people, flawed people, Jews and non-Jews searching for a way forward.

Like all of us, they were carrying the burden of the past, struggling to shoulder some parts and let go of others. As in the "Story without an End" that we began but did not finish on our last day in class, it was a journey that would never be over. Conflicts would inevitably erupt in the years to come. Age-old prejudices would continue to rear their head. Yet the efforts were continuing, and this filled me with hope — hope for the future, for Lithuania, for other countries struggling to recover from conflict, for all of us.

In the mid-twentieth century, during the dreadful times that Uncle Will and Steponas lived through, solidarity was often impossible. But other times offer the opportunity to reach beyond old divisions. As a result of my encounter with the Old World, the anthem of the Vilna ghetto had come to embody a new meaning for me. The song continued to evoke a terrible and irreversible loss — the absence of all those who are not here. But within its stirring lines I also heard a bid for all of us who will shape the future to stand together as fellow beings with the capacity for moral choice.

Zog nit keynmol az du geyst dem letstn veg,
Khotsh himlen blayene farshteln bloye teg,
Kumen vet nokh undzer oysgebenkte sho,
Es vet a poyk ton undzer trot: MIR ZAYNEN DO!

Never say that you are walking your last way,
Though leaden clouds may be concealing skies of blue.
The hour we've been yearning for is near,
And our marching steps will thunder: WE ARE HERE!

Mir zaynen do.
Mes dar esame.
We are ALL here.

Important Dates in Lithuanian History

1009   Lithuania first mentioned in Latin chronicle.

1200s   Jews arrive.

1323   Grand Duke Gediminas declares Vilnius as capital.

1387   Lithuania officially adopts Christianity.

1392–1430   Vytautas the Great rules, extends Lithuania's borders nearly to the Black Sea.

1410   Teutonic Order decisively defeated.

1495   Grand Duke Alexander expels Jews. Eight years later, he invites them to return.

1569   Polish-Lithuanian Commonwealth established.

1579   Vilnius University founded.

MID-1600s   Russian forces and Cossack raiders murder Jews, plunder Jewish communities.

MID-1700S Polish-Lithuanian Commonwealth
becomes home to world's largest
Jewish population. Hasidism, a Jewish
renewal movement, spreads north from
Ukraine, provoking Jewish opponents
(*misnagdim*) led by Vilna Gaon (genius)
Elijah ben Judah Solomon Zalman
(1720–97).

1795 Polish-Lithuanian Commonwealth ends.
Russia gains control of Lithuania. Austria
and Prussia divide up remaining lands.

1800s Haskalah (Jewish enlightenment movement) flourishes. Czar imposes Pale of
Settlement and other restrictions on Jewish life.

LATE 1800S Massive Jewish immigration to United
States begins. Lithuanian Zionist organizations founded. "Bund," Jewish Socialist
organization, founded in Vilnius.

1914 World War I begins. Fearing Jews are pro-
German, czar expels many to Siberia.

1915 Germany occupies Lithuania.

1918 Treaty of Versailles grants independence
to Lithuania. Jews gain cultural autonomy. Many Jews return from Siberia.

1920 Vilnius taken by Poland. Kaunas
becomes Lithuanian capital.

1925 YIVO Institute for Jewish Research
founded, settles in Vilnius.

1920S   "Lithuanianization" of economy begins. Rise of gentile middle class. Squeezed out of economy, many Jews leave for United States, South Africa.

AUGUST 23, 1939   Molotov-Ribbentrop Pact between Soviet Union and Germany secretly cedes Baltic countries to USSR.

SEPTEMBER 1939   Germany invades Poland. Red Army occupies Vilnius, establishes military bases in Lithuania.

OCTOBER 28, 1939   Soviet Union returns Vilnius to Lithuania; it becomes Lithuanian capital.

JUNE 1940   Red Army occupies Lithuania. Elections are organized to establish Soviet government. President Smetona flees. YIVO moves to New York.

AUGUST 3, 1940   Lithuania declared a Soviet Socialist Republic.

JUNE 14, 1941   Tens of thousands of Lithuanians (including Jews) deported to Siberia.

JUNE 22, 1941   Germany invades Lithuania, beginning occupation. Red Army flees.

SUMMER–FALL 1941   German forces and their Lithuanian allies massacre most of Lithuania's estimated 240,000 Jews. In the cities of Vilnius (Vilna), Kaunas (Kovno), and Siauliai (Shavl), Jewish ghettos are created.

1941–43   Most ghetto residents are shot or starve to death.

SEPTEMBER 23, 1943   Vilna ghetto liquidated, residents dispersed to camps.

JULY 1944   Kovno and Shavl ghettos liquidated, residents transported to Stutthof and Dachau concentration camps.

JULY 1944   Red Army retakes Lithuania. Tens of thousands of Lithuanians immigrate to the West. Out of a prewar Jewish population of an estimated 240,000, fewer than 10 percent survive. Jewish museum opens, monuments honor murdered Jews.

1944–49   50,000 Lithuanians convicted of "crimes against the Soviet Union," including collaboration with the Nazis. Jewish population numbers 10,000, including immigrants from Russia.

1944–53   "Forest Brothers" conduct guerrilla campaign against Soviet power. More than 100,000 Lithuanians deported to Siberia.

FEBRUARY 1945   Yalta agreement (among Soviet Union, United States, and England) affirms Lithuania as a Soviet Republic.

APRIL–MAY 1945   Stutthof camp liberated by Soviet troops, Dachau by U.S. troops.

1949   Stalin's "campaign against cosmopolitanism" outlaws most expressions of Jewish culture. Jewish museum closes. Monuments altered to remove mention of Jews.

1953   Stalin dies. Lithuanians begin to return from Siberian exile.

1961–65   Lithuanians who murdered Jews in 1941 are publicly tried and convicted.

1970S–80S   Many Jews immigrate to Israel. Jewish population drops from a postwar peak of 25,000 to 12,000.

1989   Jewish cultural revival flowers. Jewish museum reopens. Memorial plaques honor Jews.

AUGUST 23, 1989   More than one million citizens of the Baltics form human chain on anniversary of Molotov-Ribbentrop Pact.

MARCH 1990   Lithuania declares independence from the Soviet Union.

1991   Lithuania is internationally recognized as an independent republic. Many "anti-Soviets" who were convicted after the war are rehabilitated. Jewish emigration continues; Jewish population drops to 4,500.

1992   Museum of Genocide Victims opens, commemorates opponents and victims of Soviet rule.

1995   Lithuanian president Brazauskas apologizes to Israeli Knesset for Lithuanian collaborators with Nazis. Monuments are altered to make clear that Jews died at the hands of Lithuanians and Germans. Educational initiatives on the Holocaust begin.

1998   President Adamkus establishes International Commission for the Evaluation of the Crimes of the Nazi and Soviet Occupation Regimes.

1999   Lithuanian prosecutors bring legal action against five Lithuanians for collaboration with Nazis.

2000   Lithuanian bishops apologize for clergy's misdeeds during Nazi and Soviet eras.

2001   Vilnius Yiddish Institute founded.

2002   Simon Wiesenthal Center launches "Operation: Last Chance" to gather data about Lithuanian collaborators with the Nazis.

2004   Lithuania joins NATO and the European Union. Tuskulenai "Park of Quiet" opens.

2005   Lithuanian prosecutors open investigation of several Holocaust survivors, former anti-Nazi partisans, on suspicion of war crimes.

2008–2011   Neo-Nazi "skinhead" demonstrations take place. Jewish sites are defaced.

Author's Note

IN the time that has passed since the events described in this book, the people of Lithuania have continued to engage with their history. The Lithuanian Parliament passed legislation authorizing extensive repayment to the Jewish community for property seized by the Nazi and Soviet governments. The conflict over the Chor Shul in Vilnius came to involve legal action, and the Chabad rabbi was banned from the premises. The government made little progress in prosecuting Lithuanians who had played a role in massacring Jews during the Nazi era. In 2005, however, prosecutors began investigating several elderly Jewish Holocaust survivors — including Fanya and Rokhl, who conducted the evocative tours of Jewish Vilna described in these pages — on suspicion that, as anti-Nazi partisans, they might have been guilty of war crimes. In 2008 and again in 2010 and 2011, neo-Nazi demonstrations took place in Lithuania, and the Jewish community issued protests against these and other public expressions of anti-Semitism.

In an essay responding to some of these events, Leonidas Donskis, the philosopher who spoke with me in Vilnius, wrote, "I am sad and hurt that my homeland . . . is still intoxicated with hatred for the vanishing Lithuanian Jews." These developments saddened me, too — and made me feel that the initiatives toward education and tolerance that I saw during my visit were all the more remarkable, all the more precious.

IT is a great pleasure to thank those who helped bring this book into being.

My greatest debt is to the people in Lithuania who shared their thoughts and feelings with me — those who appear in the pages of this book, as well as others who do not. With sincerity, candor, and passion, they educated me about their country and about themselves. I am grateful to the Vilnius Yiddish Institute and its wonderful teachers, and to my fellow students there. All of the events described in the book are true to the best of my understanding, but a few names have been changed to protect privacy.

Several people were extremely helpful in connecting me with people and places in Lithuania. I am grateful to Samuel Bak, Solon Beinfeld, Shimon Davidovitch, Henry Kopelman-Gidoni, Regina Kopilevich, Tina Lunson, Ona Mackeviciene, Ina Navazelskis, Samuel Schalkowsky, Philip Shapiro, Myra Sklarew, and Rimantas Stankevicius.

As I began the project, my thinking was influenced by the work of Eva Hoffman, especially by her book *After Such Knowledge: Memory, History, and the Legacy of the Holocaust* (New York: Public Affairs, 2004). Michael Steinlauf's *Bondage to the Dead: Poland and the Memory of the Holocaust* (New York: Syracuse University Press, 1997) also helped to set me on my path. In an article in the journal *Holocaust and Genocide Studies* and in conversation, Michael MacQueen shared valuable insights about the causes of the Lithuanian genocide. I thank Saulius Suziedelis for his groundbreaking work and his generous help.

Books published by the Vilna Gaon Jewish State Museum in Vilnius were very useful to me. I am grateful to have been granted access to the Lithuanian Special Archives. At the United States Holocaust Memorial Museum, Michlean Amir was a wonderful guide to the library's Lithuania collection, and Bret Werb provided useful expertise on songs.

For help with translation from Hebrew, Lithuanian, and Russian,

I am grateful to Ilene Arnsdorf, Shimon Davidovitch, Ed Hurwitz, Regina Kopilevich, Hirsh Pekalis, Asya Shindelman, Jolita Vobolyte, and Lyn Wulfsohn. Thanks to Keith Morgan for supplying me with newspaper articles from Siauliai.

Early on, the late Ruth Gay said the magic words: "You must write this down." The late Max Rosenfeld, a beloved teacher, helped to launch my engagement with Yiddish. I owe a special debt to Rosel Schewel for her generosity in helping me to visit Lithuania, and to Susan Schewel for her friendship and her outstanding embroidery contribution.

I am grateful to Anne Dubuisson Anderson for valuable advice throughout, to Larry Blum for his help in reflecting on moral questions, and to Dick Cluster for his close reading. I thank Lois Feinblatt for her warm encouragement, Sarah Glazer for her sustaining support, Cecile Kuznitz for her generous help, Judy Smith for help with the publishing process, and Yermiyahu Ahron Taub for his compassion and insights.

Many people read all or part of early versions of the manuscript, and I benefited greatly from their thoughtful comments. I thank Jodi Beder, Solon Beinfeld, Mark Blechner, Ellen Bravo, Mary Carpenter, Andy Cassel, Carolyn Daffron, Nancy Falk, Jim Feldman, Chris Foreman, Janet Kaplan, Vivi Lachs, Erica Lehrer, Michael Lipsky, Deborah Meyer, Ina Navazelskis, Karen Nussbaum, Steve Schewel, Janet Selcer, and Natalie Wexler.

I am grateful to my Yiddish reading group, especially its wild and wonderful *kop*, Miriam Isaacs. Thanks to Clare Kinberg of *Bridges* magazine for her excellence as an editor, to Joanna Merlin for her friendship, and to Ragnar Freidank for wise advice at a key moment.

At the University of Nebraska Press, Humanities Acquisitions Editor Kristen Elias Rowley and her talented colleagues were a splendid team. Sonya Huber, Jonathan Lawrence, and Mimi Schwartz provided insightful suggestions.

I feel privileged to have known my aunt and my late uncle, Manya and William Levin, and my cousin Asya Shindelman, and am grateful beyond measure for their courage and kindness in talking with me about the past. I thank David and Daniel Levin for their generosity as well. I'm grateful to my late mother and my father, who gave me so much and who over the years laid the foundation for the journey described in this book. Thanks are due to my uncle David for his unflagging interest and affection; to my sisters and brother for being always by my side; to my son, Tim, and my daughter, Meg, for their integrity and insights; and to my husband, Jeff Blum, for his idealistic drive and generosity of spirit, his unfailing efforts to understand, and the sustaining warmth of his love.

A note about spelling: I have omitted Lithuanian diacritical marks. For the Yiddish, I have used the orthographic standards established by the YIVO Institute for Jewish Research, except in cases where alternate spellings are commonly accepted in English usage. Each choice was carefully and lovingly made.

Any errors are, of course, my own.

SOURCE ACKNOWLEDGMENTS

Several lines from the poem "Undzer yidish" by Eliezer Schindler are used by kind permission of Eva Schindler Oles.

Four lines from the poem "Blacksmith Shop" in *Provinces: Poems 1987–1991* by Czeslaw Milosz are reprinted by permission of HarperCollins Publishers and of SLL/Sterling Lord Literistic, Inc. © by Czeslaw Milosz.

The author's "poem," based on her taped interview of her aunt and uncle, originally appeared in slightly different form in *Poetica*, July 2004, 31–33. © 2004 by Ellen Cassedy.

Samuel Schalkowsky generously granted permission to quote from his translation of "Geshikhte fun der viliampoler yidisher geto-politsey" (History of the Viliampole [Kovno] Jewish Ghetto Police). The original Yiddish version can be viewed at the United

States Holocaust Memorial Museum in Washington DC, in the Central State Archives of Lithuania, General Directorate of Lithuania Archives collection, 1941–48, Fond R-973, acc. 1998, A0073.

Portions of this book originally appeared in different form in *Bridges: A Jewish Feminist Journal* 8, nos. 1 & 2 (Spring 2000): 46–52, and 12, no. 2 (Autumn 2007): 77–85. © 2000, 2007 by Ellen Cassedy.

Seven lines from the poem "A Poor Christian Looks at the Ghetto" in *The Collected Poems: 1931–1987* by Czeslaw Milosz are reprinted by permission of HarperCollins Publishers. © 1988 by Czeslaw Milosz Royalties, Inc.

The Oral History Archives at the Avraham Harman Institute of Contemporary Jewry, Hebrew University of Jerusalem (Israel), provided transcripts of interviews of Khayim Zhilinski (1972) and Gita Katsef (1973) conducted by Sima Itsiks (project files (99)3 and (99)4).

Lyn Wulfsohn generously granted permission to use her translation of selections from Eliezer Yerushalmi's *Pinkas Shavli: yoman mi-geto Lita'i, 1941–1944*, an account of the Shavl ghetto.

The lyrics to the song "Derfar, liber bruder" were written by Khane Khaytin (1925–2004?). Interested readers can locate the original Yiddish text in *Yahadut Lita*, ed. Natan Goren (Tel Aviv: Hotsa'at Am ha-sefer, 1959–84), 4:219.

The lyrics to "Zog nit keynmol," the Partisan Hymn, were written by Hirsh Glick (1922–44) in the Vilna ghetto in 1943.

DISCUSSION questions about this book are available through the website of the University of Nebraska Press (http://www.nebraskapress.unl.edu).

DISCARD

CPSIA information can be obtained
at www.ICGtesting.com
Printed in the USA
LVOW12s1154051116
511775LV00001B/39/P

9 780803 2301